One Christ — Many Religions

One Christ—Many Religions

Toward a Revised Christology

S. J. Samartha

WIPF & STOCK · Eugene, Oregon

Wipf and Stock Publishers
199 W 8th Ave, Suite 3
Eugene, OR 97401

One Christ - Many Religions
Towards a Revised Christology
By Samartha, S. J.
Copyright©1991 Orbis Books
ISBN 13: 978-1-4982-3264-7
Publication date 6/8/2015
Previously published by Orbis Books, 1991

Contents

A NOTE ON ORTHOGRAPHY   vii

PREFACE   ix

1. NEW PERCEPTIONS OF RELIGIOUS PLURALISM   1
   The Context: From the Missiological to the Theological   1
   The Roots of Pluralism   4
   New Perceptions   6
   Areas of Theological Concern   8

2. THE OTHER END OF THE DIALOGUE BRIDGE   13
   Limits of Christian-Initiated Dialogues   13
   Jewish Hesitations and Fears   16
   Muslim Responses and Initiatives   20
   Hindu Models of Dialogue   22
   Buddhist Attitudes   26
   Christians: Teachers or Learners?   29

3. RELIGIONS, CULTURES, AND THE STRUGGLE FOR JUSTICE   32
   Economic Injustice and Theological Injustice   32
   Need for New Relationships   37
   Northern Study of Southern Religions   39
   Issues for Study   42

4. RELIGIOUS IDENTITIES IN A SECULAR STATE   45
   Religions and National Life   45
   The Secular State in a Multireligious Society   47
   The Ideology of Communalism   50
   Role of Religions in the Secular State   51
   Religions in a Multireligious Society   55

5. SCRIPTURE AND SCRIPTURES   58
   The Plurality of Scriptures   59
   Hermeneutics in a Multiscriptural Context   62
   Language: "Spokenness" and "Writtenness"   64

The Quest for New Hermeneutics in Asia   66
Some Principles of Interpretation   73

6. CHRIST IN A MULTIRELIGIOUS CULTURE   76
Changes in Christian Response to Other Faiths   77
Four Moments in Interreligious Relationships in India   79
The Meaning of Jesus and the Mystery of God   82
Toward a Theocentric Christology   89

7. TOWARD A REVISED CHRISTOLOGY   92
Christology within Theology   92
From Intra-Christian to Interreligious   96
Exclusive Claims: Roots and Consequences   98
Truth and the Either/Or Mind-set   103
The Unitive Vision of *Advaita*   107

8. THE MAKING OF A REVISED CHRISTOLOGY   112
The Context of Revision   112
Helicopter Christology vs. Bullock-cart Christology   115
New Testament Witnesses to Jesus of Nazareth   120
The Buddha   124
The Historicity of Rama and Krishna   126

9. THE SUBSTANCE OF A REVISED CHRISTOLOGY   132
Faith and History   132
Marks of a Revised Christology   133
The Kingdom of God   134
The Freedom Christ Brings   135
The Cross-Resurrection Event   136
The Crucified and Risen One in a Religiously Plural World   140

10. MISSION IN A RELIGIOUSLY PLURAL WORLD   142
The Historic Context   142
Changes Since Tambaram   145
Major Issues   147
Plurality of Methods   149
Missions and Conversions   150
The Content of Mission   150
Contribution of Christian Mission   152

NOTES   155

BIBLIOGRAPHY OF WORKS BY S. J. SAMARTHA   179

INDEX   187

A Note on Orthography

The problem of rendering non-Western systems of writing into Roman letters for English and other modern European languages is notoriously difficult. Joining many publishers who do not insert diacritical marks for words such as the Sanskrit *Śūnyatā*, this book also omits them.

Scholars and others who know languages such as Sanskrit, Pali, Arabic, or Japanese do not need the diacritical marks to identify words in their original written form. And persons who do not know these languages gain little from having the marks reproduced. We recognize that languages employing different orthographic systems have a richness and distinctiveness that *are* partially conveyed by the orthographics of diacritical marks. And while we do not wish to be part of flattening out the contours of our linguistically plural globe, the high cost of ensuring accuracy in using the diacritical marks does not justify reproducing them here.

Preface

The purpose of this book is to examine the new perceptions of religious pluralism in the world today and, in the context of its implications for people in the global community, to indicate the contours of a revised christology. The conviction underlying this work is that, in a religiously plural world, a christology that is biblically sound, spiritually satisfying, theologically credible, and pastorally helpful is both necessary and possible—without making exclusive claims for Christianity or passing negative judgments on the faiths of our neighbors.

So much has been written about religious pluralism in recent years that another description or analysis is likely to be repetitive. This is why the first chapter deals with *new* perceptions of this phenomenon, its roots and characteristics, and even more important, its implications for Christians today. These may not be entirely new, but they are significantly different from some of the usual observations on the topic. Areas of theological concern such as scripture, history, theology, church and mission need to be considered afresh in the light of these perceptions.

Most interreligious dialogues during the past two decades have been invariably initiated by Christians. How do neighbors of other faiths respond to these initiatives, particularly in terms of their own theologies of religion? This dimension has scarcely enjoyed serious consideration by Christian theologians. Therefore the second chapter discusses the responses of Hindus and Buddhists, Jews and Muslims to Christian initiated dialogues.

The third chapter deals with a question that is rarely discussed in this connection. Even as there is an *economic* injustice in the relationship between the North and the South, there is also a *theological* injustice in the relationship between Christianity—which is the nominal religion of the rich and powerful North—and other religions followed by people in the poor and weak nations of the South. Is there a connection between these two forms of injustice?

Religion is not the only factor that affects life in contemporary society. There is indeed a resurgence of religions—not just in other religions but also within Christianity—which often expresses itself through fundamentalism. There is also a renaissance of religions, taking a critical look at all religions and trying to bring out their spiritual resources that sustain life and support struggles for a just society. There are Marxist and other secular humanistic ideologies that claim the allegiance of many people. The scientific temper, the rise of a technological culture, and the increasing power of the electronic revolution through computers challenge both religions and ideologies at crucial points. Within this larger conceptual framework, attention here is focused more on the religious dimension. Even though it is the most enduring element in human life, for various reasons it is the most neglected and misunderstood factor. The fourth chapter therefore focuses on religious identities in the secular state and the critical role religions play in the life of the larger community.

The fifth chapter, dealing with "scripture and scriptures," is a transitional chapter. This is a topic that has not been discussed sufficiently and is usually avoided in interreligious meetings, yet most theological claims are based on scriptural authority. In interreligious dialogues, participants invariably quote from their respective scriptures. In Europe, hermeneutics developed in a monoscriptural situation: The scriptures of other faiths did not enter into the hermeneutic circle of Christians in the West. What does it mean, then, to raise the question of hermeneutics today in a multiscriptural situation, where notions of authority, the ways in which a text becomes a scripture, the relation between "writtenness" and "spokenness," the connection between language and symbols, and the manner in which scriptures function religiously in the life of a believing community are all so strikingly different?

The next four chapters, which constitute the substance of the book, deal with the content, methodology, and substance of a revised christology in a religiously plural world. Jesus Christ is the foundation of Christian faith, the basis of Christian life, and the inspiration for Christian witness and service in the world. Christologies are formulations of this faith in God through Jesus Christ in the process of being led by the power of the Spirit in history. The missing factor in all christologies developed in the West and imported to other countries is the fact of religious pluralism, that is, the presence of other "lords" and other "saviors" in a multireligious context.

Whether Christians like it or not, no christology in the world (particularly in Asia today) can afford to ignore this factor. An attempt is made here to take this factor into serious consideration in suggesting the lines toward a revised christology. The old debate about a christology from "above" and a christology from "below" becomes thrustingly relevant here. In its attempts to land on the religiously plural terrain of Asia, a *helicopter* christology makes such a lot of missiological noise and kicks up so much theological dust that people are prevented from hearing the voice and seeing the vision of the descending divinity. A *bullock-cart* christology, on the other hand, always has its wheels in touch with the unpaved roads of Asia, for without that continuing friction with the ground, the cart cannot move at all. Moreover, a bullock-cart christology has the advantage of having its bullocks move on at a steady pace, even if the driver sometimes falls asleep. The last chapter draws out the implications of this revised christology for the life and witness of Christian communities living together with their neighbors of other faiths in a religiously plural world.

My indebtedness to New Testament scholars and theologians in preparing the christological section in chapter 8 should be obvious. As far as possible, I have indicated this through footnotes. If inadvertently some debt was not acknowledged, I ask to be forgiven. However, the critical selection of insights and conclusions from scholarly investigations, the manner in which they have been theologically used, and the larger framework within which I have situated them are my own, and even though I have been careful to avoid mistakes, I alone am responsible for any misunderstanding of their original intentions.

All christologies at any place and time need to be grounded in the New Testament. There are at least two reasons for this. First, without anchorage in the New Testament, one is inclined to make christological claims that go beyond the testimonies of the scriptures. Second, New Testament foundation is absolutely necessary for christologies to retain their ecumenical character. Christology can never be a narrow, individualistic, nationalistic, or parochial enterprise. It is the task and responsibility of the church in the world. This is not an attempt to work out an Asian or Indian Christian christology *against* the christologies of the West. An excess of nationalist zeal over Christian common sense is poor motivation for any christology. This is an attempt to respond to and articulate the mystery of Jesus Christ in an ecumenical setting, but the term *ecumenical* is understood here, in its true sense, to include not just Christians but neighbors of other faiths as well in God's *oikoumene*. However, no christology can be described as ecumenical without being particular, that is, without being rooted in the fact of Jesus of Nazareth, to whom the writers in the New Testament bear testimony as "the Christ, the Son of the living God" (Matthew 16:16).

To whom is this book addressed? There are many Christians today who are so bound to traditional christologies, so sure of the inerrancy of the Bible, so certain about the exclusive uniqueness of Christ, and so committed to mission in the sense of proclaiming the good news leading to the displacement of other religions by Christianity that they would resist even the slightest attempt to revise inherited christologies. These friends would not only reject what is said here, but are likely to be hostile to its intent, even though it should be clear that the revision called for here is not in the *substance* of the Christian faith but in its *formulations* inherited from a previous era and a different culture. There are other groups of people, however, to whom what is said here may not only be of some interest but also help for further reflections on the Christian faith in a religiously plural world.

First, there are many Christians, not just in Asia and Africa, but in other parts of the world as well, who are committed to God in Christ, who regard themselves as members of the church, who in different ways participate in God's mission, but who feel uneasy and hesitant about the exclusive claims made by Christians on behalf of Christ and Christianity. They may not articulate this uneasiness publicly, but there are many Christians, particularly younger people, who are most unwilling to subscribe to the aggressive Christian claims of exclusiveness.

Second, there are those Christians who are seriously committed to the struggle against injustice in the world, who are actively involved in movements of liberation with neighbors of other faiths, who believe that they participate in this work in the name of Christ but find it difficult, if not impossible, to accept that *only* in the Jewish, Christian and Western tradition are there spiritual resources for this struggle. When they work together with neighbors of other faiths and secular convictions, they discover "liberative streams" in other religious traditions as well, and are therefore unwilling to accept that only the Bible provides resources for "prophetic spirituality" and that "the ascetic spirituality" of Asian religions ignores issues of social justice. Neither the history of Christianity nor that of other religions like Hinduism or Buddhism or Islam or Sikhism provides any basis for such contrasting claims. To both these groups of Christians, a revised christology along the lines suggested here might be helpful, because it seeks to do justice to the values of compassion and justice in the kingdom of God—which was the content of Jesus' message—without in any way compromising or betraying Christian commitment to God in Jesus Christ.

To these must be added a third group, our neighbors of other faiths who have great reverence for Jesus Christ, his words and deeds, his life and death and resurrection, and who in different ways also follow him in their lives. Many of them are fed up with being made victims of Christian missions with arrogant and exclusive claims that are unsubstantiated by any visible evidence, either in the lives of the Christians making such claims or in the institutional Church. Without a revised christology, it is hardly likely they would respond to the deeper meaning of God in Jesus Christ or to the universal dimension in the message of Jesus Christ about the Kingdom of God. One hopes that these friends will find what is suggested here to be of considerable help, not just in their own reflections, but also in their work in society. The revised christology suggested here seeks a much broader and deeper conceptual framework, within which faith in God through Jesus Christ and the sustaining power of the Spirit do not divide people but hold them together in God's all-embracing love and justice. This christology does not set the struggle for justice over against the quest for a new theology of religions, but regards neighbors of other faiths as partners in the global community which, after all, is the object of God's love and justice.

This book has been in the making for about eight years, ever since I returned to India in 1981 after serving the ecumenical movement through the World Council of Churches for more than a decade. If theology is rooted in biography, biography is situated in geography. Being born in a country, in a given race, with a particular skin color and a received name are given factors in life which cannot be changed, but which, along with historical forces, influence the mind and heart of the individual. Those who overemphasize history miss the subtle connection between history and geography, and the dynamic interplay between the two in the consciousness of human beings. Being away from one's own country for a considerable time and returning to one's own roots becomes a transforming experience that touches the core of one's being. When such a homecoming happens toward the end of one's life, perhaps one receives the gifts of greater maturity, larger vision, and deeper insights into the mystery of life and death and the manner in which one's faith in God through Jesus Christ illumines them.

During these years I have immersed myself not only in the life of the local Christian congregation to which I belong but also in the day-to-day life of the neighborhood I share with Hindu, Muslim, Jain, and Sikh neighbors, as well as with Christians of different backgrounds—Roman Catholic, Orthodox, Mar Thoma, Pentecostal, and Adventist, as well as members of my own church, the Church of South India, which, forty years ago, united Anglican, Presbyterian, Methodist and Congregationalist denominations. Sickness and suffering, births and deaths, the joys of marriage and the celebration of different festivals are part of our daily life together in the community. I have learned a great deal from this dialogue in community.

The Karnataka Theological College, Mangalore (formerly Basel Evangelical Mission Seminary), where I began my ministry as a lecturer in theology, not only invited me to deliver lectures but on several occasions also arranged public meetings for me to address. During this period I have also been consultant to the Christian Institute for the Study of Religion and Society and a visiting professor at the United Theological College, both at Bangalore. I was also invited to teach in theological faculties in the United States, Canada, and the Netherlands. In addition, secular universities in India, such as the University of Mangalore, Karnataka, and the Madurai Kamaraj University in Tamil Nadu, the University Grants Commission of the government of India, as well as academic institutions of other religions invited me to deliver lectures. The synod of the Church of South India, the Christian Conference of Asia, the Federation of Asian Bishops Conference, and the World Council of Churches have, from time to time, asked me to present papers or deliver keynote addresses. All these have given me considerable opportunities to share and test with them most of the ideas in this book. I have immensely benefited from their observations, questions, and critical comments.

Three chapters in this volume have been previously published: "Religions, Cultures and the Struggle for Justice" in *Journal of Ecumenical Studies* (25: 3, Summer 1988); "Christ in a Multireligious Culture" (under the title "The Cross and the Rainbow") as chapter 5 in *The Myth of Christian Uniqueness* (Eds. John Hick and Paul F. Knitter, Maryknoll, N.Y.: Orbis Books, 1987); and "Mission in a Religiously Plural World" in *International Review of Mission* (78:307, July 1988). This is presented here in a revised form. I am grateful to the publishers for permission to reprint them. I have included them here because they are part of the argument of the book and were originally intended to be so when I prepared them. All the other chapters are new and written for Orbis's series *Faith Meets Faith*, dealing with issues in interreligious dialogue. The general editor of the series, Paul F. Knitter, a friend and colleague in this area of work for many years, and William R. Burrows, the managing editor of Orbis Books, have made many valuable suggestions. To these friends I express my gratefulness.

In addition, there are many others—my students, academic colleagues, scholars and thinkers of other faiths—who at various times in conversations, seminars, and public meetings have critically responded to the ideas expressed in this volume and helped me to modify, refine, and sharpen my points. To all these I am very grateful.

If this modest attempt at a revised christology in a religiously plural world should be of some help to people—not just to Christians, but also to neighbors of other faiths—and provoke some discussion leading to further critical reflection on the theme, I would be more than satisfied.

One Christ — Many Religions

1

New Perceptions of Religious Pluralism

Christian concern in religious pluralism has become an urgent and important matter for the church in the world today. The plurality of religions and cultures is an ancient phenomenon, but the *perception* of this fact has been changing during the past few decades. New historical factors have decisively influenced the conceptual framework, theological climate, and political and economic environment in which the subject is being considered today. To discuss religious pluralism without taking into account the larger context, where political and economic factors are probably as influential as the religious, would be to miss the depth and complexity of the phenomenon and its far-reaching effects on human relations in the global community.

THE CONTEXT: FROM THE MISSIOLOGICAL TO THE THEOLOGICAL

Although the larger context of history and the interconnectedness of events must be kept in mind, the focus of this discussion is limited to the chronological slice of time from the end of the second world war (1939–45) to the flow of history toward the twenty-first century. Within this time span, more attention is given in this discussion to the developments of the last two decades. It is necessary to recall both the political and economic changes that have come to pass during this period and the profound spiritual concern and emotional feelings with which people of different faiths respond to religious pluralism today.

The second world war brought immense suffering, not just to people in Europe, but also to millions of people in Asia and Africa who had no part whatsoever in the tribal quarrels of Europe. The story of millions of "colonial" soldiers who were compelled to fight in the war, almost all of whom belonged to religions other than Christianity and had no "chaplains" of their own to minister to them in their hour of need in the battlefield, and

1

who suffered and died fighting for the freedom of nations other than their own, is yet to be written. The Holocaust that took place in the country that gave birth to the Reformation, the first use of the atom bomb, and the more recent threats to humanity of environmental pollution and the shadow of nuclear annihilation have raised profound moral and spiritual questions about the credibility of Christianity. If Christianity was unable to prevent these horrors in countries over which it held sway for so many centuries, why export it to people in other countries who live by other faiths?

There is an even more powerful factor that has made an explosive entry into history during this period. This is the struggle of oppressed people everywhere—the large majority of whom belong to religions other than Christianity and cultures other than the Western—for a life of freedom, self-respect, and human dignity.

This is not just a matter of economic well-being or political adjustments in power relationships. Deep down, it is a struggle for identity, a quest for spiritual resources in the fight against injustice. The rejection of religious pluralism, the refusal to recognize that neighbors of other faiths in the world live by their own cherished beliefs and values, is a more serious form of injustice than the merely economic. This is why the demand for parity in interreligious relationships and the struggle against all forms of exploitation converge in the quest for justice in society.

Even in the colonial period, during their struggle for political independence (particularly in Asian countries like India), many people sought spiritual support in their own cultural and religious resources. This is true, for example, of Hinduism in India, Buddhism in Sri Lanka, and Islam in the West Asian countries. In India, for example, for many national leaders the *Bhagavadgita* provided the resources for a righteous war (*dharma yuddha*) against the colonial power. With the retreat of colonialism at the end of the second world war, the emerging new nations in Asia and Africa sought to build their identities on the basis of their own religious and cultural values rather than those imposed from outside. Minority ethnic groups within certain nations, like the Dalits and tribals in India, and the marginalized peoples everywhere are identifying and recovering their own folk religions and cultures in their struggle against all forms of injustice, including the religious and cultural. Thus the demand to recognize and accept plurality gets powerful support from the vast majority of the poor people in the world who are struggling for justice.

Many people would like to forget the colonial period, when the plurality of religions and cultures in the world was regarded as a bump on the road to be flattened out in the interest of Christianity and Western culture. But those who were its victims do not find it so easy to forget it, not only because its consequences are very much alive today but also because new forms of colonialism are emerging at the present time. It is not without significance that it was only a couple of decades after the dismantling of colonialism that both the Vatican (1965) and the World Council of Churches (1971) came out, rather reluctantly, with more positive statements about people of other faiths.

It is difficult to exorcise the demon of colonialism. "Colonialism is not just a matter of economic exploitation," writes Ashis Nandy. "It is the organised repression of the cultural life of a people to make them accept other values as superior."[1] The unanswered question here is about the enduring power of this illusion that enables one religion or one culture or one ideology to make exclusive claims on its behalf, thus condemning other peoples, cultures, and religions to an inferior status to be humiliated, dominated, exploited, and conquered, not just physically, but spiritually as well. That this attitude persists even to this day, and that all too often even the minds of its former victims are still colonized, should not come as a surprise. Pascal Bruckner, in a volume entitled *The Tears of the Whiteman: Compassion as Contempt*, points out that "the rhetoric of third-worldism patronises those it claims to champion, and that much of what passes as sympathy for the third world is as self-serving as yesterday's rationale for colonialism," and has thus become "one of the greatest political and moral hoaxes of our country."[2] To affirm plurality is one way of fighting against this persistent tendency. Religious pluralism thus provides resources for the survival of peoples and nations against forces that openly or covertly seek to impose uniformity on a pluralist world.

All these in their cumulative effect contribute to the new perceptions of pluralism. The conceptual framework in which this matter is being discussed is still very much Western, but efforts are being made to widen its horizon, shift its focus, and change its methodology in order to include perceptions of people to whom these religions are not just objects of study, but faiths to live by. There are quite a few theological books coming out in the West in which sections on world religions are included, something unthinkable two decades ago. This probably indicates that the study of religions is being shifted from the *missiological* to the *theological*. Both the Roman Catholic Church and the World Council of Churches have initiated new studies on this matter. The recently launched study of the World Council of Churches, "My Neighbour's Faith and Mine" (1986) with the subtitle "*Theological* Discoveries Through Inter-Faith Dialogue," would have been unthinkable in the hallowed halls of the Christian *oikoumene* twenty years ago.[3] In the "scientific" study of religions, too, there are indications that at least some scholars are willing to sniff at the academic implications of interreligious dialogues instead of looking down upon them in lofty disdain from the heights of academe. People, not religions, living faiths, not abstract religious ideas, have powerfully entered the agenda of many theologies of religion. And further, with the rise of fundamentalism and the increasing politicization of religions, not only Christians, but people of other religions and ideological convictions as well are coming to recognize the far-reaching consequences of interreligious relationships for peace and justice in the global community.

THE ROOTS OF PLURALISM

Religious pluralism is part of the larger plurality of races, peoples, and cultures, of social structures, economic systems, and political patterns, of languages and symbols, all of which are part of the total human heritage. Religious pluralism—that is, the fact that different religions respond to the Mystery of Ultimate Reality or *Sat* or *Theos* in different ways—is important because it touches ultimate questions about human life and destiny. Its roots go to the depths of human consciousness, the experience of loneliness and finiteness. Loneliness and companionship are part of the human predicament. When one is lonely, there is the longing for companionship. When there is too much company, there is the desire to be lonely. Loneliness can lead to anxiety, despair, even terror. Companionship may become difficult, suffocating, even oppressive. Religions help human beings to hold together loneliness and companionship within human consciousness. It is only within the depths of Being that the two are held together in a profound and dynamic relationship. Plurality, therefore, belongs to the very structure of reality. In theological terms, plurality may even be the will of God for all life.

The sense of finiteness in the presence of the infinite is also at the root of religious pluralism. That human beings in different cultures, at different times, and in different countries, experience and express this tension between the finite and the infinite in different ways cannot be denied. There is always a gap between what is experienced within the cave of the human heart and what is expressed through words and symbols. This should be expected, both because of the diversity of the human condition and the depth and complexity of Ultimate Reality. How can so great a Mystery be experienced in only one way and expressed through only one set of symbols? Religious plurality, therefore, is the homage which the finite mind pays to the inexhaustibility of the infinite.

Human responses to the Mystery of the Infinite are always diverse. This diversity—cultural, philosophical, and theological—is connected with a diversity of symbols interwoven into the structure of language itself. Studies in the ontology of language show how deep the original structures of speech and sound are within human consciousness. It is rooted in the human capacity for self-transcendence. A sense of Mystery provides a point of unity to all plurality. In a pluralistic world, the different responses of different religions to the Mystery of the Infinite or *Theos* or *Sat* need to be acknowledged as valid. To break down the walls of separation, even hostility, between these different responses that have petrified through centuries of isolation, a new vocabulary is needed to facilitate communication between people of different faiths. This new vocabulary, to identify, distinguish, compare, and re-express these responses in relation to (not over against) the others, is yet to be developed. This is necessary, both for mutual criticism and mutual enrichment. Therefore, what we need is: "an all embracing philosophy and theology of pluralism within which alone the fact and right of religious pluralism can be situated, and their otherness and inter-relatedness fully understood and expressed."[4]

The question of language and symbols is one of the important factors in the new perceptions of religious pluralism today. Studies in the structures of language and the sociology and psychology of knowledge show how precarious it is to depend on texts and translations to arrive at the truth behind words. There are far too many problems in the relation between "spokenness" and "writtenness," between ideas and words, between *anubhava* (experience), and *tarka* (logic), between a profound inner experience and a reasoned attempt to communicate that experience to others. The fact that studies in religions and interreligious meetings are invariably conducted in Western languages, when the languages in which the major religions are recorded are all Eastern and quite different in their ontological structures and symbolic significance from the Western, is a serious matter that is being recognized only recently. "Language," remarks Hans-Georg Gadamer, "is not just one of man's possessions in the world, but on it depends the fact that man has a world at all."[5] Jacques Derrida writes:

> Thought requires *both* the principle of reason, the *arkhe* and the *anarchy*. Between the two, the difference of a breath or an accent, only the *enactment* of this "thought" can decide ... That decision is always risky, it always risks the worst. To claim to eliminate that risk by an institutional programme is quite simply to erect a barricade against the future.[6]

Exclusive claims that seek to suppress plurality, proclaimed through a set of words in a language other than that of religions against which they are directed, and which are untested in the forum of plurality and unwilling to risk the enactment of faith in a pluralistic society, erect a barrier against future possibilities. Such claims are insensitive to the accents that come from within the silence of the heart. They miss the mood of awe and reverence and silence before the Mystery of God and close the door of hope for mutual criticism and mutual enrichment.

The connection between the plurality of languages and the plurality of religions commits people irrevocably to a dialogical stance. It also demands a rejection of exclusiveness or monologue or one-way proclamations that seek to obliterate dialogue. That the fundamental character of the religiously plural world is dialogical and polymorphic and that mutual respect is essential for living and working together are perhaps the most significant elements in the new perceptions of religious pluralism today. There is a profound connection between the diversity of religions and the diversity of languages and symbols. Dialogue is indispensable to that open society which alone serves the cause of truth and demands "a principled hospitality to difference and variety in the cultural forums of the modern world."[7]

NEW PERCEPTIONS

There are more recent developments, particularly in the West, that contribute to new perceptions of religious pluralism. It is now claimed that in science there are no certainties, only probabilities. In historiography there are difficulties in the study of "facts" and their interpretations, particularly when it is other peoples' history that is being studied. "Salvation History" (*Heilsgeschichte*), which has been and still is the bedrock of exclusive claims in a religiously plural world, is being seriously questioned, not only by Western scholars, but also by Asian and African theologians who, rather than accept the history of Israel as the norm for all history, are looking for the theological significance of their own histories. Asian theologians have questioned the relevance of "Salvation History" to Asian life.[8]

Many scholars point out that biblical criticism does not offer any firm ground for concluding that Israel's history is the "unique" realm of God's revelation or for affirming that there is only one "normative" christology in the New Testament. It is now affirmed that in the New Testament there is "one Jesus but many Christologies," which means that any exclusive or normative claim on behalf of one particular christology does not seem to have the support of the New Testament.[9]

There is also a serious disarray in theological method in the West, which some describe as "the collapse of the house of authority." There is indeed a radical revolution in theological methodologies leading to the conclusion that no single method can claim normative authority over others, including those of other religions.[10] It would be foolish to think that this is the end of the theological enterprise. On the contrary, it may be a sign of its vitality in discarding the old and seeking the new. Christian theologians in Asia and Africa, rather than depend on the shifting sands of biblical criticism in the West or on their constantly changing theological methodologies which, in any case, seek to respond to *their* needs, are developing a plurality of hermeneutics and theological methods in their attempts to discover new ways of grasping the significance of God's revelation in Jesus Christ and its relation to religions and cultures surrounding them in their daily lives.[11] That in the contemporary world a plurality of theological methods is not only legitimate, but essential, is recognized by most Christians and their neighbors of other faiths.

All this, however, does not necessarily mean that plurality in itself is a good thing. Throughout history the diversities of language and religion have led to serious conflicts between people. There are indeed "demonic" possibilities within the structures of plurality. Different religious communities within particular countries and in the world have clashed with each other, resulting in immense human suffering. There are far too many examples of this, which should prevent any uncritical glorification of plurality. The Hindu–Buddhist–Jain conflicts during an earlier period of India's history, the Hindu–Muslim clashes which unfortunately recur even at present, and now the Hindu–Sikh tensions are some examples. The Christian relationship to the Jews throughout history, in which Jews suffered grievously, the Christian-Muslim struggles in the crusades and *jihad*, which have their echoes even to this day, are reminders of the conflict potentialities of religious plurality. To these must be added the possibilities of conflict within particular religious communities. For example, the Roman Catholic–Protestant conflict within Christianity and the Sunni–Shia within Islam. Plurality therefore cannot be set up as an unqualified alternative to exclusivism. In the forum of history, both exclusivism and pluralism have failed.

While these lessons of history should make one suspicious of any uncritical claims on behalf of plurality, there are at least two points to be noted in this connection. The first is that all too often what are described as *religious* riots are, in reality, *secular* conflicts in which religions are cunningly used for political and economic purposes. Recent studies in India on Hindu-Muslim and Hindu-Sikh riots have brought out this fact very convincingly.[12] The conflicts in West Asia are not religious conflicts, but the result of political and military interests in which religions — Jewish, Christian, and Muslim — have become mere pawns in the hands of the media and global power brokers.

Second, the peace potentialities within each religion have often provided resources to overcome these tensions, sometimes before the explosions took place, and almost always to alleviate the sufferings after the happenings. This is true not just of Christians but also of Hindus, Buddhists, and Muslims in many conflict situations. There are also many instances where people of one community have helped members of other communities in danger, in spite of serious threats to themselves.

Obviously, a critical principle needs to be developed in a multireligious situation, or plurality might degenerate into a sea of relativity in which different boats flounder aimlessly without rudders. Formerly, because of their isolation from one another, each religion developed its own criteria over *against* the others. Today, when people of different religions are drawn together in the global community as never before, this critical principle has to be developed *in relation* to one another. This has yet to happen. Exclusive claims then could have validity only within a community of faith because they are confessional statements and expressions of commitment and loyalty of a particular people in a particular historical and cultural situation.

Thus understood, pluralism has several values in the contemporary world. First, it provides spiritual and cultural resources for the survival of different people in their search for freedom, self-respect, and human dignity. When nations and peoples are politically dominated, economically exploited, and militarily intimidated, what else do they have for the survival of their spirit except their religions and cultures, which can never be taken away from them? Second, as Rajni Kothari, the alternative Nobel Prize winner in India, points out, a plurality of religions, cultures, ethnic groups, and languages can be a guarantee against fascism because it will resist the imposition of any "one and only" religion or ideology on all people.[13] Third, pluralism introduces an element of choice by providing alternative visions of reality and ways of life. John B. Chethimattam, an Indian Roman Catholic scholar, writes:

> Religious pluralism presents an opportunity to liberate the individual from the arbitrary burdens laid on him by his own particular religious traditions, even long after those particular customs and traditions have lost their purpose and meaning.[14]

Plurality emphasizes that the Mystery of God or Truth or *Dharma* is too profound to be exhausted by any particular apprehensions of it. The relative may try to define Truth, but it cannot confine Truth to its own definition.

Fourth, plurality provides multiple spiritual resources to tackle basic problems that have become global today. The articulation of faith in a technological age, the quest for life in the midst of threats of death, the search for hope in the midst of despair, and the longing for peace within the human heart—all these are problems of immense dimensions. The availability of many resources to tackle these problems should not be looked upon with suspicion but accepted with gratefulness.

AREAS OF THEOLOGICAL CONCERN

Christian responses to religious pluralism vary considerably. To many people in the West, what Knitter aptly describes as "a newly experienced reality"[15] comes as a *discovery* after previous attempts to ignore or regard it as an aberration to be overcome. To people in Asia and Africa, however, pluralism provides a source for the *recovery* of their own spiritual and cultural values after long centuries of suppression. People in monoreligious situations whose countries have recently become a little more pluralist are more sensitive to the perils rather than the promise of interreligious relationships. But there are other people to whom, for better or worse, living in multireligious societies has been a matter of daily experience for a few thousand years. Thus to talk about the "emergence" or the "discovery" of religious pluralism in India is like taking a beehive to a sugar plantation. Neighbors of other faiths are often suspicious of the newfound enthusiasm of people in the West for interreligious dialogues, often because of their doubt and uncertainty about the purpose and motives behind Western Christian initiatives. The response of neighbors of other faiths to religious pluralism and to interreligious dialogue, a topic to which little attention has been given so far, will be considered separately later on.

This diversity of responses is not just because of the East–West cultural divide or the North–South economic divide, although both influence the attitudes of different communities of faith toward one another. Neither is it because of the geographic distance between Europe and North America and Asia and Africa. The line that divides negative and positive responses cuts across these borders. Quite often, theological concerns and ideological assumptions get mixed up in the debate.

There are many Christians, both in the West and in the East, who are nervous, anxious, even fearful of the new perceptions of religious pluralism thrust upon them by the pressures of history. They disturb their inherited traditions and the secure and comfortable attitudes of exclusiveness and superiority. Questions of "Truth" and "truth claims" get mixed up in defense of unexamined assumptions. There are some who regard "a creeping religious pluralism" as a threat not only to the exclusive claims of Christianity but also to what is regarded as "the Christian character" of a country. Thus John R. Stott, discussing pluralism in Britain, rejects the attitudes of "imposition" and "laissez-faire," but advocates "a strategy of persuasion by argument."[16] In a religiously plural Britain today, he defends "a Christian bias" in English education on three grounds. First, the great majority of English residents are still nominally Christian. Second, Christianity can claim preferential treatment because it has received a testing, and a consequent acceptance, in the country. And third, Christianity is fundamental to Britain's cultural inheritance.[17] What the minority communities in Britain—Hindu, Buddhist, Muslim, Jewish, and Sikh—feel about this is not mentioned. But do not these arguments apply with equal force to Hinduism in India, Buddhism in Sri Lanka, and Judaism in Palestine—all of which have been living faiths in their respective countries for a longer period than Christianity in Britain? Why try to destabilize them in the name of Christian mission? In the global community, where the destinies of different peoples are so inextricably intertwined, is any one single community of faith justified in claiming preferential treatment?

There are others, however, who not only recognize the fact of pluralism but are enthusiastic about its possible consequences to Christianity itself. Some suggest that the present encounter of Christianity with other religions may be the beginnings of "a third reformation."[18] Others point out that the present Christian dialogue with people of other faiths may lead to "a new Church, not totally new, but genuinely new."[19] The reasons for such enthusiastic expectations may have to be examined more critically in the light of actual happenings, but they are worth noting. There are others who emphasize the urgent need to respond to these new perceptions. "Pluralism is not an ultimate concern. It is something more serious. It is an immediate concern," writes Tom Driver. "Pluralism is a demand laid upon us (Western, liberal Christians) brought upon us by our own history which has largely been one of universal colonialism."[20] That this new perception is not just because of historical pressures but also because of theological reasons is openly acknowledged by others. Heinrich Ott, the successor to Karl Barth in the University of Basel, writes:

> In the future of humankind, dialogue itself must become the qualified life-form of a global pluralism — a pluralism which rests not on mutual indifference, but is constantly focussed on the question of truth.[21]

There are others who point out that theological imperatives demand a reappraisal of religious pluralism today.

> The relativity of all religions and its doctrines, plus the re-emphasis on the width of God's love, plus the inwardness of faith and love have been the theological sources of this new assessment of plurality.[22]

All this means that an emerging Christian theology or theologies of religion should take into account the meaning and significance of the new perceptions of religious pluralism today. Such a theology cannot be developed from within one's own circle without an informed understanding of other faiths and without the insights gained through the experience of actual dialogues. To ask a question such as: "Is there salvation in other religions?" is theologically illegitimate in a pluralistic neighborhood. The whole debate is vitiated by the unexamined assumption that there is only one way of experiencing salvation and expressing it, and that is one's own way. How can such a question be valid when the predicaments from which salvation is sought in different cultural situations are so different and the state of being saved is experienced and expressed in so many different ways?

In a pluralistic situation, any theology of religion, whether initiated by Christians or by neighbors of other faiths, has to take into account five areas of theological concern. Briefly stated, these are: scripture, history, theology, community, and mission. These may even constitute an interconnected syllabus within a larger global framework for cooperative studies that need to be open to mutual criticism and mutual enrichment.

There has been considerable discussion on some of these matters; for example, on theology and christology, the church, and particularly mission. That most Christians are extremely sensitive to discussions on such topics as christology, scripture, and mission is to be expected. But neighbors of other faiths are also sensitive to criticisms of their faiths, their scriptures, and their communities. How can it be otherwise in a pluralistic society? Such sensitivity makes it difficult to identify and formulate new questions that arise as a consequence of new perceptions. But unless critical questions are raised and at least tentative answers suggested, religious communities in the world will be condemned to a life of sterile coexistence.

Further, most of the debate so far has been and still is within the circle of Christianity and limited to the Western conceptual framework, even when scholars of other faiths or Christians from Asia and Africa make a bit of contribution to the debate. There are many reasons for this, some historical and theological, some political and economic. One need not be unnecessarily critical about this, because there are obvious signs that the debate is becoming wider.

The question of scripture and scriptures is so important and so sensitive that it has hardly been discussed. Is the Bible the only "true" scripture in a situation where people of other faiths also have their own scriptures? If Christians extend the authority of the Bible to apply to others, should not neighbors of other faiths also have the same freedom to extend the authority of *their* scriptures to Christians? How does a text become a scripture? The whole notion of scriptural authority needs to be examined afresh.

If the history of a particular people is given selective treatment and endowed with theological significance, what about the histories of other people? Do the histories of people in India and China and Africa and the original inhabitants of North and South America have no theological significance whatsoever in the sight of God, the creator and parent of all humanity?

The term *theology* is usually assumed to be *Christian* theology. In a religiously pluralistic world, this is insensitive, perhaps even arrogant. It precludes any insights about God's dealings with humanity found in other religions from entering into the debate. Whether the Buddhists and *advaitic* Hindus can be brought under the umbrella of "theos" is an entirely different question that will be considered later. But here the question is whether one can talk about *theo*logy at all without, at some point, taking into account the profound insights about God's dealings in nature and with humanity to which other religions and other scriptures bear witness. The work of the Holy Spirit in creation and in the lives of our neighbors of other faiths and secular convictions has scarcely entered into the debate so far.

A community of faith gives its followers a sense of belonging and a feeling of identity based on shared beliefs, symbols, ethical norms, and a network of meanings and relationships that grow deeper and stronger with the passage of time. Because of long centuries of living together, sharing the joys and sorrows of human existence, religious communities have a special place in history. As the community grows and confronts other communities, the original vision may become distorted and identities hardened over against other communities. These conflicts and their consequences are well known.

In the new global context, the church has to redefine its identity and role in history in *relation* to, rather than over *against*, other communities. What, for example, is the relationship between the Buddhist *sangha*, the Christian *ecclesia*, and the Muslim *ummah* in the global community? When every religion has within it a dimension of universality, is it to be understood as the extension of one's own particularity overcoming other particularities? In what sense can the community we seek become "a community of communities" that can hold together unity and diversity in a creative tension rather than in debilitating conflict?

The phrase *a community of communities* was first used in recent years at the Colombo multilateral dialogue organized by the World Council of Churches in April 1974, which under its auspices brought together people of five different communities of faith—Hindu, Buddhist, Jewish, Muslim, and Christian—for the first time.[23]

This leads directly to the controversial question of mission. If the new perceptions of religious pluralism are taken seriously, then mission cannot be understood and practiced as a one-way proclamation by one particular community to the rest of the world. Christians indeed have "a story to tell to the nations." But do not neighbors of other faiths also have their own stories to tell the world? Mission cannot be seen as the numerical expansion of one particular religious community leading to a corresponding diminution of other communities. The word *mission* itself, because of its colonial associations, may have to be abandoned. If mission is understood as sharing in the continuing work of God (speaking in theistic terms), mending the brokenness of creation, overcoming the fragmentation of humanity, and healing the rift between humanity, nature, and God, then possibilities of cooperation should be welcome. Such cooperative efforts are already going on between different communities in some parts of the world. The church's mission, then, is not to seek its own expansion but to seek first the Kingdom of God, to promote and practice the values of justice and peace, truth, and love which have been decisively revealed to Christians in the life and work and death and resurrection of Jesus Christ.

The pressures of history and the theological imperatives of new perceptions of pluralism demand that Christians seek new relationships with people of other faiths. It would be unfortunate if Christians fail to meet this demand and transform it into an invitation to a pilgrimage.

2

The Other End of the Dialogue Bridge

What do neighbors of other faiths think of Christian initiatives in dialogue? It is easier to ask the question than to suggest an answer. The burdens of history; a lack of clarity in the mind of Christians about their motive and purpose in dialogue; the theological distance between Christianity and other religions; the manner in which the institutions of different religions are structured; and, more recently, the politicization of religions, which influences power relations within and between nations in the world, make this topic exceedingly difficult and complex. But unless some attempt is made by Christians to purify their motives in dialogue and to take into account the responses of neighbors of other faiths, what could become the beginnings of a pilgrimage is in danger of degenerating into a tourist expedition.

LIMITS OF CHRISTIAN-INITIATED DIALOGUES

It is necessary to set some limits to the inquiry. The time span is from Vatican II (*Nostra Aetate* 1965) and the very first initiative by the World Council of Churches to initiate an interreligious meeting with neighbors of other faiths (Ajaltoun 1970). In addition to these officially sponsored dialogues, there have been many meetings organized by Christian study centers in different countries, initiatives taken by departments of religion in universities mostly in North America, and meetings sponsored by reputed journals leading to carefully documented publications on major issues in interreligious relationships.[1] In all these the initiatives have invariably been Christian, although in recent years some meetings have been organized by others as well.[2]

There are several factors which shape the character of these Christian initiated dialogues. The selection of partners of other faiths is often arbitrary and their number very small. English is invariably the language of discourse, which means that only those scholars already westernized and familiar with the Western liberal vocabulary are able to participate in these meetings, to the total exclusion of perhaps more authentic scholars who operate in the original languages of their respective faiths: Hebrew, Sanskrit, Pali, Arabic, Chinese, and many modern languages of today.

Further, the Western conceptual framework, the formulation of the theme and its treatment, and the time limit set on speakers, which favors English mother-tongue participants, make it exceedingly difficult for people of other faiths to make effective contributions to the debate. Even more serious is the almost total emphasis on religious *ideas* to the exclusion, at least in earlier meetings, of religious *life*, symbols, spirituality, and other dimensions of worship so important to all religions. This has been so until recently. The general Protestant attitude has usually been to hurl accusations of "syncretism" the moment aspects of worship enter into the agenda of interreligious meetings. This remains true even to this day. Most Protestant theologians eager to discuss theological ideas suddenly become silent or aggressively negative when aspects of meditation or worship or symbols are mentioned by partners of other faiths.

Even more serious is the question of the motives and purpose behind Christian initiated dialogues. There is always the fear of hidden agendas. A Hindu friend invited to the very first interreligious meeting organized by the World Council of Churches rejected the invitation with the following words addressed to his Christian *bhai* (brother):

> Do not think that I am against dialogue ... On the contrary, I am fully convinced that dialogue is an essential part of human life, and therefore of religious life itself ... Yet, to be frank with you, there is something which makes me uneasy in the way in which you Christians are now trying so eagerly to enter into official and formal dialogue with us. Have you already forgotten that what you call "interfaith dialogue" is quite a new feature in your understanding and practice of Christianity? Until a few years ago, and often still today, your relations with us were confined, either to the merely social plane, or to preaching in order to convert us to your *dharma*? ... For all matters concerning *dharma* you were deadly against us, violently or stealthily according to cases. ... And the pity was that your attacks and derogatory remarks were founded in sheer ignorance of what we really are, or what we believe and worship.[3]

A more recent happening brings out both the power of Christian initiatives in dialogue and the sensitivity of neighbors of other faiths to them. This was the day of prayer at Assisi on October 27, 1986, initiated by the Pope, to which about fifty Christians and fifty leaders of other faiths were invited.[4]

The importance of this meeting and its implications for interreligious relationships cannot be overestimated. There are several reasons for this. First, it conferred *legitimacy* to Christian initiatives in interreligious dialogues. When the Pope himself initiates such a meeting and acts as the host, what higher authority do Catholics need? Second, it was seen as an event of *theological* significance. "An experience of this nature and import has a theological value that should be explored and that could shed light on the whole theology of dialogue."⁵ Third, Assisi was recognized as *"an act of dialogue* in the highest degree. To prayer, which was its climate and soul, were added other manifestations of contact, respect, mutual knowledge ... This is most likely the beginning of new relationships on the universal and the local levels." ⁶ Fourth, it emphasized the *religious* nature of peace and, in doing so, recognized that not just the Christian, but other religions also have a serious contribution to make to the content and quest for peace. There is "a religious dimension to peace that is irreplaceable and essential, that is born in the heart of man as the Oriental religions insist, that is a gift of God as the monotheistic religions insist."⁷

One must be careful in assessing the significance of contemporary ecumenical events for the future, but the far-reaching importance of this event should be clear to all people committed to the promise of interreligious dialogues in a pluralistic world. And yet, as one seeks to discover what neighbors of other faiths "feel" and think about such events, two points on which neighbors have commented should be noted. One is the Pope's insistence on the centrality of Christ to the whole world as the *only* source of peace. "To one and all she [the church] proclaims that Christ is the centre of the created world and history. Precisely because Christ is the centre of the whole world and of history, and because no one can come to the Father except through Him (John 14:6), we approach the other religions in an attitude of sincere respect and of fervent witness to Christ in whom we believe."⁸ In his concluding address to all the religious leaders assembled at Assisi, the Pope said, "I profess here anew my conviction, shared by all Christians, that in Jesus Christ, as the Saviour of all, true peace is to be found 'peace to those who are far off and peace to those who are near'" (Ephesians 2:17). And further, "I humbly repeat here my own conviction: peace bears the name of Jesus Christ."⁹

Neighbors of other faiths also ask humbly, and sometimes not so humbly: What about *our* centers and *our* names? For example, would not the Buddhists be justified in saying that *for them*, the Buddha, born five centuries earlier than Jesus of Nazareth, is the name and center of peace and nonviolence? Is not Christianity connected with far more wars and violence in history than Buddhism?

The second point has caused even more disquiet to neighbors of other faiths, particularly because they accepted in good faith the invitation to Assisi to *pray together* for peace. And yet, when the time came to pray together, it was discovered that Christians had to go to one place to pray and those of other faiths to another. The geographical separation became a symbol of spiritual separation. In his speech on October 22, the Pope described the formula chosen for the Assisi gathering as "being together to pray. Certainly we cannot 'pray together,' namely to make a common prayer, but we can be present while others pray."[10]

There was considerable discussion in India on this point. Dom Bede Griffiths wrote that persons of different beliefs can pray together "because all prayer goes not to the image or the concept, but to the Holy Mystery."[11] If people of different faiths cannot pray together, why were they invited to pray together? The slippery subtleties of the English language may be useful in drafting political treaties, but they are not always helpful in interreligious meetings.

If the essential purpose was to pray together, another writer asked, why was the Dalai Lama invited? At a reception given him at Loretto Convent, in answer to a pointed question, the Dalai Lama made it clear that prayer is unnecessary to Buddhists when he said, "There is no need for God." This raises a double question: In the first place, why was he invited at all to a prayer meeting? Second, if he does not believe in prayer, why did he accept the invitation?

Swami Kulandaiswami drew attention to the handful of Hindus present at Assisi and quoted some important Hindu leaders as saying, "We are not going to be part of any prayer propaganda. Every day we offer *puja* and pray for peace. We never pray along with other religions. We fully believe in the power of our own religion."[12]

Let it be clear that these observations in no way minimize the great importance of this historic event to future relations between Christians and neighbors of other faiths. But since the subject under discussion is our neighbors' response to Christian initiatives, commitment to the dialogical principle demands that Christians should at least be sensitive to and listen to the observations that come out of the depths of others' hearts and minds.

JEWISH HESITATIONS AND FEARS

To give a systematic and comprehensive account of the response of neighbors of other faiths to Christian initiatives during these decades is an impossible task. No single individual scholar today has the scholarly information on so many religions, breadth of experience, depth of understanding, openness of mind, and sensitivity of heart necessary for the task. All that is attempted here is to offer some glimpses into our neighbors' minds and hearts as they speak out, which, because they are mostly guests, they do not always do. Sometimes their silences have to be listened to, not so much to discuss religious ideas as to share insights into the mystery of Truth. The point of view here will be that of an Indian Christian theologian with more than a decade of ecumenical experience organizing interreligious meetings and theological reflection on them. In addition, there is also my lifelong experience of living together with neighbors of other faiths in India.

The remarks here are limited to Jewish and Muslim on the one hand and Hindu and Buddhist on the other. To widen the scope would lead to an impossible task. Even as it is, it is far too complex. The Jewish and the Hindu are at two poles, quite different from each other in spiritual experience, historic understanding, and theological distance from Christianity, but they both converge in rejecting the exclusive claims of Christianity. While Jews, because of their total commitment to the monotheistic faith, find it impossible to accept the notion of Jesus of Nazareth as "God," many Hindus do not find it difficult to acknowledge the divinity of Christ. Thus the Jewish and Hindu attitudes bring out the fundamental theological and christological issues in their dialogues with Christians more sharply than any other. This is the reason why more attention is paid to them here.

The Jewish and Muslim responses to Christians are different from the Hindu and Buddhist. Historical factors, theological concerns, and the power relationships between nations involved are different. The Jewish question is primarily a matter for Christians in the West. Christians in Asia and Africa cannot ignore this matter, however, because although they are not historically involved in Western Christian persecution of the Jewish people, Christian life anywhere is spiritually and theologically bound up with the heritage of the people of Israel.[13] After the tragedy of the Holocaust and the establishment of the Jewish state, Christian-Jewish relationships can never be the same as they were in the previous centuries. It is necessary to distinguish between the Jewish people and the State of Israel. It may even be necessary for Christians in Asia and Africa to give more attention to Jewish interpretations of the Hebrew scriptures, rather than be so exclusively dependent on Western Christian scholarship of the "Old" Testament. Uncritical national zeal should not prevent Asian and African Christians from taking seriously the uncompromising emphasis of the Jewish faith on the one God, the creator of all and the Lord of all history.

It is impossible to forget that for nearly two thousand years Western Christianity has tried every means at its disposal to convert the Jews. The question of the Messiah has always divided Jews and Christians. In his book *Brother Jesus*, Schalom Ben Chorin writes, "The faith of Jesus unites us, but faith in Jesus divides us."[14] The continuation of the Jews as a people in spite of prolonged and cruel persecutions, and the persistence of their faith in history in spite of the emergence of Christianity and Islam, are regarded by Jews and many Christians as a question mark against the Christian and Muslim claims of finality. To the Jews, remarks Arthur A. Cohen, "it is as much a mystery that Christianity survived and triumphed as it is a mystery for Christianity that the unconverted Jew persists."[15]

Martin Buber discovers the roots of Jewish continuity not in the tenacity of the Jewish people but in "the reality of the space between God and ourselves." In a deeply moving passage he writes, "And we know that precisely here, in this reality, we have not been repudiated by God, that in this discipline and chastisement, God's hand holds on to us and does not let us go, holds us into this fire and does not let us fail."[16] On the christological claims of the church, Buber goes on to say, "We are incapable of holding God to any one manner of revelation. We are prevented from regarding any unique event as a definitive revelation of God, prevented by that word from the burning bush: 'I will be what I will be' (Exodus 4:14) — that is, in effect, I will exist as I will exist at any given time."[17] The concluding sentence of the essay, itself a paraphrase of the Midrash (Exodus Rabbi XIX, Sifra on Leviticus 18:5) is as follows: "The gates of God are open to all. The Christian need not go via Judaism, nor Judaism via Christianity in order to enter into God."[18] There is not much evidence that Christendom has been particularly sensitive to this Jewish desire to be left alone that seems to be less a request for tolerance than a conviction born of the experience of being sustained by God in their sufferings through the centuries.

There are Jews and Christians in Europe and North America who strongly feel that Israel and the church have different callings, that the tension between them cannot be resolved in history and the two covenants should be recognized as continuing in history till the end of time.[19] Moltmann even suggests that the Jewish concern in the World Council of Churches should be in Faith and Order rather than in Dialogue. On the occasion of the fiftieth anniversary of Faith and Order Moltmann said, "It would be a great step forward for the ecumenical movement if the Churches' conversations with Israel were conducted in the framework of Faith and Order rather than in Dialogue with Living Faiths and Ideologies."[20] The theological implications of this and similar statements are more far reaching than is sometimes recognized.

The Jews emphasize that the providence of God remains a Mystery, "perhaps the only authentic mystery for time and history" and that "the unbelief of Israel in Jesus as the Christ is not unbelief in God."[21] There is a hope, a patient waiting for the return of Christendom to the synagogue, for it is claimed that "there is no *shlamut*, no perfection until Christianity is reunited with Israel, until it has learned to transcend the Son to the Father, until it too shall have learned to say Lord and Lord alone, having been instructed to do so by the Son."[22] The Christian tendency to regard universality as the extension of its own particularity is vehemently rejected by Jews because it leads to the emptying of all other particularities. Eugene B. Borowitz argues that the notion of exclusivism based on particularity should be applied only within the limits of one's own community of faith because to discredit the claims of other religions is to discredit a universal God. Fullness of truth can come only at the eschatological redemption of all history. Until then all truth claims should be regarded as "interim and provisional."[23]

Both the Vatican and the World Council of Churches have separate departments for Christian-Jewish relations, the former through its Commission for Religious Relations with the Jews and the latter through the

Church's Committee for the Jewish People (CCJP) in the Dialogue subunit. The Jews have their own committee: the International Jewish Committee on Interreligious Consultations (IJCIC). It thus becomes officially possible to listen to Jewish responses to Christian initiatives.

When the World Council of Churches announced its theme for its 1983 Vancouver Assembly—"Jesus Christ: the Life of the World"—the Jews immediately reacted to its formulation. They made three points in this connection. First, they said,

> It is impossible for us to ignore the possibility that the strong emphasis on Jesus Christ as *'the* life of the world' could make real dialogue with people of other living faiths more difficult. The way the theme is formulated could give rise to the problematic notion that what Christians regard as a meaningful and fulfilled life begins with Jesus Christ and Him alone.

Second, they pointed out that the danger implicit in the universal way the theme was formulated was "the danger of an imperial claim for the Christian religion." Third, they wondered whether "this way of formulating the theme might not lead to a treatment of all the specific themes on the Vancouver agenda in a way which excludes the non-Christians."[24]

This last concern was also expressed by Ellen Flesseman-van Leer, a noted Christian theologian from Holland, herself having roots in the Jewish heritage. When referring to the decision to invite guests of other faiths to the assembly, she wrote, "Everything considered, it seems to me that the more the assembly concentrates on its Christological central theme, the more the guests will be made to feel outsiders."[25]

The suspicion that dialogues may be used for purposes of Christian mission is an everpresent fear among neighbors of other faiths. This is particularly true of the Jews, who have been victims of Christian mission for a longer time than any other people. Abraham J. Heschel observes:

> The mission to the Jews is a call to individual Jews to betray the fellowship, the dignity, the sacred history of their people. Many Christians do not seem to comprehend what is morally and spiritually involved in supporting such activities. We are Jews as we are men. The alternative to our existence as Jews is spiritual suicide, extinction. It is not a change into something else. Judaism has allies, no substitutes.[26]

More recently, commenting on the statements by the United Church of Christ and the Presbyterian Church in the U.S.A., Rabbi Wolf said:

> I have no complaint to register against conversionist attempts, always provided that I have the unqualified right and opportunity to show

Christians that incarnationalism and premature messianism are very dangerous to the world. . . . I recommend to Christians that they think a lot less about us, write less, apologise less and, in sum, get about their own business of saving Christians from Christianity.[27]

MUSLIM RESPONSES AND INITIATIVES

The Muslim response to Christian initiated dialogue is perhaps more influenced by historical memories, theological controversies, and power relations between nations—particularly in West Asia today—than any other response. Although during the early sixties Muslims were most reluctant to enter into any dialogue with Christians, today new factors have enabled them to relate to Western Christians in a more confident manner and to initiate dialogues with Christians on their own terms. There are varieties of Muslim response, depending on the historic and cultural contexts Muslims find themselves in today. For example, the attitudes of Muslims toward other religions are different in countries like India and Indonesia than in Pakistan and Bangladesh and the Muslim countries of West Asia. Further, in Western countries where Muslim communities live as citizens, but as religious minorities, their attitudes are different than those of Muslims who are the majority in Islamic states.

There is a strong feeling that the religious ferment within Islam today, which is primarily a grass-roots phenomenon sparked by disillusionment with Western values and way of life, is wrongly labeled by the Western media as "militancy" and "fundamentalism." It ignores the tension between popular Islam and establishment Islam in many countries and, at the same time, forgets "fundamentalist" movements within Judaism, Christianity, and Hinduism. The media tends to condemn not only fundamentalism but Islam itself.[28] Many Muslims feel, however, that fundamentalism is a way of expressing confidence in Islam at a time of moral and religious confusion. They say:

> At a time when Marxism is so debilitated that it is being shored up by capitalism, when Christianity lacks much of the missionary fire that once drove it, when Maoism is all but entombed with its founder and when democracy sounds only a muted appeal to much of the world, Islamic fundamentalism stands out as the movement on the march.[29]

Whether such a judgment on other religions and ideologies is justified or not, this confidence in the power of Islam is growing among Muslims. It is claimed that the media distortion of Islamic resurgence leads to four serious consequences. First, it blurs the distinction between "militancy" and "fundamentalism," and so unnecessarily provokes Muslims. Second, it arouses suspicion against Islam and Muslims, presenting them as a destabilizing force in society. Third, it weakens the truly fundamentalist, that is those who wish to emphasize the basic values of Islam — the secular, nationalist, and progressive people within Islam. And fourth, it confers legitimacy and a false sense of importance to the militants.[30]

Muslims do admit that there are excesses in the Islamic revival today, but they point out that such symptoms are to be found among other religious communities as well, including the Christian. Abdulla Omar Naseef, the Secretary-General of the Makkah-based World Muslim League, writes:

> The ferment that you witness in the world of Islam today and which has been variously described as Muslim resurgence or Islamic revival, is but a process by which Muslims in different parts of the world are asserting the Islamicity of their lives and rededicating themselves to the realization of the values of Islam in all walks of life. As people of faith and as groups equally committed to the vision of better life, Muslims expect Christians and Jews, above all others, to empathise with their aspirations and to seek to grasp the real impulse behind their stirrings for a new world order based on divine submission.[31]

This plea has not always been heeded by neighbors of other faiths with the seriousness and sensitivity it demands.

A significant response to Christian initiatives is the Muslim attempt to work out a theology of dialogue based on Islam, even as Christians are seeking to develop a Christian theology of dialogue. There are genuine efforts to make room for all "good people" in other communities of faith within the household of God, particularly the family of Abraham. A Muslim theology of interreligious dialogue, it is claimed, opens the way for peaceful coexistence between people of different faiths in the world. It is pointed out that this is based on four principles: peace, justice, negotiation, and kindness toward those who are not Muslims.[32] It is affirmed that the Qur'an itself offers clear guidelines to Muslims for interreligious dialogue, namely, *al-qist* (equity), *al-adl* (justice), and *al-birr* (kindness).[33]

On two questions that constantly disturb Christian–Muslim relations in dialogue — the exclusive claims based on Jesus Christ and Christian mission — Muslims make theological comments. Islam recognizes Jesus and his divine mission but has always been severely critical of incarnation and trinitarianism. The Qur'an assigns to Jesus the position of a prophet, God's Word and Divine Spirit, but withholds the conception of God-human relationship. Only God is infinite; all creatures are finite. God alone is the measurer (*Quadir*), while everything else is the measured (*maqdur*). Therefore, exclusive claims are inadmissible. Fazlur Rahman writes:

> The Qur'an's reply to these exclusive claims and claims of proprietorship over God's guidance is absolutely unequivocal: Guidance is

not the function of communities but of God and good people, and *no* community may lay claims to be uniquely guided and elected.[34]

Since both Islam and Christianity make claims that exclude each other, and since both are committed to world mission, the practice of mission has been, and still is, a serious area of tension and conflict. This is particularly true today, when Muslim countries are spending enormous amounts of money for the propagation of Islam even as, it is pointed out, during the colonial period Christianity did the same, supported by political domination and military power.

The situation is likely to become more tense in African countries and in Western countries where there are Muslim communities living as citizens. In the context of living together in multireligious societies, it is claimed that Islamic *Da'wah* (not mission) is "a witness that each Muslim is required to present in the practice of his daily life."[35] As regards the practice of *Da'wah*, the two often-quoted verses from the Qur'an are: "There shall be no coercion in Islam" (II:256) and "Reason with them in the most kindly manner" (XVI:25). Because of the shared relationship between people of the book, dialogue, it is claimed, can become "a pristine invitation for all time" (III:64) to "join hands in promoting the worship of One God and excel each other in doing his duty to mankind."[36]

To what extent this principle operates in Islamic countries where people of other faiths live as minorities and in countries where people of other faiths are in the majority and Muslims are minorities remains to be seen. Although for academic reasons it is possible to talk of Christian–Jewish and Christian–Muslim relations separately, in actual practice people of these three faiths cannot be separated, because their lives are inextricably bound up, historically, theologically, and spiritually, no less than in the political relationship among the nations.

HINDU MODELS OF DIALOGUE

The Christian–Hindu–Buddhist relationships are more recent in history and take place in a very different political and theological climate than the Christian–Jewish–Muslim. This is to be expected. Any discussion of Hindu response to Christianity has to take into account what is happening in India.

At the same time today, one should also refer to what may be called the Hindu "diaspora," the Hindu communities living in Britain, Europe, and North America as well as in the Caribbean and several countries of Africa. They are less inhibited by the constraints of orthodoxy and the caste system that are prevalent in the mother country, but have retained their religious and cultural identity as Hindus. Living as minorities in countries with large Christian majorities, it is in their interests to enter into dialogue with Christians. As citizens of the country, businesspeople, scientists, teachers, and average folk contributing to the service and values of society, they are making significant contribution to the total life of the community. Their contribution to interreligious relations in the community and to the making of Hindu theologies of religion should not be ignored.

Developments in India since political independence (1947) have made Hindu relations to people of other faiths, particularly to Muslims and Christians, far more difficult and complex. Care should be taken not to exaggerate or oversimplify these highly complex matters. Political scientists point out that there is among Hindus today a pan-Indian Hindu assertiveness, a newfound confidence in the enduring strength of the Hindu *dharma*, the continuity of the Hindu religious tradition and the power of its massive social, economic and political resources.

Sometimes Indian nationalism and the Hindu *dharma* are combined, leading to aggressive reactions against Muslims and Christians. This "neo-nationalism" asserts itself in four different ways. First, attempts are being made to widen its social base. It is now claimed that untouchability is not part of Hinduism, thus paving the way to an uneasy alliance with other castes. Second, Hindu society is becoming increasingly conscious of its Hindu identity, not just on religious, but also on political and ideological levels. Being the majority community in a democratic setup, they are politically powerful. Third, the religious and cultural elements are now combined with the vast human resources of the majority community to assert its importance to the country. The "pampering" of minorities such as Muslims, Christians, and Sikhs is now regarded as grave injustice to the majority community. Fourth, Hindu neonationalism, conscious of its economic strength and political power, challenges the secular character of the Indian state.[37] The consequences of any weakening of the secular character of the state will be disastrous for interreligious relationships, particularly to Muslims and Christians. Karan Singh, a former cabinet minister and president of the Hindu Virat Samaj, declared at a public meeting: "While having goodwill for all religions as enjoined by its scriptures, Hinduism would no longer remain a passive spectator to hostile incursions upon it ... it will act with dignity, self-confidence and courage ..."[38] Nirmal Mukarji, a former Union Cabinet Secretary, now a professor at the Centre of Policy Research at New Delhi, remarks that Hindus are "a majority community with a minority complex." But he believes they have to get rid of this way of thinking because, since they constitute 82.7 percent of the population (1985) and command enormous material and other resources, no other community can "shape the destiny of the nation the way Hindus alone can." He calls for a new ordering of relationships recognizing that minorities cannot be assimilated but need to be accommodated.

> Not unless Hindus accept the logic inherent in a plural society, that each group must have scope to express its identity in social and cultural terms, of course, within an integrated political and economic structure, and that strategies of assimilation must give way to those

of accommodation, can progressive change begin to take place in Hindu society.[39]

Nevertheless, there are others who shape the opinions and attitudes of millions of Hindus: the Arya Samaj, the Rashtriya Svayam Sevak Sang, the Rama Krishna Mission, the Sarva Seva Sangh, and many swamijis of established Hindu *maths*, etc., who feel that both Islam and Christianity are indeed threats to the continuation of the Hindu *dharma*. The Viswa Hindu Parishad proclaims that "the very survival of the Hindu way of life is in danger."[40] At a three-day conference of religions at Tirupathi, a well-known pilgrim center, Swami Chinmayananda pointed out that Hindus constitute 82 percent of the population of India and that when 82 percent of a people are seeking their religious and cultural revival, "it is not *communal*, but *national*." He went on to say, "Hindu strength is national strength and Hindu revival is national revival. There are only two communities in India today: Those who *are* Hindus and those who *were* Hindus. The poor, the sick, the diseased and the destitute constitute the minorities."[41]

Reference is made to this rather aggressive and negative reaction of Hindus to emphasize the mood of "the angry Hindu" toward Muslims, Christians, and today, unfortunately, the Sikhs as well. However, this does not mean that they are unwilling to enter into serious dialogue with Christians. They do so not only in India, but also in international meetings. Some of their religious and political leaders participate in world interreligious conferences to put forward their views with clarity and firmness. There are many others who are deeply concerned with the spiritual and cultural dimensions of religious life lived pluralistically in India and elsewhere and, through participation in carefully prepared interreligious meetings, seek to explore possibilities of growth and enrichment. Some seek resources from within Hinduism itself for meaningful interreligious relationships.

In Britain, Canada, and the United States, Hindus actively participate in such gatherings. In India the Protestants who were active in this area in the sixties are now hardly conscious of the need to continue such dialogues. The priorities of the Protestant Church in India seem to be different. But the Roman Catholic Church has officially established a secretariat for dialogue with a fulltime secretary under the Catholic Bishops' Conference in India. The Jesuits have six interreligious centers.[42] In these and other centers there are many "live-in" sessions when Hindus and Christians live together for a period, sharing religious life.

The right-wing Hindu negative reaction and the more positive response of other Hindus to Christian initiatives all over the world are both mentioned here, lest it be misunderstood that such dialogues are smooth and easy. There are Hindus, both among those in India and in the "diaspora," who are seriously concerned with the tensions and conflicts in pluralistic societies and who, recognizing that the reasons for such a situation go deeper than economics and politics, seek spiritual and theological resources within their traditions to make a more enduring contribution to life together in a pluralistic world.

Reference is made here to just a few individual Hindus from different Hindu *Sampradayas* (traditions) from India and the "diaspora" who are among many making serious efforts in this direction. V. A. Devasenapathi was for many years a professor at the Centre for Advance Studies in Hinduism, Madras, India (now Radhakrishnan Centre for the Study of Hinduism). Anantanand Rambachan, from the Caribbean, has studied in Britain. K. L. Seshagiri Rao and K. R. Sundararajan have both spent many years studying and teaching in the universities of India and have also studied at Harvard. All are personally known to the author for many years and have participated in many national and international dialogues.

Devasenapathi rejects all exclusive claims and calls for harmony between religions, but gives it a different theological twist in his position, which is based on his own tradition (*Shaiva Siddhanta*). He suggests the model of a staircase with one's own tradition as the highest step.[43] The highest step, however, is not thought of in terms of theological distance or spiritual superiority but in terms of commitment. Unless one stands at the highest step of one's own staircase, one cannot see or converse with others who are standing on their own highest steps. Only thus can differences be seen as "unique" for each particular tradition.

Rambachan has the courage to be critical of his own Hindu tradition, particularly as represented by Swami Vivekananda, who, in rejecting exclusivism, tries to fit all religions into his own *advaitic* conceptual framework. Rambachan makes two points against Swami Vivekananda. First, his position "eliminates critical evaluation of religious doctrine and practice and could become a sanction for that which is manifestly cruel, irrational and absurd." Second, arguing that "all religions are true, and that religious growth is not from error to truth, but from lower to higher truth," consigns religions other than the *advaita* to the lower levels. Such a view of religions cannot provide a basis for dialogue at the present time.[44]

Seshagiri Rao suggests that the two well-known Hindu principles of *adhikara* (spiritual competence) and *ishta devata* (chosen form of deity) may provide the basis for a Hindu theology of dialogue. Each tradition—in this case each religion in a pluralistic society—is "unique" because it fits the spiritual competence of the people who have chosen to be committed to it alone and not to the others. This position makes it possible, according to him, for "each tradition to open up a new spiritual horizon hospitable to the faiths of other people."[45]

A more carefully worked out framework for interreligious dialogue is suggested by Sundararajan, who argues that in the long history of Hinduism and its relationships with other religions there are resources that can make a *possible* contribution to a meaningful and constructive Hindu theology of dialogue.[46] During the centuries Hindus had to deal with not only different viewpoints within their own family traditions, but also with such religions as Buddhism and Jainism and, much later, with Islam, Christianity, and Sikhism.

Sundararajan's contribution to the Hindu theology of dialogue lies in the fact that he critically relates two models within the Hindu tradition, which he describes as "the closed-border model" and "the border-crossing model." The closed-border model is based on the *svadharma* (one's own way) principle. This provides no *religious* basis for interreligious dialogue, except perhaps intellectual curiosity. The border-crossing model looks promising, but in actual Hindu practice, according to Sundararajan, it merely co-opts or appropriates the others into its own system. In the process of crossing the border, "efforts are made to erase the boundary lines, to eradicate the distinctiveness and identity of the area thus appropriated. It is similar to a situation in which one claims a territory that has belonged to somebody else as one's own, and now one refuses even to acknowledge the fact of previous ownership of the territory."[47] Some examples are the way in which Hindus have tried to appropriate the Buddha and, in more recent times, to indigenize Jesus Christ. Sundararajan points out that this "imperialistic direction" of the border-crossing model makes it inadequate for interreligious dialogue. One does not always find this self-critical mood among those who claim to cross the border, an expedition which often amounts to raids for bringing captives into the fold.

What then is the value of these models? Sundararajan claims that bringing together the positive dimensions of these two models makes a contribution to a Hindu theology of dialogue. The closed-border model implies "the need for one's rootedness in one's own tradition" in order to be a participant in interreligious dialogues. The *svadharma* principle emphasizes the need for commitment to one's own faith. The border-crossing model indicates that unless one is willing to step out of one's own territory, there is no way of expanding one's vision and deepening one's self-understanding. But crossing the border can happen only through consent, and then it could even lead to "common zones" which could be shared by more than one party so that one could become a "welcome explorer" rather than an "unwanted intruder." "It is in the active interaction of these two models," concludes Sundararajan, "that I see the preparedness of Hindus for interreligious dialogue."[48]

BUDDHIST ATTITUDES

In spite of the theological distance between Buddhism and Christianity and the difficulties in power relations, Buddhist–Christian dialogues are going on at local, national, and international levels. In Japan, Thailand, Sri Lanka, and India and in Britain, Europe, and North America, where small communities of Buddhists are settled, it is obviously necessary for such meetings for the sake of harmonious relations in the larger community. In the United States, where for some time there was considerable interest in

Zen, academic dialogues between Christian and Buddhist teachers are increasing. In some ways these are a continuation of the historical encounter between Western Christianity and Buddhism, but now with a difference, because Buddhists do not always respond to the prepared agenda but make their own points during the debate.

Some observations on the different Buddhist responses to Christian initiatives may be made here. There are some who feel that Christian–Buddhist dialogues are extremely difficult. Yagi Sei'chi writes of "An Unhappy Dialogue" because of what he describes as "the problem of reversibility and irreversibility between God and human beings, Buddhists see reversibility in every relationship, i.e., mutual conditioning."[49] This, of course, refers to theological difficulties.

Other Buddhists are constantly on the alert to avoid being caught in the "trap" of being transported into a basically Western conceptual framework and being subtly persuaded to answer Western Christian questions.[50] For example, among the questions posed by a Western scholar to Buddhists are the following: Does Buddhism have anything corresponding to the Christian faith's hope of the total transformation of nature? What does Buddhism have to say about the overcoming of death, outside of the belief in an absolutely transcendent divine act of resurrection?[51] Why should Buddhists answer these Western Christian questions, which make no sense in the Buddhist context? Why shouldn't Christians answer Buddhist questions on creation, for example? Notto R. Thelle reports that when he went to a Zen master to study Zen, the master asked him bluntly, "Why do you have to study Zen when you have your own prayer and contemplation? The real question is that of being. All your speculations about Buddhism and Christianity separate you from the very basic and simple fact of being."[52]

This does not, however, lead to any hesitation on the part of Buddhists to enter into dialogue. On the contrary, recognizing that today all people, whether Buddhist or Christian, are faced with global problems, and being confident that within itself Buddhism has resources to meet these problems, they seek to make their own contribution toward the search for answers. Mahinda Palihawadana of Sri Lanka, who has taken part in many ecumenical dialogues, regards himself "as one being born and bred in an environment that is happy to regard itself as Buddhist, and as one who is happy to be the product of such an environment," thus participating in such dialogues with total commitment to the Buddhist *dharma*, emphasizing that respect for other *dharmas* and the need to listen to others have always been marks of Buddhism in a pluralistic world.[53] The Buddhist response to Christian initiated dialogues is not one of confrontation and controversy, but of responsible participation in the conviction that the message of the Buddha has a distinctive contribution to make to the world today. It is suggested that this contribution is twofold: first toward the quest for peace, and second for a more responsible understanding of the relation between humanity and nature. In recent dialogues several Buddhist participants have stressed these matters.

Peace is not just the consequence of a just sharing of economic resources or of adjustments in the power relationships between people. These are indeed important, and Buddhists are involved in sociopolitical activities to bring about changes in unjust social structures.[54] But without an inner revolution, without rejecting greed and hatred from the human heart, and without a liberation from the desire to exercise power over others, there can be no inner harmony or justice in society. The Buddha himself emphasized this and suggested ways of achieving inner peace and tranquility, even though he also worked for the elimination of the social inequalities of the caste system.[55] At an international congress of Buddhists in Turin, Italy, September 1987, about three hundred participants came together "to teach, organise and spread the lessons of the *dharma* to respond to the needs of a troubled world."[56] Among other matters the meeting emphasized that Buddhists should take "the role of the peacemaker in Europe" and that Buddhists and Christians "must learn to share a universal peace."

Equally important is the confident participation of Buddhists in dialogues touching the questions of faith and science, technology, peace, and justice. The negative criticism of Christians that Buddhists have no doctrine of God or creation is now claimed to be its strength, because it is "the critical-rational temper" of Buddhism "which is the evident common denominator between Buddhism and science and modern sociopolitical systems like Marxism." In Buddhism there is no notion of the conquest or domination of nature. Its doctrine of "conditioned genesis," it is claimed, provides a clear analysis of the existential predicament of the human situation of disease, decay and death, and also shows a way out. By rejecting the notion of creation in time, Buddhism originated basically as a human enterprise, and this makes it well suited to enter into discussions with scientists and secular people on the question of humanity's relation to nature.[57]

At the 1979 world conference on "Faith, Science and the Future" held at the Massachusetts Institute of Technology, U.S.A., in which nearly nine hundred delegates participated, a few neighbors of other faiths also made a modest contribution. Two Buddhists, one from Sri Lanka and one from Japan, presented their papers to the conference.[58] Both in the plenary debate and group sessions, some of the scientists expressed considerable interest in the Buddhist presentations. The Buddhists claimed that the climate Buddhism creates, that is, its critical rational temper that does not depend on any external source outside the human, is favorable to the scientific enterprise. However, their objection to technology was twofold: first, the way its products are turned out, advertised, and distributed traps human beings in greed and pride of possession; and second, the speed of technological progress is so fast that human consciousness does not have enough time to cope with its complexities.

In countries where it is dominant, Buddhism reacts against science and technology because they affect the *religious* quality of Buddhist life. Palihawadana points out that "... more than science itself, more than the nature of its methodology and its logic, it is the creeping materialism of new life styles that has been cutting into both the visible cultural fabric and even the intangible spiritual content of Buddhist religiousness."[59] It is not claimed that Buddhism has the answer to modern problems raised by science. No religion today can claim to have the *only* answer to such complex questions raised by the confrontation of faith and science, but in interreligious dialogues Buddhists plead that their resources should not be brushed aside in favor of the Western–Jewish–Christian tradition.[60]

CHRISTIANS: TEACHERS OR LEARNERS?

This survey of some selected responses of neighbors of other faiths to Christian initiated dialogues indicates, in spite of the fact that it cannot be systematic and comprehensive, that there is discernible ferment where people of different religions meet, more so in the world today than at any other time in history. It also makes it clear that these are not, and cannot be, just *religious* dialogues, even though efforts are sometimes made to limit discussions to theological questions. This is because political, economic, social, and cultural factors profoundly influence interreligious relationships. It is not *ideas*, but *people*, not religious systems, but living faiths, that are involved here. Unless this fact is recognized and accepted openly, the ability of interreligious dialogues to change human relationships in the global community will be minimal.

There is a further point Christians should take seriously: What have Christians *learned* through these dialogues? How do the insights gained through these meetings affect the theological expression of the Christian faith in a pluralistic world today, and in what ways do the life-style and attitude of Christians change toward neighbors of other faiths as a consequence of these accumulated experiences? Are interreligious dialogues meant to discover a more refined missionary thrust into the religious homes of their neighbors? Are they meant to sharpen the Christian profile in the pluralistic world? In interreligious dialogues is it the general Christian tendency to give rather than to receive, to speak rather than to listen, to teach rather than to learn? Tom Driver points out that "the history of Christianity is, by and large, one of not listening to followers of other spiritual roads. On the contrary it has largely been a history of combating, to the death if necessary, those who worship 'other gods'. . . the crusading mentality among western Christians is far from dead. . . ."[61]

The ferment at the intersection where people of different faiths meet in the global community, and the different kinds of response by neighbors of other faiths to Christian initiatives also indicate that the long period during which religions developed in isolation is coming to an end. A new period in global consciousness, in which different religious communities have a significant part to play, is emerging. The signs are already there, and what is needed is the spirit of discernment to see and interpret these signs for the future of humanity. In India, for example, even when it appears that because of the politicization of religions, tensions between different religious communities are growing, there are signs that the traffic across the borders is also increasing in order to build communities of compassion in the midst of cruelty, islands of hope in an ocean of despair.

The verdict that Western Christians seldom learn anything through these dialogues seems to be rather harsh, for there are many who through the years have changed their stance and made deliberate efforts to relate themselves positively to neighbors of other faiths, at times even admitting the shortcomings of a previous era. This is true not just of individuals but of official bodies as well. These may indeed be few, but they should not be forgotten, because they are signs of hope at a time when the pace and intensity of interreligious relationships are growing. Two examples may be given. At the world conference on "Faith and Science in an Unjust World," it was recognized that other religions indeed have a contribution to make to the vexed question of the relation between faith and science. The report said:

> Some of the views of other religions may prove both closer to the Bible and more appropriate to the intellectual and social needs of our time. This means that learning from neighbours of other faiths can lead to a valuable enrichment of our understanding of the Bible and to a fruitful reformulation of our theology.[62]

Even more significant is the way in which the United Church of Canada responded to the deeply felt spiritual needs of the native peoples in Canada (August 15, 1986). Calling the church to recognize "the authenticity of native spirituality," former Mohawk chief Robert Jamieson said, "We are not *Indians*. We are *natives* of the country. You gave us a wrong identity, and now you perpetuate it."[63] The response of moderator Robert F. Smith in the General Synod of the United Church of Canada, with 375 members, was very moving. He said:

> We did not hear you when you shared your vision. In our zeal to tell you the good news of Jesus Christ we were closed to the value of your spirituality ... We imposed our civilisation on you as a condition of your accepting the gospel ... We ask you to forgive us and to walk together with us in the spirit of Christ so that our people may be healed and God's creation blessed.[64]

Although there was a good deal of controversy about the matter and some Christians were unhappy about the statement, the fact that a national church could officially make such a statement is a remarkable gesture of courage, humility, and obedience to the command not just to love our neighbors as ourselves, but also not to bear false witness against them.

A sensitive understanding of neighbors' responses to Christian initiated dialogues should therefore be of help, not just to Christians but to other communities of faith as well, as humanity moves toward the twenty-first century.

3

Religions, Cultures, and the Struggle for Justice

The relationship between nations in the North and those in the South is usually discussed in terms of trade and commerce, that is, in political and economic terms. The religious and cultural components of this complex relationship are almost always completely ignored. Quite often, the religious-cultural elements are discussed in such isolation from the economic-political that their interconnectedness is seldom recognized. Thus, human life is broken and fragmented almost beyond repair. It is therefore necessary to draw attention to the inner relationship between the struggle for justice on the one hand and the quest for a more positive theology of religions on the other. This is indeed a highly complex relationship, the roots of which are not always clear. But it is important to affirm that there *is* a relationship and, if possible, to dig for the roots so that the brokenness of life can be mended and its wholeness recovered.

ECONOMIC INJUSTICE AND THEOLOGICAL INJUSTICE

That there is *economic* injustice in the trading relationship between the North and the South is obvious. When one looks at the exchange rate between their respective currencies, this fact should be clear to most people, especially those who travel between North and South. But is there also *theological* injustice in the relationship between Christianity, as the religion of the North, and the religious traditions of the South? Does this apply to Northern studies of Southern religions as well? At the moment, the Jewish-Christian-Western tradition is at least nominally the religion of the rich and powerful North. People who follow other religious traditions in the South are poor and weak, at least in economic, political, and military terms. However, religions like Hinduism and Buddhism in India and Confucianism and Taoism in China, for example, have sustained societies, cultures, and civilizations for several thousand years and are very much alive even today.

Is there then a connection between poverty and religiosity?

The notions of justice and peace are related. There can be no justice without peace and no peace without justice. But justice is not just a matter of redistribution of economic resources, nor peace a question of rearranging power relations among nations in the world. They are much deeper at the roots where they touch each other and broader where they influence relationships among people in society and nations. In every culture, whether in the North or the South, the notions of justice and peace have religious roots, even though in a technological age they are often torn away from their religious moorings. Surely, one should not minimize the secular humanistic contribution both to the clarification and practice of these notions. Nevertheless, at a time when interreligious relationships are developing in pace and depth, perhaps as never before in human history, it should be possible to affirm the religious roots of justice and peace and to recover them in order that different religious traditions can make significant contributions to the emergence of a more just global community.

To hold together the economic-political and the religiocultural components of life, one needs a much larger, more comprehensive, and genuinely ecumenical framework that is free from narrow parochial interests. True universality cannot be understood as the extension of one particularity at the cost of others. Therefore, if one particular economic pattern seeks to dominate the world, or if one particular religious tradition strives to conquer other religious traditions, peace would be disturbed and justice destroyed. This is true of political ideologies as well. Therefore, a recognition of plurality as a style of life that helps mutual criticism and mutual enrichment may be a necessary precondition of just relations between religions, cultures, and ideologies. The larger framework envisaged could be not so much a conceptual framework of ideas as a network of relationships among people who hold their particular religions and cultures to be precious and have to live together in a world where economic resources and power relations are, at the moment, unjustly distributed.

Nowhere else is the power of impersonal economic forces over human life more manifest than in the structural imbalances in the global economic system. The Non-Aligned Movement (NAM) and the group of 77 nationals (G.77) persistently draw attention to this at every international forum. It would be a mistake to think that these are merely economic forums of poor nations whose function is "to clobber" the North for its real or imaginary exploitation of the people and resources of the South. These groups also have a cultural identity within which religious dimensions play an important part, even though these dimensions do not come to the forefront. The nations of the South are also struggling to establish their cultural identity, a struggle which their economic poverty weakens, except in the case of recently affluent states in West Asia. But even though they have persistently drawn attention to the injustice in the economic relationships between the

North and the South, so far very little has been done to bring about any significant changes in this structure.[1]

North-South is not just a geographic concept. It is a spirit, a mood, an attitude on the part of nations who are accustomed to exercising power and enjoying affluence—at least during the past few centuries—toward those in the South who have succumbed to that power and who, in their helplessness, have allowed the North to continue to grow rich at their expense. They are up against a system which continues to grow powerful through a combination of economic power, political domination, overwhelming military strength, and an ideological structure in which religions and cultures are either ignored or subtly exploited to serve the powerful and the rich. Academic studies of religions therefore have an important part to play here for the sake of justice and peace.

There is also a North-South divide *within* the nations of the South. In spite of all goodwill and economic help, the gap between the rich and the poor, the powerful and the weak, the privileged and the marginalized is increasing at an alarming pace.[2] The alliance between the North in the South and the North in the North keeps the exploitative system going, particularly through transnational corporations. The investment of foreign companies in countries like India has been growing over the years, making their economy vulnerable to fluctuations outside.[3]

Because of this vulnerability the advice given by financial institutions of the North to countries in the South are less than helpful. When the President of the World Bank suggested that India, China, and Pakistan needed economic policy changes, V. P. Singh, then finance minister of India, asked how the *same* economic prescription could apply equally to countries so different in political ideology, cultural values, and religious beliefs.[4] When the International Monetary Fund advised Julius Nyerere of Tanzania to divert funds from education to "development" projects (meaning cash crops for export), Nyerere replied that he knew no form of development better than the education of a nation's youth.[5] But the tragic fact is that even when national leaders of the South know what is good for their people, the exploitative patterns within their own countries and the world economic system make it impossible for them to put it into practice.

It would, however, be wrong to blame the North entirely for the poverty and injustice within the nations of the South. The South cannot escape its own responsibility for this matter. Blaming the North for all the ills of the South is a futile exercise that lacks credibility. Writing immediately after the Sport Aid Programme, in which more than 20 million people all over the world ran in support of the project "Race against Time" (May 1986) to raise money for Africa, Professor George Aiyitty of Ghana remarks, "We Africans have made development dependent on foreign exchange, of which we have less and less, and foreign aid whose variable we cannot control." He points out that agricultural complexes in Ghana are still not working, ten years after completion. In Ghana there are more than 70 different types of tractors in various stages of disrepair at state farms. African farmers pay the heaviest confiscatory taxes. The cocoa farmers in Ghana pay 70 percent of their net produce, and Gambia's peanut farmers about 80 percent. "If these oppressive policies continue," Aiyitty writes, "no amount of aid or UN conferences can rescue Africa ... It is misplaced blame that keeps Africa in poverty."[6]

To complicate this matter further, new alignments are taking place in the world economic structure which make the North-South equation slightly out-of-date. Professor Yushi Tsurumi, president of the Pacific Foundation in New York, points out that the Pacific basin has now overshadowed the North Atlantic in terms of gross national product of the world. Whereas in 1982 U.S.-Europe trade amounted to 115 billion dollars, U.S.-Pacific trade totaled 165 billion dollars, thus ending 350 years of North Atlantic domination of the world's economy. The recent summit meeting of seven industrialized nations, including Japan, held in Tokyo (May 1986) is a pointer in this direction. But even more significant is Tsurumi's claim that Japan has now succeeded in blending Confucian cultural values with the best of the Jewish–Christian–Western values in the American capitalist system to produce a more effective blend of economy as the world moves into the twenty-first century.[7] The consequence of this new alliance is already being felt in the lives of nations in the North and the South.

That the economic factor is one aspect of the total relationship between the North and the South was accepted by the United Nations as early as 1971, when it pointed out that in the life of a nation, "the political, social and ideological aspects are inextricably interrelated."[8]

There are many thoughtful economists and political leaders who, in their struggle for just relations in economic matters, recognize that what is at stake is the well-being of people as a whole. Ajit Singh points out that "the essential purpose of any trading system should not be trade, or for that matter free trade for its own sake, but trade as a means of promoting the economic well-being of the people."[9] The former prime minister of India, Indira Gandhi, speaking of the prosperity of human society as a whole, said:

> Justice is the very condition of human survival. Its denial will be an invitation to violence. This is why market economies cannot exist without taking cognizance of social realities. That is why politics has to interfere with economics. We believe that the prime justification for all politics, all economics, and all business is the furtherance of human welfare and the removal of human want and suffering.[10]

This emphasis on the wholeness of life, the well-being of all people in the global community, touches the very core of human existence in a world threatened by violence in the continuing struggle for a just society.

Religions and cultures are mentioned together here as providing resources to strengthen a sense of the wholeness of life. In most countries of the South, particularly those in Africa and Asia, religion and culture are inextricably bound together. There are indeed forms of culture that are torn away from their religious roots, as well as a growing technological culture that is dominated by machines. In spite of this, religion and culture can seldom be discussed apart from each other. Religion is the substance of culture, and culture the form of religion. If religions are responses to the Mystery of Life, cultures are expressions of those responses—not only through words and ideas, but also through symbol and sound and color. Today, and throughout history, oppressed people everywhere express their identity, their joys and sorrows, their longings for freedom, self-respect, and human dignity through their religions and cultures.

Culture refers to "the whole complex of distinctive, spiritual, material, intellectual and emotional features that characterize a society or a social group. It includes not only arts and letters, but also modes of life, the fundamental rights of human beings, value systems, traditions and beliefs."[11] The culture of all people, rich or poor, majorities or minorities, forms part of the common heritage of humanity. Every single culture represents a unique and irreplaceable body of values through which people assert their identity and demonstrate their presence in the world. A world economic system that subordinates other people's religions and cultures to considerations of trade and commerce, or imposes an alien religion and culture on other people, goes against the freedom of the human spirit. To reject, exploit, patronize, or dominate other religions and cultures is a form of injustice that needs to be set right.

The power generated by the economic domination of the South by the North also affects its attitudes toward the religions and cultures of the South. The connection between economic power and aggressive religious militancy is not always recognized. The economic affluence of Islamic countries contributes to the expansion of Islam today, even as during the colonial period the affluence of the West contributed to the expansion of Christianity. There are many people in North America and Europe who believe that people in the South are poor *because* they follow religions other than Christianity. Thus it becomes easy for them to take a theologically negative attitude toward other religions and cultures, to patronize them, or even take a contemptuous attitude toward them in an open or hidden manner. The negative description of neighbors of other faiths as "non-Christian" is a symptom of this theological oppression of the South by the North, which is nominally but powerfully Christian in some of its ideological assumptions.

This crypto-colonialist theology of religions and cultures that lies hidden in the heart of the North prevents neighbors of other faiths from cooperating with Christians in urgent matters of justice and peace. Christians in the South are often regarded as allies of the North and looked upon with suspicion and distrust. Attempts to deal with economic poverty in the South without taking into account its religions and cultures are as one-sided as dealing with their religions and cultures without recognizing that the issue of justice is involved. Worse still, is the serious damage done to just and peaceful relations among different religions through the attitude of regarding *people* of other faiths as mere statistics—the two billion lost souls—as numbers without faces to be counted, sampled, compiled, and stored in computers to be recalled at the touch of a button and used in a game of numbers with scant regard for the freedom, self-respect, and human dignity of people.[12]

NEED FOR NEW RELATIONSHIPS

In drawing attention to religions and cultures in the context of North-South dialogue, it is not claimed that religions have answers to the desperate problems of injustice where economic and political solutions have failed. To do so would be unwise and presumptuous. Evidence in the long history of religions is against any such conclusion. Established religions have often divided people and nations and given rise to tensions and conflicts. They have held up scientific progress, resisted social change, supported the rich and the powerful against the poor and the weak, and have often added religious fuel to military conflagrations, making reconciliation more difficult. Of all the wounds human beings inflict on one another, religious wounds are the most difficult to heal. Organized religions are of little use in the struggle for justice and peace.

What is meant by the term *religions* here is not the established institutions of religion or systems of belief or boundaried social groups with their sense of separation from others. We are talking about the spiritual resources within religions, the inner experiences of the Spirit, their visions of reality, their responses to the Mystery of Truth, the liberative streams within religions that break through human limitations to reach out to neighbors in the global community.

The connection between vision and reality, between religious experience and religious institutions, is difficult to explain. But the fact that the relation between the spirit and forms of religion is complex is no reason why religions should be dismissed as having no consequence for the struggle for justice and quest for peace. Since religions have endured for a much longer period than any secular ideology, the possibility that religions might still offer resources to recover the sense of wholeness of life should at least be explored seriously, instead of being rudely rejected as of no consequence. This is urgent for at least three reasons.

First, while it is true that organized religions have often failed to provide answers to the problems of justice, the same is true of contemporary secular ideologies. In the history of religions, there have indeed been prophetic streams of justice, not just in the Jewish–Christian tradition, but in the Hindu, Buddhist, and Islamic traditions as well. In an unjust situation, justice is more a matter of willingness to share resources than evolving new economic structures. A lower economic standard need not necessarily mean a lesser quality of life. All religions call for simplicity of life, a change within, a transformation of the human heart, and therefore, a change of attitude toward neighbors.

Second, today there is a growing uneasiness about the adequacy of the secular way of life and an increasing sensitivity to the transcendent dimension of life. The speed and the manner in which politicization of religions is taking place in countries in both the North and the South brings out the dangers and opportunities in this situation. The separation of life into the sacred and the secular is being questioned today by many people, who are deeply aware of the wholeness of all life. Religious insights, particularly those that hold together humanity, nature and God in a cosmic unity, may be important here.

To these must be added a third factor which has decisively entered into the history of human relations today: the interreligious dialogues that are going on at national, international, and global levels as perhaps never before. This is being strengthened by increasing travel by people, particularly young people in different countries; by the rapid means of communication; and perhaps even more importantly, by communities of people of other faiths living in many of the Christian countries of the North. Through long centuries, religions developed in isolation from one another, often in suspicion and fear. Today, people of different religious persuasions are being increasingly drawn together as they share a common future and face problems of life and death. This should perhaps provide a sense of urgency to academic studies on an interreligious basis, with greater cooperation between scholars in the North and South.

One of the prerequisites here is to avoid uncritically negative judgments on religions in general or by one particular religious community on the religious traditions of others. Very often, there is great suspicion of the role of religions in society, particularly in countries like India, where, unfortunately, "religious" riots occur with alarming frequency. There are highly complex factors here, both economic and political, that get mixed up with religious feelings and lead to serious conflagrations. This is true of Catholic–Protestant relationships in Northern Ireland or the Jewish, Muslim, and Christian relationships in Lebanon. One must also note that in countries or cities in the North where significant numbers of people of other faiths live together with a majority Christian community, tensions between them do arise. But this should not prevent scholars and leaders of different communities from recovering the peace potentials within different religious traditions. Recent studies in India by sociologists, economists, political scientists, and theologians have brought out the fact that while religious feelings are indeed involved, they were used cunningly for economic and political purposes. Although religion was not the *causative* factor, but the *instrumental* factor in such riots, it was made to appear as the causative factor.[13] Just because religions get involved in such disturbances, the resources within religions for peace and justice should not be ignored.

Further, exclusive claims made by any one religious community lead to theologically negative judgments on the validity of other religions. This not only leads to tensions in the larger community but also affects the scholarly study of religions. When such exclusive claims are allied with economic, political, and (as has often happened in history) sometimes with military power, objective studies of religion become difficult, if not impossible. The ethical consequences of such heavily negative judgments vitiate all interreligious relationships. Perhaps a careful and systematic study of such exclusive claims by an interreligious group of scholars selected from both the North and the South could be of help in bringing out the issues in an objective manner.

In China, the gentle entry of Buddhism, far from supplanting existing traditions, coexisted with them. It had no alliance with the political powers of the country, and unlike Islam and Christianity in India, had no open or hidden economic interests. When asked why a Chinese should allow himself to be influenced by foreign Indian ways, Mou Tzu, a Chinese scholar, replied, "Why should I reject the Way of Tao, Shun, the Duke of Chou and Confucius ... Gold and Jade do not harm each other. You say that another is in error when it is you yourself who err."[14] Wing-Tsit Chan points out that in China, people of three traditions—Confucian, Taoist, and Buddhist—mutually influenced one another over the centuries. "Religions, doctrines, symbols and ceremonies, and even deities have been so intermingled that scholars cannot tell if they are of Confucian, Buddhist or Taoist origin. It is often said that the average Chinese is one who wears a Confucian crown, so to speak, a Taoist robe, and Buddhist sandals."[15]

This may not be the most creative framework to bring out the distinctiveness of each tradition, but it did provide for friendlier relationships among different religions within the nation. In central Asia, for nearly a thousand years before the sea route to the South was discovered (1497–99) by Vasco da Gama, the major civilizations of West Asia, India, and China intermingled—along with three religious traditions of the Buddhist, Chinese, and Islamic—in a critical and enriching relationship without economic or political domination, even though trade obviously was the common purpose that brought them together.[16]

NORTHERN STUDY OF SOUTHERN RELIGIONS

Perhaps the time has come to examine more critically some of the assumptions behind the Northern study of Southern religions. Scholars from the North have indeed done a great service to the study of world religions. They continue to do so. The world of scholarship should be grateful to them. They drew attention to the fundamental values within the religions of the South at a time when they were often smothered by racial, political, or missiological considerations and often went unrecognized, even by their own adherents. Also, such studies brought out the importance of religions and cultures other than European during a period when the concerns of the nations in the North were more for commerce and profit than for culture and knowledge. It is true that at certain points there were hints of a convergence between colonial interests and academic scholarship. It may be that even today there could be some connection between the research industry, largely based in the North, and the neocolonial enterprises in the South. But rather than being hurt by suggestions like this, which need to be critically examined, and instead of developing this into a full-fledged controversy that will deflect scholars from their genuine academic work, what is urgent and important is to seek ways of scholarly cooperation between the North and the South through which the resources of the religious heritage of humankind may be brought to bear upon the urgent problems facing all people.[17]

The assumptions behind the Northern study of Southern religions are based on developments during a particular period in European history. The difficulties of imposing the term *religion* on Southern *dharmas* are well known. But in using terms like *scientific* or *classical*, who selects the criteria? Surely, in a country like India, with its long history of multireligious life, Hindus did have to study the heterodox religions such as Buddhism and Jainism and later Islam and Christianity. Also, within Hinduism itself the relationships between different *sampradayas* were studied systematically by the great *acharyas* and their disciples. Most of these studies are in Sanskrit, Pali, or one or the other Indian languages, and may not be accessible to those who do not operate in these languages. But can they be totally ignored when using the terms *scientific* and *classical*? This is not to deny or minimize the significant contributions made by scholars from the South to several anthologies edited by scholars in the North, but to draw attention to the content of terms like *scientific* and *classical* in relation to these studies.[18]

Frank Whaling is certainly right in asking the question:

> What is the significance of the fact that religions outside the West have been studied in a Western way, and to a lesser extent, that religions outside Christianity have been studied in a Christianity centred way? To what extent has the pre-1945 attitude of often unconscious superiority been superceded in the contemporary situation? To what extent have Western scholars of religion subsumed the whole spiritual creation of humankind under one interpretation or religion and then absolutized it?[19]

Scholars from the South, such as Santosh Chandra Sen Gupta have pleaded that a complex religion like Hinduism should not be "misunderstood" by applying criteria derived from an entirely different culture.[20] An earlier volume by K. Satchidananda Murthy puts together readings in Indian history, politics, and philosophy that are particularly helpful because they draw attention to the conception, interpretation, and methodology of history, a topic alleged to be neglected by India's religions and cultures.[21] Subhas Anand refers to the place of women in Hindu view and way of life, a topic that is important when it is often alleged to be difficult to find women contributors to this subject.[22]

Recognizing that the historical situation decisively changed after 1945 and emphasizing that religions that developed in isolation from one another during the past are now increasingly being drawn closer together, K. L. Seshagiri Rao calls for a new departure in the study of world religions. "The future usefulness of any religious tradition," he remarks, "depends on its ability to cooperate with other traditions."[23] The *scientific* approach to the study of religions is, of course, important, and there is no call to abandon it. But when it is applied to the study of religions, it may tend to regard them as "objects" of study rather than living faiths of people.

None of the religions that are being studied "scientifically" in the North, and about which Christians theologize, originated in Europe. Nor were their testimonies written in a European language. Studies in the ontology of language have shown that depending on any translation is a serious limitation, particularly in the matter of understanding the religious and cultural life of people other than ourselves.[24]

Even the notion of knowledge (*gnosis-jnana*), its content, character, and epistemological possibilities, are different in different cultures. Van Buitenen writes, "Central to Indian thinking through the ages is a concept of knowledge which is foreign to the modern West. Whereas to us, to put it briefly, knowledge is something to be *discovered*, for the Indian, knowledge is something to be *recovered* . . . at its very origin where the absolute truth stands revealed."[25] The kind of religious knowledge which people in the South cherish depends not so much on the "writtenness" of the texts as on hearing and seeing the word. *Sruti*, that which is heard, has far greater authority than *Smriti*, that which is remembered and written down. The notion that truth stands concealed behind texts and will reveal itself through exegesis is unknown in Hindu and Buddhist religious traditions.[26] Greater collaboration between scholars in the North and South may help to complement the concern of each in the methodology, structure, and purpose of academic religious studies.

There is also the intriguing question of why the North feels so compelled to study Southern religions when the people being studied show little interest in studying the religions of the North. Should one look for reasons in the historic context of a particular period when European nations were "discovering" other peoples, religions, and cultures? The perceptions of the "discoverers" and the "discovered" cannot be the same.

A one-way study process quite often has inhibiting and sometimes negative effects on those being studied. Does the study of Southern religions contribute to the pool of religious values in the North? Does it change habits of thought, action, and attitude toward the people of the South who live by these faiths? Does it significantly influence the self-understanding of the people being studied? Or, is it because in a monoreligious and monocultural context there is greater need to know other religions and cultures than there is for people who have been living in open multireligious and multicultural situations for centuries? Or is it because of an inner compulsion to seek new ideas and extend the frontiers of human knowledge? But surely that inner compulsion for *jnana* is no monopoly of the North. It is to be found among people in the South also. These are indeed new questions and they need more careful and systematic study in the coming years through collaboration between the North and the South so that uncritical claims are not made and unwarranted conclusions not drawn.

ISSUES FOR STUDY

The academic implications of interreligious dialogues and the implications of interreligious dialogues for the academic study of religions need far more recognition and acceptance. New steps have to be taken, with more hope than caution. If one considers the relationships among religions in the world today in connection with the global struggle for justice, scholars of different religious traditions need to probe deeper into the implications of interreligious dialogues for more just human relations in the global community. There is no reason to think that such studies will deflect the academic quality of the work or undermine the sense of objectivity necessary for scholarly pursuits. There is probably a threefold task involved here: 1. to bring out, through careful study, the religious roots of the notions of peace and justice in different religious traditions; 2. to examine the inner connection between the two and draw out its ethical implications for people of different religious persuasions; and 3. to probe deeper into the relationship between humanity and nature in different religious traditions so the question of justice does not remain merely at the level of sharing the resources of nature, but also of being at peace with nature and in harmony with the cosmos.

It is not possible, and will be premature, to enter into an elaborate discussion of these matters here. The methodology, structure, and direction of such studies should be discussed by the North and South together from the beginning if what is envisaged here is taken seriously. But perhaps some of the areas of concern may be indicated.

The notions of peace and the practice of justice have religious roots. Secular and humanistic contributions are certainly recognized, but quite often these are torn away from the original religious moorings. Justice and peace are related. Without the experience of peace, there can be no practice of justice. Without the establishment of justice, peace will remain an unending quest and a distant dream. Peace, in the sense of inner tranquility, and peace, in the sense of harmony in its deepest sense, depend on just relations among humanity, nature, and God. But the content of these two notions and the manner in which they are related to each other are perceived differently in different religious traditions. If this is correct, then the perception of what exactly a just community is in a multireligious society will be affected. Any romantic notions of harmony between religions should give place to the recovery of the critical distinctiveness of each tradition. The persistence of evil and suffering within the human heart and in the structures of society makes the discussion even more complicated. Scholarly investigations into these matters might help in avoiding romantic, uncritical notions about peace and justice and in critically recovering the distinctiveness of each tradition for mutual criticism and mutual enrichment.[27]

The connection between *Shalom* and *mishpat* is perhaps more transparently seen in the biblical tradition, both Hebrew and Christian, than that between *Shanti* and *dharma* in the Hindu tradition. The connection between power and justice—power to be exercised by the king—is perhaps more strongly emphasized in Islam than in other traditions. In the shelter and protection provided by the king as "the shadow of God," justice and security are to be found. That the relationship between compassion and justice extends not just to human life but even to animals and nature is perhaps more movingly brought out by the Buddhist tradition than by others. These are indeed generalizations, and may fail to take into account the intricacies and complexities within each tradition. Nevertheless, they point to insights that need more careful study.

That the fragile gift of peace cannot be taken for granted and that one should work for peace (*Shalom*) is emphasized by Jesus (Matthew 5:9), but he also draws attention to peace as the inner quality which removes fear and enables the heart not to be troubled (John 14:27). To the Jew, the Sabbath experience opens the way to *Shalom*. To live sabbatically is to be immersed in sacred time while moving along in chronological time. The restfulness of *Shalom* is rooted in God's love and compassion, and leads to righteousness and justice in society.

Both in the Hindu and Buddhist traditions there is a strong emphasis on peace as an inward quality of life that requires discipline to acquire. The *Shanti mantra* is central to Hindu experience. There are indeed many strands within the complexity of Hindu life and practice, and one should be careful not to isolate any particular one at the expense of others. But the constant emphasis on the inward dimension of peace may be the real contribution of Hinduism to religious life at a time when *doing* rather than *being* seems to be more in demand as a mark of religious life. The compassion of the Buddha (*maha karuna citta*) expresses itself in social relationships, as well as extending it to just relationships between humanity and nature.

Although the Christian tradition regards creation as good, it seems to be less interested in nature as such than the Hindu and the Buddhist. One must examine this matter far more carefully. But it looks as if biblical tradition places stronger emphasis on the distance between God and nature, whereas the Hindu and Buddhist traditions emphasize the continuity between nature and humanity. Hints about this are to be found not just in the Upanishadic tradition of the forest meditations, but also in the theistic traditions, for example, that of Rama. Forest becomes the dwelling place of Rama, where rivers, mountains, trees, and animals seem to participate in his sufferings and struggles. Monkeys are his allies in the battle against Ravana, and even the little squirrel does its bit by rolling itself in sand and shaking itself to drop particles of sand at the location where the bridge is being built to Lanka.

Neither the notion of peace nor the practice of justice can be narrowly defined to human relationships. They need to include nature as well. Human freedom and finiteness are somehow mixed up with the relationship among humanity, nature, and God. The ecological problems that bother human life today are partly the result of technology and cannot be solved by more refined technology. Vision, values, and a recovery of the original relationships are necessary to pursue a more responsible and less exploitative attitude toward nature. The religious insistence on the stewardship of nature's resources, combined with the idea of partnership with nature, might help human beings live together more justly, with peace and harmony in the larger unity of the cosmos.

4

Religious Identities in a Secular State

The immediate focus of this chapter is on India since independence (1947), although the larger ecumenical framework is kept in mind. This is justifiable, not only because India has been a multireligious society for many centuries and continues to be so even to this day, but also because during these four decades some of the most complex and difficult questions that touch the identities of different communities and their relation to one another within the structure of the secular state have come up for serious discussion. The theological and ethical implications of this debate spill over India's geographical borders. The secular state is under serious pressure because of the competing interests of various religions and ethnic communities, languages, castes, and economic groups. A distinguished Indian diplomat remarks that today "the principal challenge to India in transition is to her spirit of tolerance, a virtue which is not without its perils and limits. For beyond tolerance is its total rejection, or its complete incorporation in true democratic pluralism."[1]

RELIGIONS AND NATIONAL LIFE

The role of religions in India is ambiguous. They have been both a blessing and a bane to Indian life. Religions have provided visions, values, and a sense of identity to different communities of people. Religions have also supported unjust and oppressive social structures, upheld superstitious practice, and have been an unending source of conflicts in society. There is hardly a single matter that touches public life in India which, sooner or later, does not become a "religious" issue.

Why is this so? To formulate the right questions about this matter is as difficult as analyzing the situation and indicating possible lines of answer. But the matter is so urgent, and human life so precious, that questions must be asked and provisional answers suggested. Are religions really to blame in the matter of communal conflicts? What role do religious communities have in a secular democratic state? Has the secular state provided opportunities for different religions to make their contributions to undergird the value bases of a nation in the making? How can people of different religious persuasions live and work together for common human purposes in a multireligious society without compromising their respective commitments?

Perhaps one should make a distinction between "faith" and "religion" here and bring out the relationship between the two. Faith is a response to the mystery of the Divine or Truth or Ultimate Reality. It has to do with visions and values. Faith is the substance of religion and precedes it. Faith can live without religion, but religion cannot exist without faith. It is the combination of the two that gives identity to a community of people and creates a tradition, but in doing so, also creates many problems and difficulties in the life of the nation.

Religion seeks to enshrine and express faith in dogmas and doctrines, rituals, symbols, and liturgy, in patterns of relationship, codes of conduct, and structures of society. And in doing so, it may distort faith and obscure the original vision. There are enough examples of this, not only in India, but in the history of other countries as well. Criticizing the manner in which a religious community lives in relation to other religious communities does not necessarily mean rejecting the intensity of its vision and the depth of its commitment which is rooted in faith. To Christians, for example, Jesus before Christianity may be more important than Christianity after Jesus.

A religious community gives people a sense of identity and belonging through shared faith, common tradition, and continuing history. It helps individuals overcome feelings of anxiety, separateness, and terror. A religious community which enshrines faith and demands ultimate commitment helps individuals overcome the tension between loneliness and companionship. Religious communities and their specific identities are important to all human beings who share the mystery of existence and seek to make sense of the complex relationship among humanity, nature, and God.

When religious communities become oppressive and are intolerant of new insights, they betray their original faith. In a recent article Swami Agnivesh remarks that "the more a religion gets formalised, institutionalised and hierarchically structured, the more it gets alienated from its own original spirit of struggle against oppression and domination."[2] In such cases faith has a critical function to perform within a religious community. To do so, faith has to break loose from its captivity to religious ideology. Faith is not just an interior attitude, but supports responsible action in society. It has a transcendent dimension that reaches beyond human beliefs, rituals, and institutions, and so provides criteria and courage to be critical of ideological distortions of religion.

In multireligious societies, therefore, the presence of different religious identities should be regarded not as an obstacle to be overcome. In the long history of religions, Christianity and Islam have tried to impose their particular brand of singularity on others but have failed to do so. Within established religions, constant attempts have been made to suppress "sects." They too have failed. The grudging recognition, if not the joyful acceptance, of this plurality in the world today is a result of this failure. The theological and ethical consequences of this perception have yet to be considered carefully by people who control the institutions of religion. One of the preconditions for harmony in the relationship among different religious communities in India or elsewhere should be the acceptance of plurality, not as an obstacle to be overcome, but an opportunity to be accepted. At the moment the plurality of religions, languages, regions, and castes appears to be a hindrance to national integration in India. But the plurality of religions is not the only cause of these difficulties. The secular state in India has failed to provide space for different religions to make their specific contribution to the pool of values undergirding the life of the nation.

There is a further point to be noted. Any notion that in a pluralistic society just one religion has the *only* answer to all the problems of human life at all times, for all peoples, and in all cultures is doubtful, despite the vehemence with which such a notion is propagated. Plurality of religions introduces an element of choice when faced with the profound perplexities of life to which people respond differently in different cultures. Alternative visions of life offer different possibilities of meaning and direction to human life. Moreover, in a pluralistic situation the possibilities of mutual criticism and mutual enrichment are greater than in a monoreligious situation. One of the lessons that has emerged during the long centuries in India is that religious life can be lived pluralistically, that commitment to one particular faith is possible, indeed necessary, within a structure of plurality, and that tolerance—not in the sense of indifference to Truth but in a mood of profound hesitation, awe, and reverence before the mystery of Truth—is the attitude people of different religious communities should take toward one another.

THE SECULAR STATE IN A MULTIRELIGIOUS SOCIETY

In 1947 India was divided into two states on the basis of religious difference between Islam and Hinduism. But in the perspective of history, the notion that religion was the only or major factor in this division needs to be revised. The burdens of history, ideological forces, political and economic factors, the power struggle between the nations of the world, and perhaps the weariness of India's political leaders such as Mahatma Gandhi and Jawaharlal Nehru after decades of struggle against the British played a part in this tragic division of the country. A more balanced study of India's past may change the Hindu perceptions of Islam and the Muslim perceptions of Hinduism.[3] All communities of faith—Hindu, Buddhist and Jain, Muslim, Sikh and Christian—have to check the legitimacy of their identities with reference to their historic roots. These identities have to be redefined, maybe rediscovered, both in relation to one another and in relation to contemporary secular society. In this process Islam and Christianity, whose historic roots and religious identities are outside the country, may need to redraw their profiles in order to make a significant contribution to the total life of the nation.

With the tragic memories of partition still fresh in the minds of people, India opted for a socialist, democratic, and secular state. There has been an enormous amount of discussion on the content and character of the "secular" state in India. So many different interpretations are given that it is almost impossible to define it. It is enough to say that the secular state in India, sensitive to the lurking violence beneath the surface of a multireligious society, seeks to be impartial in its dealings with different religious communities, particularly its religious and ethnic minorities. In a multireligious country this is indeed justified, for only a secular political framework can provide neutral space for people of different religious persuasions and ideological convictions to make their contributions to the value bases of the nation. A theocratic state based on one religion or ideology would be unbearable in a multireligious country. Therefore, the secular character of the Indian state has to be cherished, nurtured, and supported by all communities of faith against any theocratic tendencies on the part of any single religion or ideology.

However, during the past four decades the secular state, fearful of all religions, has failed to provide creative space for religions to make any serious contribution to the moral life of the nation. Unlike in Britain[4] (which is fast becoming a multireligious society), where there is room for teaching and learning about different religions in educational institutions and the media, in India the study of religions has been unfortunately banished from schools and colleges. Generations of students have been brought up with scarcely any informed understanding of their own religions or those of their neighbors. This may be one reason for today's erosion of moral values in personal and public life. The secular state and the secular ideology behind it have generated "equal indifference" toward all religions.

Let it be understood clearly that this is not an uncritical defense of religions. The role of religions in history has always been ambiguous. Established religions have often sided with the rich and powerful against the poor and the oppressed. Under the slogan "religion is in danger," they have often resisted the human rights of individuals in the community. They have legitimized unjust social structures, resisted social change, exploited superstitions and dogmas, and often been concerned with power, prestige, and comfort rather than with service, humility, and sacrifice.

While this is true of most religions in history, it is equally true that there are liberative resources within religions which have inspired individuals and groups to fight against tyranny and injustice.[5] This fact has been almost completely ignored by the secularists. They have failed to recognize the finer distinctions within religions by rudely dismissing religions from the high roads of modern life. Moral values and emotional commitment to public life as a vocation are derived from religious roots. "Therefore," remarks Surinder Suri, "to reject religious beliefs as unsecular is to empty public life of its moral and social base."[6] To displace religions from the formal as well as the informal arena of political life and relegate them to the sphere of personal belief and private commitment shows very poor understanding of both religion and society.[7]

Sometimes in a mood of lofty condescension born out of prejudice, ignorance, and an almost total lack of sensitivity to the profound dimensions of religious life, secularists succeed in giving genuinely religious people an inferior political consciousness. They give the impression that only secularists who reject religions are truly nationalist. Genuinely religious people are made to feel like crows that have wandered by mistake into a conference of swans.

One consequence of this attitude is the encouragement given to hypocrisy in public life. Even some of those who claim to be guided by the "scientific temper" consult astrologers in private for auspicious moments. Political leaders find it profitable to mix agnosticism and religiosity in various proportions, depending on the occasion. Religions are used as handmaidens to political interests. Some leaders are secular in public but religious in private. Others are religious in public but are really agnostics in their personal lives.

Among the leaders of India, Nehru was secular both in private and in public. "Instead of committing himself to the hopeless task of banishing religion from politics while expanding democratic participation, he dared to seek a politics which would be infused with the right kind of religion and be tolerant."[8] Mahatma Gandhi was religious both in private and public life, combining in himself the life of a saint and a politician without any tension. In spite of this, Nehru and Gandhi worked together for the freedom of India.

But today, unfortunately, the secular credo seems to be coming to its end.[9] The rise of fundamentalism, the politicization of religions, and the communalization of politics, when coupled with the reign of experts and technocrats, are weakening the secular state. "The new convergence of a technocratic model of the state and a communal model of the nation has been the striking feature of the past two or three years," remarks Rajni Kothari.[10] This means that the political process is being bypassed and the participation of the poor, the weak, and the marginalized in their own development is neglected. Religious people who emphasize not just compassion and justice but also human rights cannot afford to ignore this. Fundamentalism, communalism and the politicization of religions have to be resisted for the sake of authentic religious life itself.

At the moment (1988) the political problem of India is not so much the conflict between tradition and modernity or authority and democracy as an excessive concentration of power at the center, in the hands of people who seem to have little respect either for the participation of people in the political process or for values of public morality that have their roots in the religious culture of India. Hindu civilization, unlike that in the West, has never accorded the state autonomy against society. It has always seen the state as an *adjunct* to society, not *against* it. *Rājadharma* (the duty of the king) was regarded as one among others, coexisting with *prajādharma* (the duties of the people).

In the contemporary struggle between Kautilya (symbolizing power) and Gandhi (standing for *dharma*), the latter seems to be losing. There are at least three reasons for this: the weakening of the liberal tradition after political independence and its erosion after Nehru; the inability of Indians to build the effective autonomous institutions needed to check state power, such as religious bodies, universities, press, judiciary, and voluntary organizations; and the unhappy tendency in Indian political and social life to identify institutions with personalities. Religions, banished from public to private practice, have yet to recover those genuine values which can serve a critical and prophetic function in society.[11]

THE IDEOLOGY OF COMMUNALISM

Perhaps the most serious argument against recognizing any role for religions in India's political life is the charge that they breed and promote communalism. Probably no other single factor has so strongly militated against the role of religions in public life in independent India as the charge of communalism. The horrors of communal riots make a mockery of the principle of tolerance. The wounds they inflict on society take generations to heal, if they heal at all. Unfortunately, in India since 1947, the incidence of communal conflicts and violence is growing. Recent studies have shown that in the fifties there were 381 communal riots with 153 fatalities; in the sixties, 2,689 with 3,246 killed; and in the seventies a slight decrease, with 2,608 incidents and 1,108 deaths. But during the eighties during the first five years alone (including the 1984 riots after the assassination of Prime Minister Indira Gandhi) there were 2,771 riots with 2,772 people killed.[12] To this must be added the enormous destruction of property, the immense suffering caused to families of those killed, and the seeds of suspicion, hatred, and revenge sown in the hearts of people.

One must be careful, however, not to blame religions alone for these troubles. Studies by sociologists, political scientists, economists, and theologians bring out the fact that to single out religions as the only cause of these conflicts is to oversimplify a highly complex matter. It is pointed out that all too often these are secular riots in which religions are cunningly used for political or economic purposes.[13]

Bipan Chandra points out that communalism is an ideology that should be fought at every level. He draws attention to three stages in the growth of communal ideology in India.[14] First, a feeling is promoted that people who follow the same religion have not only common religious beliefs, but also common economic, political, and cultural interests. From this arises the ideology of a religion-based community. In the second stage, it is emphasized that the secular interests—that is, political, economic, and social interests—of one religious community are *different* from those of another religious community. This quickly leads to the third stage, when people are made to believe that these interests are not only different among different religious communities, but are also *antagonistic* to one another.

Over the years different elements that constitute this ideology have been floating around in the country, becoming hardened beliefs through the inner logic of repeated communal riots escalating through violence. Communalism cannot be suppressed by force but has to be fought against in the realm of ideas. This is because the roots of this ideology are to be found not just among religious fanatics, but also in the minds of secular intellectuals. Therefore, remarks Bipan Chandra, the struggle against communal ideology has to be fought "not only with the help of intellectuals, but first of all among the intellectuals."[15] This is not to underestimate the role of religions in communal conflicts but to point out that ideological factors certainly are mixed up with the religious factors in provoking such conflicts.

What we now witness in the country are mostly *secular* riots, justified later on in nonsecular terms, blaming religions for the benefit of the victims and the instruments of violence. Truly religious people do not want their religious faith to be politicized. In fact, those who are strongly rooted in their faith are not easily roused to fanatical actions. It is those who are insecure and uncertain about their faith who are easily roused by the slogan of "pious secularists" that religion is in danger. Religions do not need, nor should they seek, state patronage. But the state has the duty and the responsibility to provide creative space for dialogue in order that a climate of profound tolerance might grow in the life of the nation.

ROLE OF RELIGIONS IN THE SECULAR STATE

The increasing politicization of religions is a disturbing feature of contemporary Indian life. Politicization is the use of religion by political or religious leaders for the benefit of one community at the expense of others. Religion and politics were always mixed up in the long history of the country. Buddhism, at least partly, was a protest movement against the domination of the upper castes over the rest of the people. The conversion of Ashoka to Buddhism had political consequences. The entry of Muslims for purposes of trade and the later establishment of Muslim kingdoms in Delhi, led to tensions between Hindus and Muslims, the consequences of which are with us even to this day. Although the Portuguese and British came to India mainly for trade, Christianity was not far behind. Many reform movements within Hinduism were a reaction against Western missionary expansion, and had political repercussions. Sikhism, a religion born out of the confrontation between Islam and Hinduism, is now becoming increasingly militant.

Although religion and politics were thus closely related in the history of the country, what is new today is the intensity of communal passions that go against the very spirit of religion. The politicization of religions threatens the secular character of the state, hinders the process of national integration, gives rise to anxiety, fear, tension, and conflicts in society, and has global implications as well, because the major religions of India extend beyond the frontiers of the country.

One of the marks of Indian life today is that in spite of secular developments and the influence of science and technology on human life, people take religious life seriously. The visible expression of religion in the daily life of the people is in marked contrast to life in Europe. Catholic and Protestant churches are crowded. Whether in the village or in the city, Sunday worship in the churches is very well attended. Mosques are crowded on Fridays. The daily *puja* in Hindu temples is regularly done by thousands of people. Birthday celebrations of Rama, Krishna, the Buddha, and Mahavira are celebrated joyfully in public meetings in which thousands of people participate. Millions of people go on pilgrimage every year, and enormous amounts of money and gold are offered by people to well-known pilgrim centers all over the country.

In recent years, particularly after 1984 (after the assassination of Prime Minister Indira Gandhi), the politicization of religions has become a crucial factor in the increase of communal feelings and violence. Politicization of religions takes place when leaders of political parties, of the state, or of particular communities remain silent when they ought to speak out against superstitious or barbaric acts in the name of religion or incite people over minor incidents when they should remain silent. Short-term electoral gains have tragically led many politicians to remain silent when human rights— particularly those of women and ethnic minorities—are violated. Crimes against backward caste people today described as *Dalits*, whom earlier Mahatma Gandhi called *Harijans*, are increasing. There are so many examples of this in recent years that it is unnecessary to single out any one.[16]

In a multireligious society, the politicization of religions is not only an obstacle to national integration but is also harmful to the genuine values of all religions. A 1987 report on an Indian workshop observes that the political use of religion "divests it of its spiritual content, which would essentially expand the sympathies and human compassion to encompass the entire creation." The report observes further that politicization makes religion into a tool of distinction, placing the followers of one religion in confrontation with members of other religious faiths. Thus the religious community is made into a political community, and that is why the demand for separation of religion from politics came into being. "While there should be full freedom to preach and practice religion," the report says, "this freedom cannot be extended to identify a religious entity with political entity."[17]

The politicization of religions in India has at least three serious consequences. First, it becomes a hindrance to the task of building the nation. With so many dividing factors such as language, caste, and region working against national integration, bringing the religious factor to the forefront of politics arouses deep passions. Communal riots inflamed by religions have always been an unfortunate feature of multireligious societies.

Second, politicization is a threat to the secular, democratic, and socialist character of the Indian state. Organized large-scale conversions can bring about structural changes in Indian society, drastically altering its voting patterns and political balance. In the international context, the success or failure of the Indian state as secular will very much depend on how this issue of conversions is handled, not just by the government but by the different religious communities as well. The dangers of a theocratic state are obvious. In any case, in a multireligious society it is only an open secular state that can provide freedom to people of different religious and ideological convictions to make their critical contribution to the growing life of the nation.

Christians should also consider responsibly what kind of "mission" it is to which they are committed in a pluralist society. Does Christian mission mean the extension of the Christian community and the extinction of all other religious communities? What if Hindus and Muslims also decide on the same procedure? The fact that not just Christians but Muslims and Hindus too have their "missions" demands that the whole matter of the content and practice of mission has to be reconsidered, maybe with all three coming together in dialogue. Earlier than other religions, the Buddhists too had their mission and continue it even to this day, although in very different ways than the Muslim or the Christian.

Third, the politicization of religions in India has global consequences. Christianity, Buddhism, and Islam are not confined to the boundaries of India. Now Hinduism too has its "diaspora" communities and "missions" in other countries. With the resurgence of Islam along with its economic power and with Pakistan and Bangladesh becoming Islamic states in the neighborhood, more tensions are generated. Other countries also get involved. The possibility of the religious factor intensifying conflicts between nations that have strong religious communities cannot be easily dismissed.

That international issues and interreligious relationships are often related is belatedly being recognized by others as well. In countries where the church and state are constitutionally separate, people forget that in other countries, and sometimes in their own, religious beliefs and political attitudes get mixed up. The theologically negative attitudes taken toward other religions and cultures inevitably affect the political perceptions and attitudes of Christians toward nations where the majority of people profess religions other than Christianity. Ideological, economic, and political concerns are undoubtedly important in international relationships. But it would be a serious mistake to ignore the consequences of religion on political attitudes, not just in India, but in other countries of the world as well. In Arab-Israeli and Iran-Iraqi wars, the tragic conflicts in Lebanon and Northern Ireland, and in the tensions between India and Pakistan, the religious dimension adds passion and fervor to a great deal of violence.

The connections between religion, culture, and nationalism create difficulties in the secular state. The notion that each religion has a separate culture of its own and that each religious culture has the potential identity of a nation has led to the evolution of a communal consciousness. This has gradually led to the consolidation of a particular religious community as a political identity, leading to the demand for separate electorates. From this the road to a nation-state based on religious identity is not far. This is what happened to Muslims in India, leading to the establishment of Pakistan as a separate nation. Today it underlies the demand of Sikhs for Khalistan. "Never before was communal consciousness so keen, so assertive, nay so aggressive, as within the last fifty years of British rule," remarks Krishnan Kant. "The concept of composite culture born of multi-religious identities developed into multi-religious nationalisms. In a democratic system where we have adult franchise, multi-religious nationalisms build up mutual confrontation leading to domination of majority nationalism or chauvinism."[18]

But the relationship between religion, culture, nation, and state is far more complex than the theory of "composite culture." People of different religious persuasions may share in the same cultural values, and people who belong to the same religious community may be culturally different. In spite of the religious plurality of India for a few thousand years, Hindus, Buddhists, Jains, and later on, Sikhs, share basically the same cultural values, even though today the dalits and tribals opt out of it. Islam and Christianity, as religions that entered India from outside, were already allied to different cultures, but when one takes into account the fact that a large majority of these are "converts" who often retain the languages and customs they are used to, the notion that people of different religious communities have different cultures—and therefore may even be considered separate "nations" requiring separate territory for expressing themselves—breaks down. Islam, as a religion, failed to hold together Pakistan and Bangladesh as one theocratic state. People in Pakistan, Bangladesh, and Nigeria share the same religion but are culturally different. There are Roman Catholics in Northern Ireland, the Philippines, France and in Latin American countries, but culturally they are different. At a time when India as an ancient civilization is still a nation in the making, it is necessary to recognize that religion and culture are not synonymous and that it is possible for people of different religious communities within a nation to share in basic cultural values.

All this means that every religion in a multireligious society and a secular state has to rediscover its role in the changing situation. There is urgent need for theological reorientation, reform of religious education of the younger generation, drastic revision of syllabus for the study of religions in theological colleges and seminaries, and for developing links with other religious communities, so all religions may make genuine contributions to the value basis of the nation and the growth of public morality. As Ariarajah points out, perhaps

> the time has come to "institutionalise" the reconciling potential of religion as well. Inter-religious councils, multi-religious fellowships of religious leaders, peace education, studies in peaceful methods of conflict-resolution, education for justice and peace, exposure to each other's prayer and spiritual practices, etc., may have to be the new "institutions" that supplement the institutions that brought education, healing and service to communities. Peace does not come about by wishing it; we have to be *peace-makers*. One has to work for and build peace, and strive to preserve it.[19]

RELIGIONS IN A MULTIRELIGIOUS SOCIETY

This leads to the question of the role of different religious communities in a state with a multireligious society. One should recognize that the character of the state and the degree of plurality differ in different countries. Some countries have been multireligious for many centuries. In some, plurality is a more recent phenomenon, rather reluctantly accepted by the majority community. In Western countries, Christians are in a majority with pockets of other religious communities sharing the larger life of the nation. In countries of Asia, with the exception of the Philippines, people of other religions form the majority; for example, Hindus in India, Muslims in Pakistan, and Buddhists in Sri Lanka and Thailand.

So too the political character of the states in the world is different. Some are secular and, after many years of struggle, have succeeded in keeping state and religion separate. Some are theocratic, where religious belief determines the character of the state and the attitude toward religious minorities. Indonesia is based on the *pancasila* principles. It is necessary to recognize this complexity and variety, lest people offer simplistic religious solutions to complex political problems. But whatever the political complexion of the state and the degree of plurality in multireligious societies, unless there is religious freedom and creative space, people of different communities cannot, as citizens, make their specific contribution to the larger life of the nation.

There are at least three areas where religions can make significant contributions to the life of the nation. One is through exercising what may be described as a "prophetic-critical" function in society. The other is to encourage the emergence of new communities of concerned individuals cutting across visible religious boundaries who, with courage and conviction, can work for fuller life in society. And the third is to draw attention to a transcendent center that serves both as the source of all values and the norm to judge all human conduct, personal or public. Whether this is called God or *Sat* or *Dharma* or Ultimate Reality is less important than for all religious communities to point to a sacred symbol that transcends loyalty to one's own religion, tribe, caste, or language. Secularism empties life of this content; faith recognizes and accepts it.

The negative role of religions has been stressed so much (and indeed with good reasons) that the positive function of religions in society is almost wholly forgotten. To say that politics and religion should be kept separate is understandable, especially at a time like ours. But what it really should mean is that politicians should not use religions for short-term political ends and religious leaders should not use politicians for narrow communal gains. But surely, every religion has a social and public dimension. To say that religion should be a private affair is to misunderstand both religion and politics. Justice, as a social virtue, has religious roots. When religious leaders became corrupt, when kings forgot to be just, and when the powerful exploited the poor, individuals, at great risk to themselves, have publicly protested against them in the name of religion. There are enough examples of this, not just in the Jewish–Christian–Western tradition, but also in Hindu, Buddhist, Muslim and Sikh histories. There are liberative streams, revolutionary urges, and prophetic voices in the history of every religious community.[20]

The prophets of the Hebrew scriptures, and Jesus Christ himself, criticized corruption and called for the cleansing of public life. The leaders of Hindu reform movements such as Raja Ram Mohan Roy, Swami Vivekananda, Sir Aurobindo, Mahatma Gandhi, Balagangadhar Tilak and many others were profoundly religious, with a public conscience. The resources for the struggle against such practices as *Sati*, untouchability, and child marriage were not just secular but also deeply religious. Buddhism has a long history of rebellion against all kinds of oppression and corruption in public life. The *mahā karuna citta* of the Buddha was not a private affair; it extended to all life, including the animal.[21] Throughout the history of Islam, there are many examples of revolts against all kinds of oppression, and these were born out of religious imperatives. Sikh gurus have become martyrs opposing Muslim oppression of their Hindu brethren. With such powerful examples in the history of every religious community, genuinely religious people should not abandon their critical function in society. They should avoid fanaticism and resist "secular" leaders from giving them an inferior political consciousness. The time has come for people of different religious persuasions to come together to discover ways and means of exercising their critical function to cleanse political life of its evils and shape rules for public morality.

There are already groups of people, both secular and religious, who have joined together against the evils of communalism, political corruption, and social and economic oppression. Some of them are rejected by their own communities of faith. There are instances when Hindus have rescued Muslims in danger of death during communal riots and Muslims have come to the help of Hindus caught in similar situations. There are Hindu mothers who have tried to save Sikh boys from being killed and Sikh families sheltering threatened Hindus. Such acts of compassion and defiance against religious fanaticism cannot be done without courage and a profound faith in human life. A new vocabulary of communication needs to be developed so that people of different communities can genuinely converse with each other on deeper matters of faith and so build new communities that cut across the walls of separation.

In an age dominated by science and secularism one of the tasks of genuinely religious people is to draw attention to the Mystery of transcendence, a center of values, a source of meaning, an object of loyalty beyond the smaller loyalties to one's particular caste, language, or religion. Whatever the manner in which faith responds to this Mystery and expresses it in different cultural ways, this sense of the Beyond in our midst, of the Mystery that touches life at all points but is not confined to it, helps people to come together for common human purposes in society, not just for pragmatic reasons, but for deeper reasons of faith and commitment.

None of these functions can be exercised effectively without the spirit, mood, and attitude of dialogue. Opening the gates of hospitality to neighbors of other faiths is far more urgent than strengthening the fences that separate religious communities from one another in a multireligious society. There can be no true community unless strangers become friends and travelers become pilgrims on the road to the city of God.

5

Scripture and Scriptures

In a religiously plural world, a plurality of scriptures is to be expected. Where different religions respond differently to the mystery of life, and where the identities of different religious communities are mixed up with political and economic, social and cultural factors, the question of "authority" becomes inescapable. What is the source of authority for the claims and counterclaims of different communities of faith? What happens when there is a clash of authorities in the larger community? The meaning, practice, and purpose of hermeneutics in a multiscriptural context has yet to be taken seriously by people concerned with interreligious relationships today.

Several questions arise in this connection. In a multireligious community there are different scriptures which are accepted as authoritative by their respective adherents. But can the authority of one scripture be extended to operate over other communities of faith who have their own scriptures? Who decides? Further, the notion of authority itself, particularly religious authority, is being questioned today. In the West the church had to develop its hermeneutics in response to developments in science, philosophy, historiography, and other secular movements. The church in the West had no scriptures of other faiths to take into account. Therefore, its hermeneutics inevitably had to be a monoscriptural hermeneutics. Today, however, Christians in a multireligious world cannot ignore other scriptures that provide spiritual support and ethical guidance to millions of their adherents. Christian hermeneutics today has to respond to a double challenge, namely, from the side of scientific enterprise on one hand and the scriptures of neighbors of other faiths. The manner in which christological affirmations are expressed in a multireligious society depends very much on the way in which the Bible, particularly the New Testament, is interpreted in relation to other scriptures. Christologies developed in the monoscriptural situation in the West, in response to Western challenges, may indeed be helpful to Christians in Asia and Africa, but they cannot be "normative" to them,

58

because they have yet to develop new hermeneutics in a multiscriptural society.

THE PLURALITY OF SCRIPTURES

To Christians it is astonishing that neighbors of other faiths also have written scriptures. The notion that the Bible is the "true" scripture and all other scriptures are "false" is so stamped in the minds of many Christians that any discussion on scriptural authority becomes almost impossible.[1] It is therefore necessary to draw attention to different scriptures in the world which provide the living sources of authority to millions of people of other faiths.

The life of the people in Asia has been nourished for a few thousand years by the scriptures of religions other than Christianity. The Hindus have their *prasthana-traya* (triple canon) of the *Upanishads*, *Brahmasutra*, and the *Bhagavadgita*. The Buddhists have the *tripitaka* (the three baskets of the canon), and the Chinese have their classics of Confucianism and Taoism. Over and over again in the history of Asian people, when powerful renewal movements emerged, they were nourished by profound reinterpretations of their scriptures. It is the *Bhasyas* (commentaries) that have pointed out new directions to the *Sampradayas* (ways, traditions, movements) in India. Sankara and Ramanuja did not write treatises on theology but commentaries on the triple canon, bringing fresh meanings out of the texts. During more recent times, Radhakrishnan (1888–1975), the Indian philosopher president, in addition to his other works, produced his own translations and commentaries on the *Upanishads*, *Brahmasutra* and the *Bhagavadgita*. During the days of India's freedom struggle, almost every Hindu nationalist leader—Tilak, Bhave, Gandhi, and many others—wrote commentaries on the *Bhagavadgita*. In fact, the *Gita* became the gospel of action supporting a *dharma yuddha* (righteous war) against the British.

During nearly a thousand years of Muslim presence in India, Pakistan, and Bangladesh, Muslim scholars of the Qur'an have produced important volumes on the interpretation and exposition of texts. Over the years these scholars have gained a reputation in the world of Islam that gives them recognition for their distinctive hermeneutic contributions to the interpretation of the Qur'an. In Indonesia, too, which has the largest Muslim population in the world, the work of Indonesian Muslim scholars has continued to nourish the lives of Muslims. Perhaps one should note that Islam, as a religion belonging to the Semitic family, is different in its approach to hermeneutics than the ancient religions of India and China.

Without sufficient information, it is difficult to make convincing observations about the religious situation in China. But there is no reason to believe that in spite of decades of Maoist ideology the classics of Confucianism, Taoism, and Buddhism have lost their hold on the hearts and minds of people. Confucius (born 551 B.C.) deeply influenced the life and thought of the Chinese as a transmitter, teacher, and creative interpreter of ancient culture and literature. The Confucian classics, including the *Analects*, "are not the canon of a particular sect but the literary heritage of a whole people."[2] The book of *Lao Tzu*, translated into English as *I Ching*, the Book of Changes, goes back to the third century B.C. and is the foundation of Taoism. Although little is known of the two fathers of the sect, Lao Tzu and Chung Tzu, what is important is the book, which is "one of the shortest, most provocative, and inspired works in all Chinese literature ... the quietism, mysticism, and the love of paradox that distinguish this work probably represent very old strains in Chinese thought. ..."[3]

Buddhism originated in India, but in terms of its influence in China and Japan, the Lotus school is important. It is based on a text from North India, the *Saddharma Pundarika* or the *Lotus of the Good Law*. It is the interpretation given to this text by the great Chinese monk Chih K'ai (or Chih-i, A.D. 538–597) that forms the basis of this school. He lectured for years on its written text, "minutely examining every detail of language and subtlety of meaning, and giving special attention to the methods of religious practice embodied in the Lotus."[4] In recent years the Rissho-kosei kai, one of the most powerful new religious movements in Japan, is based on the *Lotus*, and a number of commentaries on it have been published recently in Japanese and English.

In developing new hermeneutics there are at least two considerations which Christians in a multireligious world cannot ignore. One is the attention given to the study of scriptures in the *original* languages, the meticulous attention given to texts, their interpretation in particular contexts, and the exposition of meanings (*artha, tatparya*) in the life of the people. Second, Christians must recognize that neighbors of other faiths in Asia, whether it is Hindu and Buddhist neighbors in India or Confucian, Taoist, and Buddhist in China, have developed their own hermeneutics in their own setting, without depending on external sources. For example, the hermeneutics of Buddhism developed in India in response to Indian situations was not uncritically accepted by China or Japan. One of the frequent objections raised by Confucianists and Taoists against Buddhism was: why should a Chinese allow himself to be influenced by Indian ways? Chinese Buddhists answered this question in various ways. Mou Tzu said:

> If a gentleman-scholar dwells in their midst, what business can there be among them? According to the Buddhist scriptures, above, below and all around, all beings containing blood belong to the Buddhist clan. Therefore, I revere and study these scriptures. Why should I reject the way of Tao, Shan, Confucius, and the Duke of Chou? Gold and jade do not harm each other. Crystal and amber do not cheapen each other. You say that another is in error when it is you yourself who err.[5]

According to official tradition, Buddhism reached China from India in the first century A.D. Because of Chinese aversion to foreign languages, Buddhist texts were translated into Chinese. The book *Disposition of Error,* or *Li-hoc-lun,* as it is known in Chinese, written probably during A.D. 420–587, appears to be an apologia for Buddhism. "The author takes the stand that there is no fundamental conflict between the Chinese and Buddhist ways of life and that the great truths of Buddhism are preached in somewhat different languages, by Confucianism and Taoism as well."[6]

Hermeneutics as the disciplined study and interpretation of scriptures is neither recent in Asia nor the monopoly of Western biblical scholars. The question in Asia is not so much rules of interpretation as the perception of Truth or *Sat* or Reality or *Dharma* or the Tao itself. How Reality is to be perceived is a concern prior to questions of rules of interpreting the scriptures. To the Hindu *Sruti,* that which is heard is prior to and more authoritative than *Smriti,* that which is remembered and written down. The perception of Truth through *anubhava* (inadequately translated as "intuition" or "experience") is basic to any knowledge to which the scriptures bear witness. The Sanskrit word for "word" is *Sabda* (from which is derived *Sabda pramana,* one of the three Hindu criteria for interpretation), which means both *sound* (that which is heard), and *word* (that which conveys meaning). Thus by instantly attracting one's attention through hearing and in communicating a particular meaning through words, a relationship is established between the source of the word and the word itself. In the sacred syllable AUM, the sound produced by uttering it is as important, if not more, than the word itself. It overcomes the dichotomy between the knower and the known, between the subject and the object. Communication therefore becomes communion. "He who knows the Brahman becomes the Brahman."[7]

Confucius speaks of the unitary principle that runs through everything (*Analecta* IV, 15; XV:2). The teaching of *Lao Tzu* is based upon the way of Tao, the one great underlying principle that is the source of all being, which must remain essentially indescribable and known only through a kind of mystic intuition. "The Tao that can be told of is not the eternal Tao: the name that can be named is not the eternal name . . . It is the Mystery of all mysteries! The door of all subtleties."[8] The "uncarved block" is a favorite figure in Taoism, referring to the original state of complete simplicity which is its highest ideal. *Lao Tzu* says, "Truly a great cutter does not cut."[9] There is an underlying mood or feeling or attitude which recognizes that true knowledge (*Satyasya Satyam* — the truth of the truth, *Brihad.* I:16) is not a matter of exegesis of scripture but a transformation of the knowing subject. *Tarka* (logic) does not lead to truth. It is the person whose mind is purified through discipline who can *hear* or *see* the Truth. The essential point constantly affirmed is that hermeneutics by itself cannot yield truth in its fulness without purification of the mind, transformation of the heart, and discipline of the body.

HERMENEUTICS IN A MULTISCRIPTURAL CONTEXT

A plurality of scriptures raises highly complex questions. The way in which a text becomes a scripture, the relation between "spokenness" and "writtenness," the manner in which a scripture functions religiously in the life of a community, and the notion and practice of authority itself are different within different communities of faith.

The notion of scriptural authority itself is understood differently by different religious communities. To most Hindus primary authority lies in that which is *heard*, not that which is *remembered* and written down. To the Buddhist, scriptures have an *instrumental* authority, like that of a boat that helps one to cross the river but which, after reaching the other shore, becomes unnecessary. It is sometimes said that to the Muslims the Qur'an is what Christ is to the Christians. The difficulty in that comparison indicates the striking differences in the notion of authority between the two. Although all Christians accept the normativity of the Bible, scriptural authority is understood differently in the Roman Catholic, Orthodox, and Protestant traditions. Within the Protestant tradition itself, not all accept the "inerrancy" of the Bible. These differences mean that the criteria derived from one scripture cannot be applied to judge other scriptures. In addition to these is the fact that scriptures serve not just as sources for doctrinal formulations but also for personal devotion and the spiritual formation of the community. How does an oral tradition become a text and a text become scripture in the life of a community? Two examples may be given, one from the Hebrew and the other from the Hindu tradition.

Wilfred Cantwell Smith points out that originally the *Song of Songs* was a secular love song sung in taverns in the first century A.D.[10] How then did it get a place in the Hebrew canon? Rabbi Solomon ben Isaac described it as depicting the love of God for the Jewish people. But for this, and the attribution of its authorship to Solomon, it probably would not have found a place in the canon. Bernard of Clairvaux interpreted it as the love of Christ for the church. A modern commentary with very elaborate exegesis relates it to contemporary issues such as the correlation between love and death, women's liberation, and others.[11]

A more recent article (1986) brings out the connection between Eros and language, between the "Pleasure of the Text and Text of Pleasure."[12] In interpreting Origen's commentary on the *Song of Songs*, Miller points out that to Origen the *Song of Songs* was an *epithalium*, a song sung before the bridal chamber, which then becomes "a drama of love" in which the bride is described as *sponsa verbi*, the Bride of the Word who is espoused to Christ described as a *philtron*, "a saving wound." In this process, language and love are intimately related. "Speaker and lover have been fused, and the reality over which the speaker-lover presides is linguistic."[13] To Origen the *Song of Songs* was also mystical and contemplative. To contemplate is to desire, to long for the loved one, and words give expression to it. The name of love is the substance of language itself. Love seduces language. It hurts and wounds, and yet in the pain of wounding is also the pleasure of healing.

The manner in which the *Bhagavadgita* (hereafter the *Gita*, ca. fourth century B.C.) was used and interpreted through the centuries is a different example of the evolution of scriptural authority in a very different setting, namely, that of Hindus in India. Originally embedded in the epic *Mahabharata* very early in its history, it was lifted from the *Smriti* context (secondary authority) and placed among *Sruti* (primary authority). A striking change in its status took place by its being invested with higher authority. There are over 2,000 editions of the *Gita* in about 75 languages.[14] Sankara, (eighth century A.D.), the well-known teacher of *advaita*, interpreted the *Gita* not as a gospel of action but of *moksha*, release. Sankara subordinates the way of action and devotion to that of *jnana* (knowledge).[15] On the other hand, Ramanuja (twelfth century A.D.) interprets the *Gita* in a different way, emphasizing the devotional aspect of the book, drawing attention to a merciful God of grace who can be fully known only through love.[16]

A striking change took place in the twentieth century during India's freedom struggle against the British. The *Gita* was once again regarded as the gospel of action, this time for a *dharma yuddha*, a righteous war against the oppressive foreign power. Many political leaders such as Aurobindo, Tilak, Mahatma Gandhi, Bhave, and others have written commentaries on the *Gita*. Balagangadhar Tilak's commentary is one of the most outstanding in this connection.[17] To Tilak, Arjuna, the hero, was essentially a man of action, a *karma yogin*, and he interprets the message of the *Gita* to be an encouragement to act in such a way that one ultimately attains *moksha* through the way of action.

Radhakrishnan brought out his commentary of the *Gita* in 1948. It was dedicated to Mahatma Gandhi, who was assassinated that year.[18] By the time his book was published, political freedom in India had become a reality. Radhakrishnan's purpose in writing the commentary "was to restate the truths of eternity in the accents of our time because it is the only way in which a great scripture can be of living value to mankind."[19]

The latest book on the *Gita* by Krishna Chaitanya (1987) is a very different volume from others, in that it takes into account a far wider range of concerns, and is more acutely aware of the imminent disaster through nuclear holocaust and so seeks to bring out the message of the *Gita* to the inner anxieties of modern people. The book is illustrated with nineteen reproductions, five in color, of some of the most impressive works of Indian painters and sculptors, ancient and modern, as visual correlates of the themes of different chapters. Thus, "hearing" the text and "seeing" the paintings combine to produce a strikingly new "integrative vision" of the message of the *Gita* very different from earlier works.

Thus scriptures function differently at different times within particular religious communities. In the case of the *Song of Songs*, a purely secular poem is gradually invested with sacred authority and, at different times, deeper meaning is read into it in different ways. In the case of the *Gita*, a scripture embedded in a source of secondary authority is lifted into a higher plane, and over the centuries, serves as the source of theological strength, spiritual solace, and ethical guidance.

Several points are involved in this process of a text becoming a scripture. There is obviously sensitivity and openness to new perceptions on the part of individuals. Unless individuals have the freedom and courage to bring out the new, no fresh developments can take place. Without Rabbi Solomon, the *Song of Songs* would have remained a secular song. The perception of the sacred in the secular, of divine love in human eros, is indeed a profound insight. Without Tilak's interpretation of the *Gita*, the freedom struggle in India would have probably remained purely political, without any spiritual, theological, and ethical undergirding. Further, the acceptance of individual insights by the community invests authority on new insights and interpretations. No text can function religiously in the life of the community unless the new interpretations meet the specific needs of a community at a particular time. An uncritical attachment to inherited notions may prevent a community from considering fresh interpretations. Thus people brought up in the notion that their scripture is "the only true scripture" might refuse even to consider the suggestion that neighbors of other faiths cherish their own scriptures and are sustained and nourished by them.

But there is a third dimension in addition to individual sensitivity and community acceptance that should not be forgotten. This is what may be described as the transcendental element involved in all sacred scriptures. It may appear that in the case of the *Song of Songs*, because of its original secular character, this dimension is missing. But the whole Bible is witness to the divine initiative to which human beings respond and to which they bear witness in the scripture. In the case of the *Gita* this is more obvious, particularly because of the central importance of the vision of Krishna to Arjuna as the Lord of the whole universe. Thus in the history of religions an oral tradition becomes a text through a long process, and a text becomes a scripture, and provides not only *formal* authority but also *becomes* authoritative in new situations through new interpretations. The sensitivity and openness of individuals, the responsibility of the believing community to reject or accept new interpretations as authoritative, and the needs of the community as it faces the profound mysteries of life, birth and death, love and suffering, loneliness and companionship, time and eternity are all involved in this complex process. This means that the authority of one scripture cannot, and should not, be imposed on other scriptures.

LANGUAGE: "SPOKENNESS" AND "WRITTENNESS"

The connection between "spokenness" and "writtenness," along with the question of language, introduces another element into this discussion.

Scriptures have played different roles in the religious life of different communities in history, sometimes within a particular religion. In Protestant Christianity in the West, the desire to look for an authority other than the Pope brought the authority of the Bible into greater prominence. Further, the invention of printing and the translation of the Bible into languages of the people gave them greater accessibility to the scriptures. When Western missionaries brought the Bible to multiscriptural Asia, the authority of the Bible that had been formulated against other authorities in Europe was set against the authority of other scriptures. This attitude, unfortunately, continues even to this day.

But the attitude toward written texts is very different in other religions. In cultures such as the Hindu and the Buddhist, even though scriptures were written very early, it was the recital and the hearing of the scriptures that operated as authority among the people. The profoundly *spoken* character of scripture in India, particularly the emphasis on the *mantra*, indicates this. What becomes important is not so much the rational intelligibility of the written texts but the power of the original Word (*Sabda*). The holiness of the words is intrinsic. One participates in it not just through reading and exegesis and interpretation but by reciting and hearing it.[20] This is by no means to minimize the importance of written scriptures that function religiously in the life of the people.

"Writtenness" introduces an element of rigidity into the freedom and fluidity of the spoken word. Between speech and writing a rupture takes place which can seldom be bridged by later readers. Writing, therefore, is "a detour of speech."[21] Writtenness also introduces a serious limitation on fluid, free-flowing speech by imposing a form, a structure of logical precision. Quite often, it misses the symbolic meaning that speech conveys. The scientific temper seeks precision and clarity and is therefore impatient with symbols and metaphors. It uses language as an instrument to define, control, and manipulate Truth, which is considered a liability to be overcome rather than a gift to be treasured.

"We dismiss realms of meaning beyond the literal either as confusion to be cleared up by logicians or as emotional embellishments to be kept in check," remarks Paul Ricoeur, who goes on to say that for people in the West, it is hard "to see scriptural language full as it is with figure, vision and myth, as having to do with Reality."[22]

This note about the limitation of written words is meant as a caution against claiming final authority for the literalness of what is written, but it does not minimize the importance of scriptures. Hindu scholars have always emphasized the primary importance of the Word that is *heard* (*Sruti*) which, of course, is later on written down. The notion of separate individual letters forming a word and a cluster of words being shaped into a meaningful sentence introduces a profound sense of unity. The great *acharayas* (teachers) of Hindu *dharma* speak of *ekavakyatva* — "one-sentence-ness" — that holds diverse elements together within itself.[23]

The particular formation of words and sentences in different religions and cultures indicates different ways of thinking about Truth and expressing it. There has been a great deal of discussion in India on the nature of language, the relationship between words and sentences, and the relationship between verbal and nonverbal words.[24] In the Hindu and Buddhist traditions there is a strong feeling that by merely reading texts and analyzing them one does move nearer Truth, that wisdom is not synonymous with knowledge, and that one should not too quickly identify wisdom and authority with written forms and techniques of communication.[25] Therefore to quote inadequately translated texts from a particular scripture without taking into account the original context in which it was spoken and impose it in place of other scriptures as the only true authority is neither charitable nor reasonable. This leads to a discussion of the manner in which Asian Christians are seeking to interpret the Bible as they live with neighbors of other faiths in a multireligious context.

THE QUEST FOR NEW HERMENEUTICS IN ASIA

At a time when scriptures cannot be regarded as the monopolistic possession of any one particular people but should be accepted as belonging to the heritage of the whole world, the hermeneutic question may be stated thus: How can the Bible, a Semitic book formed through oral and written traditions in an entirely different geographic, historical, and cultural context, appropriated and interpreted for so many centuries by the West through hermeneutic tools designed to meet different needs and shaped by different historical factors, now be interpreted in Asia by Asian Christians for their own people? In what ways does biblical authority help Asian Christians confess Christ in a multiscriptural context? Christians in Asia are heirs to a double heritage—that of the Bible and that of other scriptures. If this fact is taken seriously, Asian Christians could provide a bridge through which the insights of different scriptures might be shared in the larger community.

To enter this multiscriptural situation with the claim that the Bible "is the only written witness to God's deeds in history"[26] is to cut off all conversation with neighbors of other faiths. This attitude makes it impossible for Christians to develop "their own hermeneutics." In a continent like Asia a claim for the supreme authority of *one* scripture can be met by a counterclaim for similar authority for *another* scripture. It ignores the relation between "words" and "events," spoken languages and written texts, the text and what or who is behind the text. "Biblicism" should not be equated with being biblical. Further, the notion of "correspondence" between contemporary situations and biblical situations fails to see the gap between then and now and results in alienating the text from both its own historical context and our context today. What if there are situations that obviously do *not* correspond to those in the present? Is the limited and narrow experience of Israel with its surrounding nations or one sermon by Paul to the Athenians sufficient grounds to pass heavily negative theological judgments on neighbors of other faiths in Asia today? One gets the impression that too often the search for "similar situations" and "applicability" of texts reduces "the Kerygmatic content" of the Word of God to which biblical writings bear witness.

There are other trends in biblical interpretation in Asia which are more helpful in holding onto Christian commitment and developing new relations with neighbors of other faiths. The quest for new hermeneutics in Asia, although at present in its initial stages, is a significant movement. Too much should not be claimed for it. A comprehensive and systematic analysis and evaluation of the various trends in Asia is yet to be done.[27]

The concern in Asia here is not so much to formulate rules of interpretation as to bring out the insights, guideposts, and directions to which the Bible points, in order to illumine the path of Christian obedience in Asia today. The images, stories, and particular traditions of the Bible—carefully studied with considerable knowledge of the original languages and the formation of oral traditions and written texts—together with an understanding of historical contexts, form the basis of interpretations of God's Word for the life of the churches in Asia today. Some Asian theologians even seem to reject the formal authority of the Bible in order to come under the *living* authority of the Word. They point to a certain measure of plurality in the Bible, both in ways of knowing and defining the ultimate goals of life. Thus, for example, when two living religious traditions such as the Hindu and the Christian meet in the experience (*anubhaya*) of the interpreter, the *pramāṇas* (criteria for interpretation) of each tradition might help each other—by way of mutual criticism and mutual enrichment—encounter the reality behind the texts. So, too, in defining the ultimate goal of life salvation as *reconciliation* with God or as the *realization* of God, the meeting of the two traditions—not in a formal academic way, but in the profound sharing of experiences (*anubhaya*)—should help the entry into "new modes of being." The meeting point or points between the Bible and scriptures of other faiths have yet to be discovered.

There are two related questions here. One is the plurality of languages into which the Bible has been translated in Asia; the other is the question of the nature of language itself. There is "nothing more authentic than language itself ... language itself is understanding."[28] In the Bible, *event* and *word* are born together. They form a unity. The preachings of Jesus are language events. Once we recognize this, the gap between then and now, between biblical times and our times, is bridged because there is "a merging of horizons."

Asia is diversified into at least seven linguistic zones, the most that any continent can boast of.[29] Biblical languages are Hebrew and Greek. Almost *all* Asian theological writing is done in English, that is, a language other than the mother tongue of Asian people. Suppression or domination of the languages of a people is one of the most common and far-reaching methods of colonialism, with consequences that last for generations. The decolonization of speech is far more difficult than the decolonization of the land. Asian theologians and biblical scholars face a serious dilemma here. On the one hand, without using their own particular mother tongues, their encounter with the language events of the Bible can hardly be authentic. On the other, without using English, they cannot communicate with one another in the larger community of the Asian world.

Furthermore, a great deal of the preaching of the Word is done in the languages of the people. This is particularly true of a multilingual country such as India, where in a large number of village congregations the Word cannot be heard except through the mother tongue. The implications of preaching in the mother tongue for biblical interpretation and the manner in which theological training in English affects the minister's ability to communicate the message and encounter the language events of the Bible with the congregation have yet to be carefully studied.

There are other Asian theologians who, while based in sound biblical scholarship, move beyond its boundaries into the realm of symbols and images. They ignore the line of demarcation between biblical scholarship and theological reflection and move back and forth across the boundaries with ease and sensitivity. To them these boundaries cease to be hindrances but become thresholds into the realm of meanings to be discovered where biblical realities and the life situations of Asian people meet in the inner experience of the interpreter. Almost all of them have had experience in teaching, and quite a few of them are still related to theological seminaries. Perhaps their large ecumenical experience enables them to lift images from the Bible and transpose them into Asian situations without doing violence to the text or the life situations of the Asian people.

Selecting a few among many such people is not easy. A certain representativeness, both geographical and confessional, has been kept in mind. Kosuke Koyama is a Japanese theologian well-known for his Bible studies. Choan-Seng Song, from Taiwan, combines a deep knowledge of Chinese classics with fresh Christian biblical insights. Mar Gregorios is a bishop of the Syrian Orthodox Church in India widely known for his Bible studies and other theological writings. At present (1987) he is one of the presidents of the World Council of Churches. D. S. Amalorpavadass is a Roman Catholic scholar in India well-known for his liturgical experiments in inculturation. He is one of the few Christian scholars who has given serious attention to the authority of nonbiblical scriptures. The concern here is not so much with the theological content of their writings as with their methodology of interpreting the Bible, although the two cannot strictly be kept separate.

Koyama's Bible studies are noted for the striking way in which he *contrasts* biblical images with images taken from contemporary life. One finds a methodology that is not always articulated but is implied in his writings.[30]

Although a large number of his references are to Hebrew scriptural images, there is a certain christocentric emphasis in his writings, particularly those on the cross. He points out that we learn of Jesus Christ through studying the Bible, particularly the New Testament, identifying ourselves with the community of faith.[31] The "crucified" mind is contrasted with the "crusading" mind, the Good Friday mind with the Easter mind. The lunchbox and the briefcase have convenient handles to carry them; the cross has no handle to carry it.

There are other illustrations. The hand of Buddha is open; that of Lenin is closed (clenched fist); that of Jesus Christ is open, but pierced through with a nail.[32] In *Three Mile an Hour God*, Koyama contrasts the slowness of God in educating his people during forty years in the wilderness with the swiftness of modern technology. There is the technological straightness of the pipe and there is the natural "curvedness" of the bamboo. A car is smooth, sleek, and fast. A bullock cart is rough, cumbersome, and slow. The wilderness to which God led the people of Israel is open on all sides; a modern city is closed on itself, without a sense of spaciousness. There is a "tourist" approach and a "pilgrim" approach to other people and other cultures. We need to move away from hostility to hospitality.[33] Most of these come from short, rather quick Bible studies presented mostly to Western Christian groups and are meant to convey a mood rather than demand sustained reflection. In a long Bible study entitled "Adam in Deep Sleep," Koyama works on a dialogue between "Adam awakened" and "Adam in deep sleep" in the life of Asia.[34] K. C. Abraham, in his response to this study, which was presented to an Asian Christian consultation, remarks, "I feel Dr. Koyama's paper, with all respect to his creative contribution, is still basically Western. All the central categories and concepts are taken from Western thinkers ... This is not a criticism but an observation!"[35] Koyama succeeds in conveying an Asian flavor to his Western hearers. His method is communication by contrast—contrast between biblical images and those in a technological Western society. Its possibilities for biblical interpretation in Asia need to be explored more critically where Christians live together with their neighbors of other faiths and ideological convictions.

Breaking away from literalist interpretations of the Bible, C. S. Song provides an important, perhaps more Asian, alternative to connect what is truly biblical with what is authentically Asian. He does this by going beyond the structures of languages to the meaning of symbols that provide openings into a transhistorical world. Meaningful selections from the Asian cultural heritage, particularly from Chinese—poems, stories, legends, myths, dramas, and proverbs—are placed alongside significant chunks of biblical material, challenging the imagination and touching the spirit of the readers, who are constantly invited to go beyond the written words to the symbolic meaning behind them. This is particularly true, for example, in his booklet *The Tears of Lady Ming* and the article "Opening the Stone Gate of Religion with a Golden Key." In the inner experience of the interpreters whose hearts and minds are opened to the meaning of symbols, the hermeneutical circle is closed, not short-circuited.[36]

A literalist interpretation of the Bible, according to Song, destroys the power and meaning of revelation. There cannot be "a verbatim correspondence" between what is written down and what transcends history. "Human language has to be stretched beyond its normal logic to capture something that transcends human rationality. Scriptures can thus be interpreted symbolically."[37] One cannot become sensitive to the power of symbols without a spirit of "transposition." This is an important principle in Song's method of interpretation, which he elaborates on at considerable length. Transposition is "a shift in space and time" from the biblical world to the Asian world, even "a theological leap." It is an effort "to respond to that mysterious and powerful bond of life with which the compassionate God creates, redeems and recreates a family and a human community."[38]

This calls for sensitivity and creative responses to vibrations coming from the depths of the human spirit that are outside the familiar realm of everyday life and may at first appear alien to our religious consciousness. Asia, with its vast number of peoples, religions, and cultures, demands a spirit of transposition "and invites us to a hermeneutical and theological adventure."[39] Song constantly notes that one has to go beyond the rules of interpretation to the heart of a self-revealing God who continues to redeem all people. Changes in present-day realities in Asia oblige us to reinterpret the Word of God afresh. Asian hearts need to be open to new insights as Asian Christians stand at the intersection where the Word of God and the reality of life in Asia constantly meet and react. "The Christian Bible which follows God's search from the time of Adam and Eve to its culmination on the cross, gives us profound insights into God's work: the recovery of the human heart."[40]

Mar Gregorios brings a distinctively Indian and Orthodox contribution to the quest for biblical interpretation in Asia.[41] He is very impatient with Western historical criticism of the Bible. Few people are so proud of their Indian heritage, so unmistakably Orthodox in their Christian commitment, and so unreservedly critical of the West and of Western Christianity as Mar Gregorios. It is easy to disagree with him, but difficult to ignore him. Europeans "short circuit" hermeneutics, remarks Gregorios. Instead of asking the question, "How do I perceive reality and how can I improve the way I perceive it?" they ask, "What are the rules to interpret the Bible and how do I improve my way of interpretation?"[42] This appears to be a little too harsh. But many Asian students, including Indians who have done their biblical studies in the West, are so trapped within the hedges of European biblical criticism that they are unable to move beyond their restricting limitations into the realms of original Asian theological reflection.

One should note that Asian religious traditions such as the Hindu and the Buddhist do not believe that one can develop a scriptural hermeneutic which will yield truth by itself. True knowledge is not the fruit of logical investigation or the exegesis of scriptures, but a transformation of the knowing subject. Gregorios connects this with the Eastern Orthodox tradition. Both Indian philosophy and the Eastern tradition, he says, generally hold the view that one can know reality only when one's whole life becomes pure. Gregory of Nyssa emphasizes the need to cleanse the mind and control the passions in order to "see" God. The basic hermeneutic principle is that of *"apatheia"* or a personality that is not only free from passions which dominate the mind and from all evil inclinations, but is also positively developed to conform to the image of God.[43] This emphasis on the discipline of the body, mind, and heart (*sadhana*) as a prerequisite to any hermeneutics is too often neglected by Asian Christians.

To this Gregorios adds two further points. One is the importance of tradition, that is, the ongoing life of the believing community within which scriptural interpretations take place. Community plays a much greater role in shaping our perceptions of truth than we imagine. His other point is the necessity to be open to the Spirit of God. Sharpening the intellectual tools of perception is only a minor part of hermeneutics. Being open to the Spirit is the major part. However, the moment we mention the Spirit of *God*, we must take into account the larger human community, particularly because in Asia the Christian community is a small part of a much larger multireligious and multicultural community. "The Bible is an important element in the operation of the Spirit in the community. But we will certainly need to know more about the larger operation of the Spirit not only as a whole, and in fact in the whole universe, before we can understand what the Spirit is saying to the Churches."[44]

This emphasis on tradition (*sampradaya*), which is the principle of continuity in the life of the church, is accepted both by Orthodox and Roman Catholic scholars. Protestant scholars do not ignore this dimension, but their concern with biblical interpretations has been part of their quest for a source of authority independent of, or at least critical of, the authority of the institutional and hierarchical church. This is understandable when one takes into account the history of the church in the West during the Reformation and after. In Asia, however, with its many powerful religions, cultures, and scriptures, the story of the Bible has to be retold in a different context. When all the three major traditions of the church—Roman Catholic, Orthodox and Protestant—are present in Asia, the *Christian* concern with the Bible has to be more ecumenical in its deepest sense. The dynamic interplay of scripture, tradition, and reason within the Christian church should influence and be influenced by the hermeneutical struggle of neighbors of other faiths as well.

There are many Catholic scholars in Asia writing on the subject of biblical hermeneutics. Some tend to see it as a tool or instrument of theology. Biblical scholars are often regarded as technicians, selecting and sharpening the tools for the architects and engineers of theology. Thus Carlos H. Abesan remarks that "theologians need the help of the exegetes and biblical scholars." He speaks of different kinds of biblical scholars. Some, according to him, regard the Bible as "an arsenal of incipient dogmatic truth." Some see biblical study as "a handmaid" to dogmatic theology. Others reconstruct the meaning of the Bible against its literary and historic contexts.

> Finally, there are the Biblical scholars, who, as they do vigorous exegesis, open each book of the Bible as they would different doors, and as they do, open up to themselves and to others a whole panorama in which to contemplate the whole history of salvation with its past and its promise for the future. These last are the *technicians* the theologians are looking for.[45]

The question inevitably arises: What is the authority of the Bible, not so much *against* as *in relation to* the authority of scriptures which are cherished and held in deep respect by our neighbors of other faiths, even as Christians cherish and respect the Bible? D. S. Amalorpavadass, the well-known Roman Catholic scholar in India, has given considerable attention to this question. There are also other articles by other scholars.[46] Protestant biblical scholars have not paid serious attention to this matter. The volume Amalorpavadass has edited is the fruit of a consultation which gathered together Roman Catholic, Orthodox, and Protestant scholars to consider this matter, although one must note that the Roman Catholics were the majority group that provided substance and direction to the discussion.

Amalorpavadass recognizes that the question of the authority and inspiration of nonbiblical scriptures is important and urgent for the church in Asia. He prefers the term "non-biblical" to "non-Christian," because the latter has negative connotations. He points out that Christians are already using selections from nonbiblical scriptures in their meditations, prayers, and sometimes even in the liturgy. The enrichment Christians receive from them is accepted. Further, in the growing experience of interreligious relations, the question of the authority of scriptures becomes increasingly important. It cannot be ignored anymore. Christians in Asia should recognize that this is a new problem for the church, because neither the early church nor the church in the West had to face this question as Christians do in Asia today. To the church in the multireligious countries of Asia, the matter is even more important and urgent. He remarks, "It seems that the Church in India is destined by Divine Providence to contribute as its specific share to the theology of the religious traditions of humankind, more specifically to that of non-biblical scriptures."[47]

The notions of revelation and inspiration are changing within Christianity itself. One cannot therefore approach the scriptures of our neighbors with absolute notions of the exclusive inspiration of the Christian scriptures. The scriptures of any religious group are the objectification of the faith experience of that particular community. Therefore, scriptures have to be regarded not as an absolute creation, but an actualization, a re-creation of the experience. Inspiration can be meaningful only in the context of the faith experience of the believers.

In the statement that emerged out of the consultation, at which no less than thirty-two research papers were considered, two attitudes toward nonbiblical scriptures are apparent. One is to regard them as preparing the way for Christ. Thus the Hindu scriptures, it is claimed, "give us many openings into the mystery of Christ." The mystical love of the *Bhagavadgita* foreshadows the love of Christ. If we can speak of "the Unknown Christ of Hinduism," we can also speak of "the half-known Christ of Islam."

But this view is hardly new. It retains Christian scriptures as the norm and either uses other scriptures to justify its supremacy or co-opts them into its own structure in a patronizing way. Many people at the consultation expressed uneasiness about this position and argued for a theocentric approach rather than "a Christomonistic" one. This attitude emphasizes that the mystery of God revealed in Jesus of Nazareth and attested to in the Bible is expressed in different ways in other religions such as Hinduism or Buddhism. Therefore, the scriptures of other religions should not be subordinated to the Christian but regarded as valid and authoritative to those who accept them, because they are based on their own particular faith experience.

Obviously, this whole question needs to be studied more carefully by Asian scholars in the years to come. Protestant scholars who have not given sufficient attention to this question need to grapple with this matter, together with their Catholic and Orthodox colleagues. Whether biblical hermeneutics is a separate and distinct discipline or whether it can benefit by sharing the general hermeneutical task with neighbors of other faiths is a matter that needs further discussion. In any case, this task cannot be done satisfactorily without accepting the fact that interreligious dialogue in Asia is no longer the concern of a few but part of the experience of the church in Asia as a whole. Out of this experience and critical reflection on it, Christians should become sensitive to new insights and fresh perspectives. The Christian community can speak meaningfully of the inspiration of the scriptures of other religions only insofar as its experience of itself is no longer that of a closed group but of a community that is open and moving toward the formation of a new, wider community that would be as wide as God's economy of salvation.

SOME PRINCIPLES OF INTERPRETATION

In this discussion on scripture and scriptures in a religiously plural world, certain tentative conclusions may be noted here.

1. There is indeed a *plurality* of scriptures. This is a fact of history to be accepted, not a theological point to be discussed. This should be openly acknowledged by people of all religious traditions. Each particular tradition

cherishes its own scripture, holding it as sacred and authoritative. To ignore this fact amounts to blindness and self-deception.

2. Scriptures *function differently* in the life of different religious communities. The manner in which an oral tradition comes to be written down, the ways in which a text becomes a scripture, and how a scripture functions religiously in the life of a believing community are all different, depending very much on cultural differences and historical circumstances. The notion and exercise of authority itself is understood differently in different communities of faith. Therefore the criteria derived on the basis of one particular scripture cannot be used to pass judgment on other scriptures.

3. There are certain *exclusive* elements within each scripture leading to truth claims by each community of faith. Thus the *Gita* talks of many *avataras*; the New Testament speaks of Jesus Christ as "the way, the truth and the life"; the Qur'an describes Mohammed as "the seal" of the prophets; and the Torah is still waiting for the Messiah to come. These claims are important for the self-understanding and identity of each community of faith in the larger community. These should not be relativized, but accepted as legitimate *within* the boundaries of particular communities of faith. They cannot be extended to other faiths. How these claims based on scriptures are to be related to one another will become an important question. Premature conclusions made unilaterally by one community of faith would preempt discussions in a multireligious world.

4. The language of religion does not depend solely on *texts* but also on *symbols* that are not an end in themselves but point to something beyond that is deeper, larger, and more mysterious. The language of religion is a language of love and commitment. It would be most unwise to draw logical conclusions from the language of love. An exclusive claim expressed in religious language has the character of commitment, not of rejection. A negative judgment on other commitments based on one's own particular commitment is unwarranted. The relationship between different truth claims in the larger community is yet to be discussed. Charges of relativism should not be hurled against those who recognize other commitments in a religiously plural world.

5. In every living religion, scriptures are not just sources of doctrine, but also of personal devotion, spiritual sustenance, and help in times of trouble, perplexity, and suffering. Therefore the *devotional* use of *other* scriptures by people of a particular tradition should not be rejected or looked upon with suspicion. In the lives of many people, reading from other scriptures is enlarging horizons and deepening inner life without in any way disturbing, diluting, or betraying one's own commitment.

6. All life, including the religious, has a *pilgrim* character. We are always *on the way*. Every arrival is a point of departure, and every journey looks for a new destination. This means that scriptures should not be regarded as "petrified texts" written once for all, or that the entire religious life of humankind is limited to a continual hermeneutical exercise seeking to inter-

pret texts handed over from the past. That would amount to ignoring the leading of the Spirit into new realms of truth and blocking the possibilities of new insights being recognized to sustain life on the way. The major religions in the world today, the Semitic and the Indian, originated in isolation from each other. The formation of particular scriptures and the development of the canon took place without reference to what was happening in other places and at other times among other people. Today, when the nations of the world are being drawn together as never before and people of different religious beliefs share a common destiny, the different scriptures should not be regarded as passport documents that divide different nationalities but as signposts that point to a more promising future.

In order to avoid any misunderstanding, it must be stated firmly and in as unambiguous terms as possible that the cumulative effect of these points does not in any way minimize or weaken the authority of the Bible for Christian life and thought, but puts it in a larger perspective that is theologically appropriate in a religiously plural world. The Bible remains normative for all Christians in all places and at all times, because it bears witness to God's dealings with the whole World and to Jesus Christ, his life and death, and resurrection, his deeds and teachings, thus providing the basis for Christian theological reflection. The dynamic interplay among the Bible, tradition, and reason—whatever the differences between Roman Catholics, Orthodox, and Protestant—is very much part of the Christian hermeneutical process in all situations. But to be "biblical" it is not necessary to claim that every letter and word in the book is true or to ignore and condemn the scriptures of neighbors of other faiths. All christological reflections take place on the basis of the authority of the Bible and the strength of Christian tradition, which is the cumulative experience of the believing community in history. Today, however, in a religiously plural world, the interplay among scripture, tradition, and reason has to be far more dynamic and theologically imaginative than ever before.

6

Christ in a Multireligious Culture

Although most Christians today are unwilling to take a totally negative attitude toward neighbors of other faiths, there seems to be a good deal of hesitation on the part of many to reexamine the basis of their exclusive claims on behalf of Christ. The place of Christ in a multireligious society becomes, therefore, an important issue in the search for a new theology of religions.

It is important to realize that I seek not to attack the "truth" of classical christological doctrines, but to discuss ways to avoid negative consequences that follow when such doctrines are narrowly interpreted and lead to cramped psychological and spiritual attitudes among Christians. In such cases, it can be argued, the classical formulae *defeat* the purposes for which they were originally articulated.

Theological claims have political consequences. This is particularly true in contemporary India, where the exclusive claims made by any one particular community of faith affect its relationships with members of other communities of faith. Such claims make it difficult, if not impossible, for persons belonging to different religious traditions to live together in harmony and cooperate for common purposes in society. Such claims, open or hidden, also raise basic theological questions concerning God's relationship to the whole of humanity, not just to one stream of it. Thus both historical pressures and theological imperatives demand a reexamination of all exclusivist claims.

Through the incarnation in Jesus Christ, God relativized himself in history. Christian theologians should therefore ask themselves whether they are justified in absolutizing in doctrine one whom God has relativized in history. Today's questions regarding the relationship of Jesus Christ to God are very different from those asked in earlier centuries. In many ways, they are new questions that need new solutions. These new solutions, however, must be theologically credible, spiritually satisfying, and pastorally helpful.

A process of rejecting exclusive claims and seeking new ways of understanding the relationship of Jesus Christ to God and humanity is already underway. From what may be described as "normative exclusivism," Christians are moving toward a position of "relational distinctiveness" of Christ. It is *relational* because Christ does not remain unrelated to neighbors of other faiths, and *distinctive* because without recognizing the distinctiveness of the great religious traditions as different responses to the Mystery of God, no mutual enrichment is possible.

Such efforts toward a new Christian theology are taking place in India. Christian theological reflection in India obviously cannot be carried on in isolation and must take into account what is happening in different parts of the world church. But at the same time, Indian theologians cannot go on as if, in the long centuries of religious life in India, there had been no theological reflection whatsoever on issues of interreligious relationships. More precisely, the Hindu response to religious pluralism should become a part of Indian Christian theological reflection. Thus, the interplay of these two factors—the ferment within the world church and the experience of religious life lived pluralistically in India—provide the context for the following reflections.

CHANGES IN CHRISTIAN RESPONSE TO OTHER FAITHS

During the last two decades significant changes have taken place officially in Christian attitudes toward neighbors of other faiths. The well-known declaration of the Second Vatican Council, *Nostra Aetate* (1965), is regarded as "the first truly positive statement" of the Catholic Church about other religions.[1]

Founded in 1948, the World Council of Churches moved rather slowly and somewhat reluctantly on this issue until, in 1971, it accepted an interim policy statement on other faiths. After nearly a decade of hard work, often marked by controversy, the W.C.C. accepted in 1979 a theological statement and adopted a set of *Guidelines on Dialogue*, "welcoming the degree of agreement and mutual understanding represented by it among those who held different theological views." With regard to neighbors of other faiths, the statement said: "We feel able with integrity to assure our partners in dialogue that we come not as manipulators but as fellow-pilgrims. . . . "[2]

These attitudes are indeed strikingly different from those the Christian church persistently held during previous centuries. It is precisely at this point, however, that there now seems to be considerable hesitation as to what steps the church should take next in a continuing pluralistic world. It looks as if, having opened the door slightly, Christians are afraid that the strangers, long kept outside, might indeed turn out to be fellow pilgrims after all. What if the forbidden frontier turns out to be a welcoming threshold?

Since the mid-1960s there have been many developments in the Catholic Church and in the churches affiliated with the World Council of Churches. But many internal tensions have also developed. There are Catholic scholars who feel that the tensions regarding other religions are rooted within the official magisterium:

> The failure adequately to explain what Vatican II means, and to square it either with Scripture or with the strong theological tradition that has seen other religions as idolatrous is serious. Unless the magisterium can do so convincingly, it will be under fire . . .[3]

Roman Catholic scholars in India also feel that there is now a stalemate in interreligious dialogue, with participants repeating the same alternatives in various combinations, unwilling to move ahead.[4] Pope John Paul II recently convoked an extraordinary Synod of Bishops "to relive in some way the extraordinary atmosphere of the ecclesial communion during the Council [Vatican II]" and "to foster a further deepening and acceptance of Vatican II in the life of the church, especially in the light of new demands."[5] Inasmuch as some of the new demands are precisely in the area of relationship with neighbors of other faiths, one would hope for a more decisive turn in the attitude of the Catholic Church.

Within the World Council of Churches, given the variety and complexity of its membership and the very different theological positions represented within its wide spectrum of opinions, the tensions are even stronger, though not always openly articulated. With the many evangelicals represented within the fellowship of the World Council of Churches, there is an unavoidable tension between mission and dialogue. Yet the problem is even more complex than it appears, for there are tensions *within* the perceptions of mission itself and dialogue itself.

"Though it might *seem* that the tension between 'mission' and 'dialogue' has been resolved," writes Allan R. Brockway, "the real tension remains."[6] The massive studies now underway in ecumenical and evangelical circles on "Gospel and Culture" are important, but they can also become a way of avoiding the challenge and invitation of other religions by diverting resources toward a topic on which a great deal has already been said.[7] What is the substance of *culture*, particularly in Asian societies, without its *religious* dimensions? An essay on the elephant without reference to its ivory is incomplete, and can even be positively dangerous. Even though the theological issues have already been identified and questions for the study of other faiths formulated, there seems to be great reluctance to move ahead.[8]

With regard to conservative evangelicals, it is difficult to talk about *next* steps when even the *first* steps have not been taken. One cannot ask a door to be opened *wider* when it is already latched from within and chained. Given the evangelical assumption of the inerrance of the Bible, it is hardly likely that any positive approach toward neighbors of other faiths will emerge in the coming years. Evangelicals' recent talk about "dialogue," with its seeming openness to members of other faiths, is misleading. Dialogue is understood by them as a means of communicating the message.

"The dialogic method is necessary if those who witness to Christ are to engage the minds of their listeners."⁹ In "true" dialogue and encounter, it is claimed, "we seek both to disclose the inadequacies and falsities of non-Christian religions and to demonstrate the adequacy and truth, the absoluteness and finality of the Lord Jesus Christ."¹⁰ It is the *instrumental* use of dialogue rather than its *intrinsic* worth as a living way of seeking new relationships in the household of God that is emphasized.

There are many reasons why, in this matter of interreligious encounter, Christians are unwilling to move beyond the positions they have already taken. Sometimes political and economic factors influence the attitude of one religious community toward others. Quite often, unexamined ideological assumptions prevent Christians from critically examining their traditional positions. But the major reason for the present impasse is the unresolved theological tension within the consciousness of the church about other religions.

To ask theological questions about this matter is to go to the very roots of our pluralistic existence today. To truly confront these questions, the study of religions has to be shifted from a *missiological* to a *theological* framework, particularly in our theological colleges and seminaries. The question is not *what* to do with so many other religions that claim the loyalty and devotion of millions of followers in the world, but *why* are they so persistently present, providing meaning and direction to the lives of millions of our neighbors. What does this mean theologically—that is, for our understanding of God and God's relationship to the whole created *oikoumene*, of which Christians are not the only citizens? Can it be that plurality belongs to the very structure of reality? Or can it be that it is the will of God that many religions should continue in the world?

These are difficult questions indeed, and it may take a long time for the church to arrive at clear and unambiguous answers to them. The Western church took quite some time to come to terms with Copernicus and Darwin, with Freud and Jung, with science and technology, and is still struggling with Marx and Mao. The challenge and invitation of other religions may take even longer to elicit firm and clear answers. But beginnings have to be made, lest the church look like a fortress to be defended rather than the household of God where strangers and sojourners can become fellow citizens.

FOUR MOMENTS IN INTERRELIGIOUS RELATIONSHIPS IN INDIA

In contemporary India a radical change in the Christian stance toward neighbors of other faiths is both an existential demand and a theological necessity. It is desperately needed when the unity and integrity of the country is in danger of being torn apart by forces of separation that are often influenced by the claims and counterclaims of diverse religions. And yet the search for new relationships among different religious communities is not just a matter of political adjustments or a redistribution of economic resources. Deep down, it is a theological question seeking to relate different responses to the Mystery of Truth.

By blaming the highly visible religious communities for the political and social ills of the country, one avoids a serious discussion about the spiritual and theological resources available within religions for the critical renewal of community life. No one would deny that religions have exploited persons and have contributed to much of the social injustice in India (as well as in other countries). In the struggle for a just society, established religions have often been on the side of the rich and the powerful, not that of the poor and the oppressed. Religions have been unable to tame political passions and, quite often, have added religious fuel to political conflagrations. Yet recent studies on communal clashes between Hindus and Sikhs (after the assassination of Mrs. Indira Gandhi), have brought out the point that religion "is not the *causative* factor but the *instrumental* factor in such clashes. ... it is made to appear as the causative factor."[11]

A secular "emptying" of religions in light of the role of religion in the real or imaginary ills of society would lead to a tremendous loss of creative power. It is very necessary to accept "the normative plurality" of India's life and to provide space for dialogue among religious, linguistic, and ethnic groups. The contemporary contribution of India as a civilization to the meaning and content of democracy could be in the way India tolerates this initial Babel of multicultural encounters that can lead to the creation of new communities, myths, and languages. The acceptance of plurality can well be an answer to fascism.[12]

Through long centuries of pluralistic existence, India has developed a particular attitude toward religious dissent. A systematic and sympathetic study of this mood of tolerance is yet to be made.[13] But a few moments in India's long history can be profitably noted.

As early as the Vedic period (about 1500 B.C.E.), Brahmanism tried to solve the clash between the One and the many by suggesting that while *Sat* (Truth, Being) is One, sages call it by different names. It was not by eliminating the gods or by conquering them, but by relating them to the One, and therefore to one another, that they were held together in a structure of difference rather than similarity. The One was greater than any of the gods or even than the sum total of the gods. And even when the distinctiveness and legitimacy of different gods were recognized within an existential relationship, the ontological substance remained above and beyond the gods. Without recognizing and accepting this Mysterious Center (the *Satyasya Satyam* — the Truth of the Truth), genuine plurality is impossible.[14]

It took many centuries for Brahmanism, and later Hinduism, to "overcome" the challenge of the Buddha who rejected the authority of the Vedas, the superiority of the Brahmins, and the necessity of the sacrificial ritual. Now, however, the Buddha is "co-opted" into the Hindu structure of the *avataras*.¹⁵ Later on, the *sampradayas* (traditions connected with Vishnu, Siva, and Sakti) within Hinduism were held together in a larger framework, despite the tensions caused by different kings who followed different *sampradayas*.¹⁶

If one takes a leap across the centuries, one encounters moments when Islam and later Christianity, armed with their exclusive claims and allied with military, political, and economic power, rudely intruded into India's delicate balance of relationships. This created deep disturbances within Indian consciousness, the consequences of which are with us even to this day. The Hindu arguments against any claim of "uniqueness," "finality," or "once-for-allness" for one particular way are well known. Westerners, together with Indian Christians, are familiar with the English works of Ram Mohan Roy (1772-1833) and S. Radhakrishnan (1888-1975) on this subject.¹⁷ The "neo-Hindu" emphasis on the equality of all religions (*sarva dharma samanvaya tattva*) was probably more a *political affirmation* of the relationships between different religious communities at a time when political tensions were developing in the country rather than a *theological statement* on the relationships between religions. Perhaps, therefore, one should not attach too much theological significance to this emphasis. On the other hand, there is a body of writings in Sanskrit and other Indian languages that reflects more strongly the tolerant mood and feelings of the people in general. These writings remain a closed book to those who restrict themselves to the English language.¹⁸

It is worthwhile to note these orthodox Hindu arguments because they are influential even to this day. Basing themselves on two principles—*mataikya*, the unity of all religions, and *matavirodha*, their noncontradictoriness—the pandits advanced three arguments against the claim of Christian superiority. First, the plurality of religions is "intrinsic and purposeful" because of *dharma*. The basic differences in humankind make it natural and inevitable that there should be plurality, not singularity, in religion. In other words, plurality is rooted in the diversity of human nature itself.

Secondly, there is the principle of *adhikara* (which may be translated aptitude, competence, eligibility), which makes plurality necessary. Birth is never accidental. It is the result of *kārmic* repercussions. Therefore one is born in a particular religion because of the *sādhana* (discipline) possible for that particular person. Thirdly, this *adhikara-bheda* (differences in aptitude or competence) is not a matter of choice but is a "given" element, even the will of God, and it allows persons to choose different *margas* (paths or ways). God defines one's *adhikara* by the attraction (*ruci*) one feels toward a certain *marga*. Hindus are Hindus rather than Christians because they have aptitude and eligibility only for their *dharma* and not for Christianity.

Therefore the question of superiority or uniqueness of any one *dharma* over others does not arise. Criticism of one religion based on criteria derived from another is unwarranted. Conversions are unnecessary. The

Hindus are not asking Christians to give up their commitment to God in Christ. Rather, they are pleading with Christians not to ask Hindus to give up their commitment. One should note that these arguments, so different from the later "neo-Hindu" affirmation of the equality of all religions, are echoed even to this day and have a pervasive influence on general Hindu consciousness.

Perhaps it is worthwhile to recall an even more recent moment in the history of India just after the nation's political independence (1947). Despite fresh memories of how their country was divided on religious grounds and torn by massive human sufferings, Hindus as the majority community were generous toward their minority neighbors—Muslims and Christians. In the Constituent Assembly, working on a constitution for the Republic of India, Loknath Mishra introduced an amendment that would delete the words "to propagate" from the Article on Fundamental Rights: "to profess, practice and propagate" one's religion (Article 25:1). During the debate, such well-known leaders as Pandit Lakshmikant Maitra, T. T. Krishnamachari, K. M. Munshi (vice-chancellor of the Bhavan University), and several others argued for retaining the words "to propagate" as a recognition of a fundamental right of minority communities. Without the support of Hindu leaders, the clause would have never passed. Soli Sorabji, a distinguished jurist, remarks, "One cannot but be struck by the broadmindedness and the spirit of tolerance and accommodation displayed by the founding fathers of the majority community towards their Christian brethren."[19] In no other country, does the claim for the uniqueness of one particular religious tradition or the assertion of the normativeness of one particular faith over others sound so rude, out of place, and theologically arrogant as in India. Such assertions contradict India's whole ethos and tear at that fabric of interreligious relationships so carefully woven during centuries of conflict, tension, and massive sufferings by the people.[20]

THE MEANING OF JESUS AND THE MYSTERY OF GOD

In this context of ongoing life in India, where Christians live and work together with neighbors of other faiths, where a deep-seated theological tolerance coexists with social intolerance, can a christology be developed that is free from the burdens of the past but is unmistakably Christian and recognizably Indian?

Any attempt to formulate such a christology should take into account at least two factors that have emerged out of India's long history of multireligious life. One is the acceptance of a sense of Mystery; the other is the rejection of an exclusive attitude as far as ultimate matters are concerned. Mystery is not something to be used to fill the gaps in rational knowledge. Mystery provides the ontological basis for tolerance, which would otherwise run the risk of becoming uncritical friendliness. This Mystery, the Truth of the Truth (*Satyasya Satyam*), is the transcendent Center that always remains beyond and greater than apprehensions of it, or even greater than the sum total of those apprehensions. It is beyond cognitive knowledge (*tarka*), but it is open to vision (*dristi*) and intuition (*anubhava*). It is near yet far, knowable yet unknowable, intimate yet ultimate and, according to one particular Hindu view, cannot even be described as "one." It is "not-two" (*advaita*), indicating thereby that diversity is within the heart of Being itself and therefore may be intrinsic to human nature as well.

This emphasis on Mystery is not meant as an escape from the need for rational inquiry, but it does insist that the rational is not the only way to do theology. The mystical and aesthetic also have their necessary contributions to theology. Mystery lies beyond the theistic/nontheistic debate. Mystery is an ontological status to be accepted, not an epistemological problem to be solved. Without a sense of Mystery, *Theos* cannot remain *Theos*, nor *Sat* remain *Sat*, nor can Ultimate Reality remain ultimate.

In religious life, Mystery and meaning are related. Without a disclosure of meaning at particular points in history or in human consciousness, there can be no human response to Mystery. The history of religions shows that these responses are many and varied, sometimes even within a particular religious tradition. Quite often these differences are due to cultural and historical factors. Although each response to Mystery has a normative claim on the followers of that particular tradition, the criteria derived from one response cannot be made the norm for judging the responses of other traditions.

One strand of Hinduism, for example, has described this Mystery as *sat-cit-ananda* (truth-consciousness-bliss). This is one way of responding to Mystery in a particular cultural setting, but it is very different from that of the early Christian centuries. Christians believe that in Jesus Christ the meaning of this Mystery is revealed in such a way as to constitute a revelation of God and provide a way of salvation for all human beings. The doctrine of the Trinity, which describes God as Father, Son, and the Holy Spirit, is an attempt to make sense of this Mystery through the meaning disclosed in Jesus of Nazareth, identified with Christ, and using categories from Greek thought alien to the Indian context.

Both the terms "Brahman" and "God" are culture conditioned. One could as well use the term Mystery, which may be more acceptable. In this case the statements that "Brahman is *sat-cit-ananda*" and "God is triune, Father, Son, and Holy Spirit" could be regarded as two responses to the same Mystery in two cultural settings. One cannot be used as a norm to judge the other.

The limitations of language are obvious here. Feminist theologians have already objected to the "maleness" of the trinitarian formula. If cultural obstacles could be overcome, they might be persuaded to accept the Hindu notion, which avoids this problem. In any case, neither *sat-cit-ananda* nor Trinity could, in linguistic terms, adequately describe the inner ontological working of Mystery. One could ask, therefore, on what grounds can it be claimed that the trinitarian formula offers a truer insight into the nature of Mystery than does *sat-cit-ananda*? At best, the two formulations can only be symbolic, pointing to the Mystery, affirming the meaning disclosed, but retaining the residual depth.

No one could have anticipated in advance the presence of God in the life and death of Jesus of Nazareth. There is an incomprehensible dimension to it. That Jesus is the Christ of God is a confession of faith by the Christian community. It does indeed remain normative to Christians everywhere, but to make it "absolute singular" and to maintain that the meaning of the Mystery is disclosed *only* in one particular person at one particular point, and nowhere else, is to ignore one's neighbors of other faiths who have other points of reference. To make exclusive claims for our particular tradition is not the best way to love our neighbors as ourselves.

If human responses to the revelation of Mystery are plural and are articulated in different ways, the same observation applies to the experience of salvation and to the manner in which it is articulated by followers of different traditions.

In multireligious situations such as in India, notions of salvation and of what we are saved from are understood differently. This is to be expected. The question here is not whether there *may be* plural ways of salvation. In multireligious situations the fact is that there *are* plural ways of salvation, experienced and articulated in different ways. Both the context and expression of salvation are different. When the questions asked about the human predicament are different, the answers are bound to be different. How can it be otherwise? Even in the New Testament, salvation through Jesus Christ was experienced and interpreted differently by the Aramaic-speaking Jewish Christians; the Hellenic Jews of the diaspora, who were much more open to other peoples among whom they lived; and non-Jewish Christians, such as the Greeks, Syrians, and Romans, who had no part in the Jewish history of salvation. And yet, there was no doubt about the root of this experience of salvation in Jesus Christ.

Whereas Christians use the term sin to describe the human predicament, Hindus might use *avidya* (ignorance) and Buddhists *dukkha* (sorrow) as the condition from which deliverance is sought. The notions of *moksha* and *nirvana* as the ultimate goals of deliverance are conceived differently, as are the *sadhanas*, the ways of discipline advocated as necessary to attain these goals. In addition, today one must also take into account the desperate desire of millions of human beings for salvation of a different kind: liberation from oppression, exploitation, and injustice. In this context, many feminist Christian theologians decline to accept as normative the notion of a revelation and salvation through a male person that excludes more than half of humanity.

When alternative ways of salvation have provided meaning and purpose for millions of persons in other cultures for more than two or three thousand years, to claim that the Jewish–Christian–Western tradition has the *only* answer to all problems in all places and for all persons in the world is presumptuous, if not incredible. This is not to deny the validity of the Christian experience of salvation in Jesus Christ, but to question the exclusive claims made for it by Christians—claims that are unsupported by any evidence of history, or in the institutional life of the church, or in the lives of many Christians who make such claims. If salvation comes *from God*—and for Christians it cannot be otherwise—then possibilities should be left open to recognize the validity of other experiences of salvation.

The nature of Mystery is such that any claim on the part of one religious community to have exclusive, unique, or final knowledge becomes inadmissible. Exclusiveness puts fences around the Mystery. It creates dichotomies between the divine and the human, between humanity and nature, and between different religious communities. It leaves little room for the nonrational elements in religious life—the mystical and the aesthetic, rituals and symbols, prayer, worship, and meditation. It is not surprising that very often Christian theologians ready to discuss religious ideas with others feel extremely uneasy when it comes to matters of worship or art in interreligious meetings (*satsang*—fellowship or truth). Further, those who make open or hidden claims of exclusiveness find it impossible to live together with neighbors of other faiths, except on very superficial social levels. A one-way, exclusivistic proclamation is like a stone hurled into a flowing stream. It makes a little splash, and then remains submerged, making no difference whatsoever to the waters flowing past it. Someone might even pick it up and hurl it back to where it came from.

Very often, claims for the normativeness of Christ are based on the authority of the Bible. Exclusive texts are hurled back and forth, as if just by uttering texts from scriptures the problem is settled. The authority of the Bible is indeed important for Christians. In multireligious situations, where there are other scriptures whose authority is accepted by neighbors of other religious traditions, how can the claims based on one particular scripture become the norm or authority for all? Here, too, the plurality of scriptures is a fact to be accepted, not a notion to be discussed.

But there are even more important factors to be recognized. For example, what does one make of the fact, hardly recognized by Christian theologians, that none of the revelations on which Christians theologize today took place in a Western European context or were written down in a Western European language? Recent studies in the ontology of language point out how precarious it is to depend on texts and translations when it comes to the question of authority in matters of faith.[21]

Even notions of authority are different when it comes to interpreting holy scriptures. To the Hindu and the Buddhist, the authority of the scriptures does not depend on the "writtenness" of the text, but on *hearing* and *seeing* the word (*Sabda*). Texts are indeed important. But a Hindu or Buddhist would reject the notion that through the study of texts one can encounter the truth behind them, or that merely by quoting texts one can encounter the truth within them, or that merely by quoting texts truth is communicated to hearers. Knowledge of God is not something to be discovered through the study of written texts. It is to be *recovered* through *hearing*. The holiness of words is intrinsic. One participates in it not through understanding but through reciting and hearing it.

The Western notion of editing an original text is an intrusion into Eastern situations. One has to go behind the written texts to the *sound* of the Word, recited and heard over long periods of time by the community, in order to see how words have functioned in matters of faith. This question of hermeneutics in multireligious situations needs careful study. In India, around 35–32 B.C.E., Buddhists were the first to commit their sacred oral texts to writing. Attempts are now being made by Indian Christian biblical scholars to study Hindu and Buddhist hermeneutical theory as it has developed over the centuries and to work out the implications of Eastern hermeneutics for the Indian Christian theological enterprise.[22]

If the great religious traditions of humanity are indeed different responses to the Mystery of God or *Sat* or the Transcendent or Ultimate Reality, then the *distinctiveness* of each response, in this instance the Christian, should be stated in such a way that a mutually critical and enriching *relationship* between different responses becomes naturally possible. Exclusiveness regards universality as the extension of its own particularity and seeks to conquer other faiths. Inclusiveness, though seeming generous, actually co-opts other faiths without their leave. Both exclusiveness and its patronizing cousin inclusiveness may even be forms of theological violence against neighbors of other faiths and, when combined with economic, political, and military power (as has often happened in history) becomes dangerous to communal harmony and world peace. It is not without significance that only after the second world war (1945), when, with the dismantling of colonialism, new nations emerged on the stage of history and asserted their identities through their own religions and cultures, both the Vatican and the World Council of Churches began to articulate a more positive attitude toward peoples of other religious traditions, although both church bodies remained reluctant to recognize the *theological* significance of these other faiths.

In moving beyond exclusiveness and inclusiveness, Christians must come to a clearer grasp of the uniqueness of Jesus. The distinctiveness of Jesus Christ does not lie in claiming that Jesus Christ is God. This amounts to saying that Jesus Christ is the tribal god of Christians as compared to the gods of other peoples. Elevating Jesus to the status of God or limiting Christ to Jesus of Nazareth are both temptations to be avoided. The former runs the risk of an impoverished "Jesusology" and the latter of becoming a narrow "Christomonism." A theocentric christology avoids these dangers and becomes more helpful in establishing new relationships with neighbors of other faiths.

A theocentric (or Mystery centered) christology is not a new fashion.

The Bible continually emphasized the priority of God, and Jesus himself was theocentric. In recent years, within the Indian and the broader world church, discussion of this question has begun. The issues were earlier hinted at or articulated by certain Christian theologians in different parts of the world. Both in the Catholic Church and in the churches affiliated with the World Council of Churches, new dimensions of this christologico-ecumenical issue are taking shape. On one level, the discussions seem to be within a parochial Christian ecumenical framework, seeking to accommodate different Christian viewpoints. On another level, however, the implications of these new christological insights go far beyond the narrow confines of Christians, to the deeper and larger ecumenism that embraces the whole of humanity. In discussions in different parts of the world, a new hermeneutics is developing, a hermeneutics willing to read and hear biblical texts about Jesus in ways quite different from those of the West.

In the West, the International Theological Commission appointed by the Pope admits no distinction between christology and theology. And yet it states that *"confusion* between christology and theology results if one supposes that the name of God is totally unknown outside of Jesus Christ and that there exists no other theology than that which arises from the Christian revelation." The commission thus opens the possibility of recognizing theologies other than Christian. The statement goes on to call the church to cooperate with others in order "to participate in building a civilization of love."[23]

Also in the World Council of Churches, fresh discussions have started on "the inner core" of its basic affirmation that "the Lord Jesus Christ is God and Saviour." Throughout the council's history, questions have been raised about the adequacy of this formulation. On the one hand, New Testament scholars have pointed out that the statement identifying Jesus Christ with God goes beyond the witness of the New Testament. On the other, Catholic and Orthodox theologians have felt that the statement is narrowly "christomonistic and needs a full-fledged trinitarian emphasis." More recently, additions have been made to the original phrasing.[24] In the present discussion, two factors have become important. The christological question is being raised against the background of renewed dialogue with adherents of other faiths and of cooperation with persons of secular convictions who are struggling against the forces of death and destruction. The ontological equation of Jesus Christ with God as traditionally understood runs the risk of impeding any serious discussion with neighbors of other faiths or with secular humanists.[25]

Throughout the Bible the priority of God is taken for granted. The affirmation that God is the creator of all life and all humanity puts Christians and their neighbors of other faiths together at the very source of life. God breathes life into humanity (Genesis 2:7) and in doing so entrusts to it responsibility for all created life (Genesis 2:15). God lets men and women share in the divine power to create life (Genesis 4:1). Life is God's gift, and human beings have the duty and responsibility to cherish and guard it.

This belief in the ontological priority of God is also taken for granted by Jesus Christ and his hearers in the New Testament. He started his ministry by declaring that "the time is fulfilled, and the kingdom of God is at hand" (Mark 1:15). New Testament writers emphasize God's initiative over and over again. "God so loved the world that He gave His only begotten Son" (John 3:16). "God was in Christ, reconciling the world to Himself" (2 Corinthians 5:19). God set forth in Christ "a plan for the fullness of time, to unite all things in Him" (Ephesians 1:10). "And when all things are subjected to Him, then the Son also will be subjected to Him who put all things under Him that God may be all in all" (1 Corinthians 15:28).

This acknowledgment that God is the Creator and Redeemer of all life enables the entire world, the whole of humanity, to be included in the struggle for life and to feel responsible for its preservation and its continuation. God, in the sense of *Sat* or Mystery or the Transcendent or Ultimate Reality, is the ultimate Horizon over the ocean of life. God's covenant with all humanity, of which the rainbow is a timeless symbol, has never been abrogated.[26]

A theocentric christology provides more theological space for Christians to live together with neighbors of other faiths. "Christomonism" does not do full justice to the total evidence of the New Testament, nor does it give sufficient emphasis to the trinitarian dimension of the Christian faith. It tends to minimize the work of the Holy Spirit in the lives of others. The Orthodox rejection of the *filioque* clause in the description of the procession of the Holy Spirit in the Nicene Creed (A.D. 451)—that is, its insistence that the Spirit proceeds from the Father and *not* from the Son—has far-reaching ecumenical significance. To draw attention to these points is not to minimize the centrality of Jesus Christ in Christian faith, but to put him more clearly into the structure of trinitarian faith. New insights contributed by biblical studies and research on the great christological councils of the church (Nicea, A.D. 325, and Chalcedon, A.D. 451) help us better understand how God is in Jesus Christ and how Jesus Christ is related to God. Christocentrism without theocentrism leads to idolatry.

A theocentric christology provides a basis for retaining the Mystery of God while acknowledging the *distinctiveness* of Jesus Christ. It makes commitment to God in Jesus Christ possible without taking a negative attitude toward neighbors of other faiths, and at the same time it offers a more comprehensive conceptual framework for dialogue with these neighbors. Removing the threat implicit in one-way proclamations, it offers an invitation to all to share in the abundant riches of God. It makes dialogue a normal way of relationship between persons of different faiths, instead of artificially contriving to make it a mode of communication. It helps shift the emphasis from a *normative* to a *relational* attitude toward neighbors of other faiths. New relationships may have to be sought through recognizing *differences* rather than through seeking *similarities*. It helps avoid the dichotomies between "we" and "they" or those on "the inside" and those on "the outside."

The theocentric circle includes the christocentric circle. It makes it possible to recognize the theological significance of other revelations and other experiences of salvation, a point that for many Christian theologians is frightfully difficult even to admit. Theocentrism allows for an evolving quest for the meaning of Jesus Christ in which neighbors of other faiths can also participate, as in fact they already do, thus opening for Christians undreamed-of possibilities of enriching others and being enriched by them. Further, theocentrism does not ground cooperation on expediency, but on *theology*, providing a vision of participating with all human beings in God's continuing mission in the world, seeking to heal the brokenness of humanity, overcome the fragmentation of life, and bridge the rift between nature, humanity, and God.

TOWARD A THEOCENTRIC CHRISTOLOGY

Exclusive claims isolate the community of faith from neighbors of other faiths, creating tensions and disturbing relationships within the larger community. But when the *distinctiveness* of a particular faith is stated in a manner that avoids open or hidden exclusiveness, then meaningful *relationships* between different communities become possible. This has been happening throughout the history of different religions in the multireligious life of India. It is unfortunate that Christian theologians, including Indians, have failed to recognize the significance of such relationships for the shaping of an emerging theology of religions.

Perhaps one reason for this failure is the stranglehold of propositional theology and its methodology on the minds of most Christian theologians. This is not to minimize the need for and the importance of serious, rational theological work. Rather, it points out that to exclude the cultural, the mystical, and the aesthetic from the experience of interreligious relationships is to seriously impoverish theology. Such a claim is based on an understanding of theology as critical reflection on God's relationship to humanity and nature, history and the cosmos.

Nowhere else than in India, perhaps, is the importance of the aesthetic more manifest, for here we find that the distinctiveness of Jesus Christ is expressed through art by persons who do not necessarily belong to the visible Christian community. India might well be the only place where persons of other faiths, without crossing over the visible boundaries that separate them from Christians, have related themselves to Jesus Christ through art, thus breaking down the walls of exclusiveness. These artists, standing outside the confines of institutional Christianity, make evident that it is not the dogmas and doctrines about Christ or the institutions of the church that have touched the heart and mind of India, but the life and teachings of Jesus of Nazareth, his death and resurrection, the illumination he has brought into the Mystery of God, and the transforming power he has introduced into human life as he invites all persons to move from self-centeredness to God-centeredness. He is indeed *jivanmukta,* one who is truly liberated in life, and therefore able to liberate others.

Visitors to India are often struck by the responses that followers of other faiths have made to Jesus Christ through the religious dimensions of art— literature, poetry, and drama in the different languages of India (including English), as well as painting, movies, and television. Jesus Christ seems to move beyond the structures of the church, with its dogmas and doctrines about his person, in order to establish new relationships with adherents of other faiths. There seems to be an "unbaptized koinonia" outside the gates, which the church is most reluctant to recognize or even talk about. One must indeed be careful not to exaggerate such phenomena. But neither should their importance be minimized nor their theological significance for developing new relationships with neighbors of other faiths be rejected rudely and hastily.

Over the centuries there have been many examples of this influence of Christ beyond the confines of the church. Among the more recent ones is Manjeshwar Govinda Pai, a noted Hindu poet who won the national award for literature some years ago. His well-known and lengthy poem *Golgotha* is marked by literary beauty, depth of religious perception, and a sensitive understanding of the crucifixion of Jesus Christ.[27] Muliya Keshavayya, a Hindu lawyer, wrote a drama on the life of Christ with the title *Maha Chetana (Great Energy),* bringing out the compassion of Christ toward the poor and the power of his cross and resurrection.[28] Gopal Singh, a well-known Sikh scholar and diplomat, wrote a poem entitled *The Man Who Never Died.*[29] The poet has the risen Christ speak these lines:

> But he said unto those that believe
> that nothing dies in the realm of God—
> neither seed, nor drop, nor dust, nor man.
> Only the past dies or the present,
> but the future lives for ever.
> And I am the future of man.
> To me, being and non-being were always one,
> I always was and never was! [30]

Many Hindu and Muslim artists have been inspired by themes in the life of Jesus Christ, particularly his sufferings, death and resurrection. According to Jyoti Sahi, a noted Christian artist, Indian Christian art was initiated not by Christians but by Hindu artists. For example, there is the well-known painting of the Last Supper by Jamini Roy of Calcutta. More recently, well-known Hindu and Muslim artists such as Hebbar, Panikker, Hussain, Khanna, and others have painted many themes from the life of Christ.[31] All this might well be regarded as signs of the increasing traffic across the borders, helping to develop new relationships among persons of different religious communities and bringing out new meanings in christology.

There can be no exclusiveness in art. By evoking feelings of reverence and joy and gratefulness, it transforms human feelings and gives to those who participate in it a sense of inner peace (*shanti*). It liberates persons from feelings of possessiveness. Some of these examples, and there are many more, make it clear that although Christianity belongs to Christ, Christ does not belong to Christianity. This kind of art by Hindu or Sikh or Muslim neighbors mediates the mystery of Christ to Christians in new ways, different from those of the West, and builds deeper relationships among members of different faiths. This form of art should be regarded as at least one of the new ways of bringing out the relational distinctiveness of Jesus Christ, the theological implications of which have yet to be worked out. But to ignore it would be disastrous to future interreligious relationships.

When theological debates end in sterile apologetics; when social relationships between different religious communities become superficial or degenerate into sullen coexistence; when economic sharing becomes a matter of profit and loss; and when political cooperation in the life of a nation becomes difficult, if not impossible, because of narrow communal interests, quite often it is aesthetic experience that provides the bridge for deeper relationships among persons of different faiths. This does not always happen, but when it does happen, it is mostly by the few on behalf of the many. Nevertheless, art combines truth and grace and, in generosity of spirit, through color and sound and symbol and image, it mediates Mystery to a broken humanity. Through participation in art focused on Christ and the experience of enjoying it, the walls of exclusiveness are broken down and new relationships established among persons of different faiths in the larger community.

7

Toward a Revised Christology

Jesus Christ is the center of Christian life and is the substance of Christian faith. Christologies are human attempts to articulate the meaning and message of Jesus Christ to the church and the world. Every christology is a quest to grasp the content and explain the meaning of the mystery of Jesus Christ, to discover and articulate how God is related to humanity and how humanity is related to God in Jesus Christ.

Jesus Christ is "the same yesterday, today and tomorrow" (Hebrews 13:8), but christologies need to change, redefine, and revise themselves constantly to make sense to the church and the world at different times and in different cultural situations. Such revisions have gone on at different times in the history of the church. They should be regarded as signs of vitality and the renewing power of the Christian faith in the world. At present, religious pluralism should enter into any christological discussion in the world. Christian commitment however, is not to particular christologies, but to God in and through Jesus Christ. Christian theology is the task of the church, and its purpose is to glorify God and serve the people in the church and in the world.

CHRISTOLOGY WITHIN THEOLOGY

Although christology has to do with Jesus Christ, christological reflections are concerned not simply with the question of Jesus Christ, but at the same time, with the meaning of God or Ultimate Reality for human existence. Therefore the question of God and the question of Jesus Christ are intimately related. There can be no christology without theology. There can be no *Christian* theology apart from Jesus Christ.

But at the same time, in a religiously plural world, there can be and are theologies without reference to Jesus Christ. To ignore or deny this fact is to be insensitive to the faiths of our neighbors. To confuse christology with theology, or to seek to displace theology with christology, is not only to impoverish Christian theology but also to do grave injustice to the theologies of neighbors of other faiths. A christology which claims that God has been revealed in order to redeem humanity *only* in Jesus of Nazareth, and that this revealing and redeeming activity of God took place *once-for-all* in the first century, runs the risk of contradicting another strand of Jewish and Christian theology which affirms that God is the God of love and justice as creator, sustainer, and redeemer of all creation. A central issue facing us, then, is whether such "lower" christologies do not provide an important asset to us in our attempts to seek revisions in doctrine that will be both soundly Christian and conducive to honest dialogue. If, according to the earliest tradition of the New Testament, Jesus Christ always points to God and is therefore himself theocentric or God centered, then the only way to be Christ centered is to be God centered, but in a religiously plural world, being Christ centered is not the only way to be God centered.

What I attempt here is not to articulate a systematic, full-fledged christology, but an attempt to indicate *possibilities* for christological developments in a religiously plural world, taking into account the Asian (more particularly the Indian) situation. This is justified because the major religions of the world have originated in Asia, and for several thousand years the thoughts and lives of millions of Asian people have been shaped by these religions.

The need for a *revised* christology in this context should be obvious. Christologies in the West have been redefining themselves over the centuries, particularly during the last two, in response to developments in history, philosophy, art, language and literature, and even more important, in science and technology, which have challenged not only the Christian worldview and way of life, but the foundations of Christian faith itself. Christian faith has retained its power, vitality, and credibility because of the tremendous work done by Western theologians over the centuries. It is these theologies and christologies, developed in very different historical and cultural situations, that have been brought to other countries during the past few centuries.

The major element that is missing in all christologies that have been exported by the West to the rest of the world is a theological response to the powerful presence of other religions. The theological implications of this fact are often ignored by theologians not only in the West but of other countries also. Asia is the most religious and the least Christian of all the continents. The major religions of the world originated in Asia. No other continent—Europe, America, or Africa—has such a powerful presence of other religions—with their culture and civilization, scriptures, institutions, philosophy, ethics, social structures, and art—as Asia. Any christology in Asia that fails to take into account this fact cannot touch the hearts and minds of people. Christologies based on a Europe-centered history, a too narrow or deductive Christ-centered theology, and a church-centered mission tied to classical dogmas about the person of Christ and theories of atonement, which respond to Western needs, are not only irrelevant to the life of the people but often obstruct the life and witness of the church in Asia. The fact that at this historic period the countries in Asia are economically poor and militarily weak should not obscure the spiritual depth, theological strength, and ethical power of Asian religions. The realization of the inadequacy of Western christologies to Asia is one reason for the quest for new christologies.

But the longing for new christologies is not just the desire for freedom from bondage to Western christologies. It would be both ungrateful and irresponsible for theologians in Asia to regard nearly two thousand years of Western Christian theology as of no consequence to their own theological enterprise. Without recognizing the continuity of Christian life and thought, and without a critical attitude toward both Western and Asian religions and cultures, Asians cannot make a serious contribution to ecumenical theology. What we are looking for is not an inclusive Christ to replace an exclusive Christ. We need christologies that respond to the needs of Asia today. There is not much point in seeking to free ourselves from bondage to the West only to be bound to Asian or African or Latin American christologies.

For Indian Christian theologians, for example, to reject violently "Brahmanical christology" only to be enmeshed in "Dalit christology" or "People's theology" or "liberation theology" or "feminist theology" is to exchange one bondage for another. It is necessary to rise above these dividing lines and seek a larger ecumenical framework in which Christian theology would remain distinctively *Christian* theology but at the same time respond to different needs of people in different situations without betraying Christian commitment to God in Christ. "We must contain all the divided worlds in ourselves," remarks Thomas Merton, that venerable sage, who was so much at home in the spiritual depths of both the West and East, "and transcend them in Christ."[1]

Christological reflections entered into on these pages may be of some interest to three groups of people. First, there are many Christians, not just in Asia but in the other parts of the world as well, who are committed to God in Christ, who regard themselves as members of the church, who in different ways participate in mission, but who feel hesitant and uneasy about the exclusive claims made by Christians on behalf of Christ and Christianity. They may not articulate this unease openly, but in Christian congregations there are many, particularly younger people, who are unwilling to subscribe to the aggressive Christian claims.

Second, there are those Christians who are seriously committed to the struggle against injustice in society and who are actively involved in movements of liberation, people who believe that they participate in this work in the name of Christ, but who find it difficult, if not impossible, to accept that *only* in the Jewish–Christian–Western tradition there are spiritual resources for this struggle. When they work with neighbors of other faiths and those with secular convictions, they discover "liberative streams" in other religious traditions as well. They are therefore unwilling to accept the claim that only the Bible provides resources for "prophetic spirituality" with a social concern, whereas the "ascetic spirituality" of Asia ignores issues of social justice. Neither the history of Christianity nor that of other religions such as Buddhism and Islam and Hinduism and Sikhism, provides basis for such claims. Both these groups of Christians seek a revised christology which can take into account the values of justice and righteousness in different religious traditions without in any way betraying the Christian commitment to Christ.

Third, there are many neighbors of other faiths who not only have great respect for Jesus Christ, his teachings, his life, his cross, and his resurrection, who also, in different ways, try to follow him. Many of these people are weary of being made victims of Christian mission with arrogant exclusive claims that are unsubstantiated by any visible evidence in the lives of the Christians who make such claims, or in the life of the church in the world. Thus they are prevented from reflecting more deeply on the meaning of Jesus Christ and the universal dimensions of his message.

Without a revised christology it is most unlikely that the renewing activity of God in Christ and the creative and sustaining power of the Spirit can make a serious contribution to interreligious dialogue on the one hand and to the struggle of people of all faiths for a just society on the other. My attempt at articulating elements for such a revised christology seeks a broader and deeper conceptual framework in which Jesus Christ does not divide people but holds them together in God's love and righteousness, in which the struggle for justice is not set against the quest for a theology of religions, but regards neighbors of other faiths as partners in the larger community which is the object of God's love and redeeming grace. The conviction behind this quest is that in a religiously plural world, a revised christology that is biblically sound, spiritually satisfying, theologically credible, ethically responsible, and pastorally helpful—not just to Christians but also to neighbors of other faiths—is both necessary and possible without making exclusive claims on behalf of Jesus Christ and without making negative judgments on the faiths of our neighbors. This does not mean an uncritical acceptance of all religions as they are, but rejecting the a priori notion that Christ is *against* any religion and that the struggle between truth and falsehood is between Christianity and other religions. That struggle is going on constantly within every religion, and Christians participate in it in the name of Christ.

The way to a revised christology, however, is not through diminishing the centrality of Jesus Christ to Christian life or diluting the christological substance in theology. It can only be through a recovery of the depth of God's being in love and justice and through a much greater sensitivity to the working of the Spirit within human consciousness in history and in nature. What can be less heretical and more orthodox than involving the Trinity in such a complex matter as the relationship between Christians and neighbors of other faiths? But, at the same time, to ignore the depth of God's being behind the Trinity to which the Trinity points symbolically is to forget that christology is not the whole of, but *a part* of, theology. To tread the thin line between heresy and orthodoxy as demarcated by the classical dogmatic formulae is both a risk and an adventure, and those who complain that Asian Christian theologians have not even produced a decent heresy should not cast the first stone against those who wish to risk the adventure or prevent them from hoping and dreaming.

FROM INTRA-CHRISTIAN TO INTERRELIGIOUS

The most serious obstacle on the way toward a revised christology is the exclusive claim made by certain groups of Christians on behalf of Christ and Christianity. One gets the impression that there is great unwillingness, even a refusal, to discuss the validity and ethical implications of this attitude for human relations in the larger community. This leads to a total rejection of the religious beliefs and convictions of neighbors of other faiths and, in the name of aggressive Christian mission, seeks to replace all religions with Christianity. All too often, these claims are mixed up with ideological assumptions backed by economic affluence and political power. This exclusive mood makes it impossible to have any serious debate between Christians who hold different views on the subject and, even more serious, between Christians and their neighbors of other faiths in the community.

The consequences of this attitude are disastrous, not just to Christians in Asia, but to the church in the whole world, and lead to a serious impoverishment of ecumenical theology. Therefore an open and critical examination of all exclusive claims is very necessary as a preliminary step toward a revised christology. At present, in countries like India, where evangelism is marked by an aggressive verbal proclamation of the gospel and where the struggle for a just society is carried on chiefly in political and social activism, there is hardly any serious debate among Christians on this matter. To avoid such a discussion is to impoverish seriously the life and witness of the church.

Obviously, Christians in Asia and Africa are not free in the matter, because such a debate is tied up with forces and attitudes in the world church—among Roman Catholics, "ecumenicals," and the "evangelicals." The last two labels are imprecise and unfortunate, but since they are being used at the highest level to indicate different points of view and approaches toward other religions I use them here. But the exclusive attitude cuts across these boundaries.

Conservative evangelicals are in the forefront of a strident and aggressive rejection of other religions and have a powerful hold on their followers in Asia and Africa. Nevertheless, although there is a *seeming* openness toward neighbors of other faiths in the statements of the Vatican and the World Council of Churches, there are many Christians among them who are as exclusive as the evangelicals. This is one reason why there is such unresolved tension within these bodies whenever this matter comes up for serious debate in world meetings. Thus, during the recent (1988) Central Committee meeting of the World Council of Churches, when a suggestion was made that people of other faiths might be involved in the preparatory discussions on the theme of the next Assembly (1991): "Come, Holy Spirit—Renew the Whole Creation," there was reluctance, hesitation, even hostility to the suggestion. How a theme like the Holy Spirit, whose very character is freedom (wind and fire), and who is called upon by the Assembly to renew the *whole* creation, can be discussed *only* by Christians, ignoring the rest of humanity created by God—or how a topic like "Peace, Justice and the Integrity of Creation" can be considered by Christians while ignoring the spiritual resources available in the different religions of the world—is beyond the comprehension of ordinary mortals like this writer.[2]

David Jenkins, formerly Director of Humanum Studies in the World Council of Churches and now Bishop of Durham, writing for the Lambeth Conference 1988, exhorts his fellow Christians in the West "to move consciously away from a backward looking late mediaeval, Mediterranean model of the Church with triumphalistic overtones to a forward looking *federal* model with overtones of service which is centred on a broader ecumenicism related to God's new covenant for a world-wide humanity."[3] But within the parochial Christian *oikoumene* at present there does not seem to be any serious attempt to build a theological bridge between the exclusive and federal models within the larger and true *oikoumene* of God, which includes Christians and their neighbors of other faiths as well.

It is not necessary here to make any elaborate analysis of the attitudes of these three Christian groups and their differing attitudes toward people of other faiths. Recent studies have adequately brought out both the theological differences between them and the variations in their attitudes toward other faiths. Paul Knitter distinguishes three groups among the evangelicals.[4] David Bosch, discussing "Evangelical-Ecumenical Relationships" in recent years identifies six different strands.[5] Very wisely he puts a question mark against what he describes as "a growing relationship?" Charles J. Fenshaw analyzes the Evangelical-Roman Catholic Dialogue on Mission, which has obvious implications for Christian attitudes toward neighbors of other faiths.[6] It is rather striking that each of these traditions within world Christianity claims to have nonnegotiable items of faith and conviction which do not prevent them from having what appears to be friendly bilateral dialogues. If this is so, should not the same freedom and right be conceded to neighbors of other faiths who also have their nonnegotiable items of faith, particularly when these refer to such profound and complex matters as revelation, salvation and the practice of mission?

Fenshaw writes, "My argument has been that Evangelicals and Catholics do have *different visions of salvation*, but there is an overlap of vision sufficiently large enough to allow for further development in dialogue."[7] If two groups of Christians can affirm *two different visions of salvation*, should not a far greater difference in the visions of salvation be expected between Christians and neighbors of other faiths? And would not the Creator God, the Parent of all humanity, in grace and mercy, allow for at least some overlap of these visions to make dialogues beyond intra-Christian to inter-religious possible?

Pointing out that the major obstacle to establishing a relationship between ecumenicals and evangelicals is pride, Bosch writes:

> One cannot, I guess, argue people into humility and into a posture where they see the relativity of their own view and the validity of those of others; yet this is what is needed. We are often forbidden in scripture to judge others; nothing is said to discourage us from self-examination and confession.[8]

If evangelicals and ecumenicals are encouraged to see the *relativity* of their own views and the validity of those of others, cannot the same principle be extended by Christians to neighbors of other faiths, especially when the application of the scriptural injunction not to judge others is not limited to Christians? If not, why not?

Obviously, one recognizes that this jump from intra-Christian to inter-religious cannot be made without a valid theological bridge. But that cannot even be attempted without rejecting the open or hidden exclusivist claims. This is another reason which cries for a revised christology in a religiously plural world. There is not the slightest suggestion that this is to be done by diminishing Christ or by diluting the substance of the Christian faith. It is not a matter of restructuring the Christian faith in order to accommodate neighbors of other faiths, but of critical reflection on the God–human encounter in Jesus Christ in a situation where new perceptions of religious pluralism cannot be ignored anymore. This factor, for obvious reasons, did not enter into the making of christologies either in the West or in most countries of Asia and Africa until very recently. One must be willing and ready to distinguish between truth and truth claims, between Jesus Christ and the Christian claims about Jesus Christ, between Jesus before Christianity and Christianity after Jesus. The way toward a revised christology is through acknowledging the mystery of God, rediscovering the meaning of the God–human encounter in Jesus Christ, and by becoming more sensitive to the working of the Holy Spirit today leading hearts and minds to new avenues of truth.

EXCLUSIVE CLAIMS: ROOTS AND CONSEQUENCES

With the rise of fundamentalism all over the world and its consequences on community relationships, it becomes urgent to examine the seed of exclusiveness that lies embedded in the soil of all fundamentalism. Every commitment in life has a certain element of exclusiveness in it. Commitment to truth excludes all forms of falsehood; to justice, all involvement in structures of injustice; to compassion, any cruelty to human beings or animals. There are many instances where such a choice between alternatives is quite clear and, even if the right choice is not always made, people do feel some unease within their conscience because of wrong choices. But there are other commitments where not rejection, but acceptance, not isolation, but relationship, is called for. Commitment to one's family or community or nation does not exclude recognizing similar commitments on the part of our neighbors. In such situations, recognizing the commitments of others becomes the only guarantee of the validity of one's own commitment. This is true of all religious commitments. When different commitments clash in society, it becomes necessary to examine where they differ and to discover ways in which they can be related in the larger framework of life.

Religious commitments are much more complex, stronger, and deeper, not only because they touch ultimate matters of faith, but also because history, tradition, and emotional factors—along with the self-identity of the believing community—are all involved. And when, during the course of time, social, economic, and political factors also get mixed up with religion, the relationship among different religious commitments becomes even more complex and difficult. In a pluralist society, unless it is accepted that in such a profound matter as Truth or God or Ultimate Reality different human responses are not only possible but also valid, and that no single vision of Truth can claim finality, there is always the temptation to regard any recognition of other commitments as compromise or betrayal of one's own commitment. In a pluralist society a critical attitude is called for, not only toward expressions of one's own commitment, but also toward those of others, in order that a pluralist stance does not lead to a shallow, uncritical relativism, a soup in which all pieces of toast eventually become soggy.

There seem to be three elements involved in all exclusive claims. First, there is the powerful initial vision or experience or response to Truth, which, because it is the total response of the person, often needs no further corroboration. This is more than just a conviction. Within the core of every religion there lies this powerful *anubhaya* (experience) or *darshana* (vision) that becomes a nonnegotiable item in the life of the believing community. True religion begins at the point where the push of human longing meets the pull of God's grace.

Second, in certain cultures this feeling of certainty, which may begin instantly and then grows with the life of the group, leads to a feeling that other commitments in the larger community are not only different but also false or wrong. There may even be a feeling, a hidden fear, that unless one charges that other commitments are false, the truth of one's own commitment might be in danger. Those who make exclusive claims seek scriptural support and theological argument to affirm why their commitment is the only true one. When such teaching starts in the home and the family and continues in the Sunday schools or educational institutions, and even in theological colleges and seminaries, this attitude becomes hardened and often brooks no further discussion. It generates a sense of insecurity, even fear, about discussing such matters in the open.

From this, the jump to the next stage is not too difficult, namely to a zeal to eliminate other commitments as false and propagate one's own as the only true one. Error has no right to exist. Therefore, other religions, regarded as false, absurd, and wrong, must be eliminated, conquered, displaced, in the interest of Truth itself as received and understood by the exclusive community. Having been possessed by Truth, the community now regards itself as possessing the Truth. The gap between Truth and truth claims is eliminated. The ontological, theological, epistemological, and existential dimensions of Truth, and the highly complex relationship between them in the apprehensions of the believing community, are mixed up in a totalitarian claim for exclusiveness. When, during further developments, this attitude is mixed up with sociological factors, political considerations, and particularly economic affluence—that is, when power factors get mixed up with exclusive claims—attitudes become hardened, with serious consequences to life in the pluralistic community.

It is often forgotten that exclusive claims in the Hebrew scriptures and in the New Testament are in the nature of a "minority language," a "survival language." A minority community was seeking to guard its identity in relation to a large and powerful majority. When that minority language and exclusive claim got mixed up with the power and pomp of the Roman Empire under Constantine (and in a similar way during the colonial period, when political domination, economic exploitation, and military strength allied themselves with exclusive claims), such attitudes led to serious ethical consequences in a religiously plural world. The relationship between Christianity and Judaism, between Christianity and Islam—and during the colonial period, between Islam and Christianity on the one hand and the religions of China and India on the other—illustrate this point. It should be recognized that not just the question of Truth but also that of peace and justice among different nations, peoples, and cultures in the world are at stake here.

One must be careful not to caricature or distort the commitments held seriously and sincerely by fellow Christians. But this theological politeness is required not just of Christians towards each other—Roman Catholic, ecumenical, or evangelical—but also of all Christians toward neighbors of other faiths.

The roots of evangelicalism are not in Asia or Africa, but in the West. They are to be found in the history of Europe and America during a particular period. Evangelicalism was a protest against what were considered to be certain liberal tendencies in Western Christianity. At one point, it was also a powerful voice against certain fascist ideologies which deliberately sought to mix Christian faith with state ideology, particularly in Nazi

Germany. Against these "syncretistic" tendencies, the evangelical cry of "No Other Name" than that of Jesus Christ was certainly justified. But to transfer that attitude uncritically to Asia and Africa and propound a "Christ against religions" attitude, backed with Western economic power, military strength, and political subjugation of nations was and continues to be a disaster to the cause of Christ in the world. For Asian and African Christians to themselves retain such attitudes inherited from missionaries is more than a disaster, it is a tragedy. It isolates Christ from people and alienates Christians from their neighbors. It draws attention to the finger (attached to the mailed fist) that points to Christ and so prevents people from seeing Jesus Christ himself. It has transformed neighbors of other faiths into enemies to be conquered. The crucified Christ becomes the conquering Christ. Jesus the servant becomes Christ the King. Evangelism becomes a one-way proclamation on a take-it-or-leave-it basis. Invitation to the wedding feast becomes a proclamation to be baptized. Mission becomes an organized effort to "convert" people into members of the Church. Statistics become the measure and criterion of success in mission and evangelism.

Although some missionary societies now avoid the term *mission*, perhaps because of its colonial associations, and call themselves "overseas ministries," and although many evangelists from the West now apply for and receive tourist visas, a crypto-colonial exclusivist attitude still lurks in the hearts of many Christians, not only in the West but also in Asia and Africa because the latter have inherited it from the West and seem to hold on to it with more enthusiasm than critical sense. Loyalty to the past often prevents emergence of the new and clouds the vision of hope for the future. There seems to be an excess of christological confidence over theological common sense in this matter. Anyone who suggests that this attitude must be rejected in order that Jesus Christ may be seen without the benefit of Western Polaroid glasses, or that the good news of the Kingdom of God he preached and toward which he constantly pointed should be received without the syncretistic mixture of Western *masala* (mixture of selected spices) in its original purity, runs the risk of being accused of compromise or betrayal. But unless this question is discussed openly with courage and conviction, a revised christology is impossible in a religiously plural world.

Being born in a particular country or a particular community of faith is a given factor in human life. Through no fault or merit of one's own, one is born in the affluent North or the poor South, black, brown, or white, a nominal Christian or Hindu or Buddhist or Muslim or Confucian or Taoist. Why punish people with eternal damnation for accepting the given factors of creation and human life? This does not mean that people are not free to change from a nominal commitment to a more decisive faith or from self-centeredness to God centeredness within their own religion. Also, people should not be bound for all time to the religion in which they are born. People should be free to respond to the different visions of life, to choose and be enriched in their life.

In a pluralistic world, an exclusive claim for any one particular religion introduces an element of theological injustice into God's creation. Interactions and mutual criticisms should take place for the sake of mutual enrichment. This has always happened. The long history of religions has plenty of examples of such mutual relationships. At a time when the limitations of both secularism and a technological culture are becoming increasingly obvious to people in the West and in the East, this mutual interaction among religions and between religions and the secular-scientific temper is even more necessary. This process is already underway, with far-reaching consequences for the future of humanity. Christian theologians and missiologists cannot afford to ignore these developments.

Any exclusive claim leads to four negative consequences in a multireligious society. First, it divides people into "we" and "they," those who are "saved" and those who are "not saved," those on the "inside" and those on the "outside." This is one reason why, in a country like India, in spite of all talk about Christian participation in nation building, Christians, with the probable exception of Kerala, are so isolated from the mainstream of national and community life.

Second, it makes cooperation among different religious communities difficult, if not impossible, for tackling common human problems in society. In countries like India, resources supporting most of the social-service projects of the church come from outside the country. Claiming that only one religious community has the spiritual resources to tackle, for example, the problem of injustice in society, isolates and alienates people who make such claims from their neighbors. Christians are not the only people in a country like India, for example, who are concerned with the urgent problem of injustice in society. The government, secular movements, a large number of voluntary organizations, and institutions supported by other religious communities with resources from within are also working among the poor and the oppressed.

Third, exclusive claims, combined with economic, political, and military power, lead to tensions and conflicts in society. Since Christianity and Islam have worldwide connections with affluent nations, tensions within a country are easily internationalized and may threaten world peace.

Fourth, exclusive claims raise serious theological questions which no amount of intellectual juggling or sophisticated exegesis can resolve. What answer is there, for example, to the question of what happened to the millions of people who died before Jesus of Nazareth was born, if salvation is *only* in Jesus Christ? Does not a christology claiming that God has been revealed to save humanity *only* in Jesus Christ (*once-for-all* in the first century) contradict a theology affirming that God is the Creator, Sustainer, and Redeemer of all humanity and that God's love and justice embrace all people at all times? What right have human beings to limit God's freedom to intervene in history to a single moment in the stream of time?

Such an exclusive claim weakens God's outreach to all humanity, underestimates the humanity of Jesus of Nazareth, trivializes the human situation, and makes mutual interaction among people of different religions and cultures impossible. "By stressing the absoluteness and otherness of the Biblical kerygma to the point of allowing for no significant dialogue between it and the great and little streams of culture," remarks Julius Lipner, "Jesus Christ becomes a rootless wonder."[9] Surely, a christology that leads to such negative ethical consequences in society needs revision, and any attempt to do so, however inadequate it may be at the moment, should not be looked upon with suspicion and fear but approached with courage and hope for the future of human relationships in the world.

TRUTH AND THE EITHER/OR MIND-SET

There is a deeper and perhaps a more complex question that needs to be touched upon here: what has been described as the either/or mind-set at the root of exclusivism. This is sometimes contrasted with the both/and mind-set. It is also related to the question of truth. Very often the question is raised whether the desire for friendly relations with people of other faiths is a matter of expediency rather than of theology. Is it right to seek friendliness at the cost of truth?

It is neither possible nor necessary to enter into an elaborate discussion on Truth here. So much has been written about this matter, particularly on truth in interreligious contexts, that any summary of arguments would be repetitious.[10] But the connection between certain notions of truth, the either/or mind-set, and exclusive claims should be noted, because the possibility of a revised christology depends on this. If christologies developed in the either/or context have certain limitations, the question should be raised whether the framework of both/and may provide a different context for revised christologies. Maybe a dynamic interplay between the two in a growing cross-cultural hermeneutics could help to shape a larger conceptual framework, which may help to hold together a plurality of christologies, always acknowledging that while there is only one Jesus, there can be many christologies.

What is truth? How do we know truth? How do we know what we know to be true? What are the ethical consequences of knowing the truth for human conduct, particularly for interreligious relationships in a pluralist society? In Asian situations, where *Sat* (Truth) is both being and truth, the goal of the quest for truth is to close the gap between thinking and being. In one strand of Hinduism, *Moksha* is not just knowledge of the Brahman but participating in the being of the Brahman. "He who knows the Brahman becomes the Brahman" (*Brahmavid Brahmaiva Bhavati, Mundaka* III, ii, 9).

In an either/or mind-set, however, there is a desperate attempt to keep "being" and "knowing" distinct, because of the high value placed on the individual ego. One must be careful not to contrast unnecessarily the Western mind as advocating the either/or attitude toward Truth and the Eastern mind the both/and approach. These are overly simplified generalizations of highly complex matters, resembling those of a previous era which talked of "life-affirmation" and "life-negation" or "ontocratic" and "theocratic" or more recently of "prophetic spirituality" and "ascetic spirituality." Such oversimplifications do injustice to a highly complex subject and to the diversities within particular traditions. They also fail to take into account the enormous amount of interaction that has taken place between scholars of the East and West in recent years. The intellectual attitudes and habits of the heart of quite a few historians of religion and theologians, not only Christian but of other faiths as well, have been deeply influenced and shaped by cross-cultural forces. Therefore an uncritical contrast between Europe and Asia that fails to take into account new developments in the global scene in history, science, and religious understanding will only lead to a serious impoverishment of ecumenical theology, and should be avoided. Paul Knitter points out that growth in historical consciousness, developments in science and technology, and new perceptions of religious pluralism are pushing people both in the East and the West to look for new models of Truth.[11]

Truth is no longer defined in terms of exclusion. A religion that defines itself as true by excluding others is outmoded. In science there are no certainties, only probabilities. "Salvation history" is not limited to one people. Within a global consciousness where different peoples and cultures are being drawn together into one community, and where the destinies of different people are bound together, there is a plurality of historic consciousness. Truth is not a static substance but a dynamic process. Truth is not concerned with an "Unmoved Mover" waiting to be discovered, but with a "Moving Mover" involved in the historic process, but transcending it.

Truth is a matter of discerning and relating oneself to a "Moving Mover." Therefore the apprehension of truth at a given point in history cannot claim exclusive validity. It can indeed be valid, but not exclusive. No particular response to or formulation of truth can claim to be unique, final, or absolute. We need to *grow* into truth. This means that the truth as received by a particular community of faith at a given time can prove itself to be true not by rejecting, but by reacting to and relating itself to the truth as perceived by neighbors of other faiths.

To Christians this truth is decisively manifested in Jesus Christ. No one asks them to dilute or betray this faith. But the function of christology in a pluralistic world is not to claim uniqueness for Christ by proving that others are wrong or false, but to confess, explain, and help Christians live in obedience to the truth manifested to them in Jesus Christ. Therefore christology becomes both a joyful acceptance of the truth revealed in Jesus Christ and a pilgrimage toward the fullness of truth (John 14:16-17).

The inner demand for clear-cut formulations of truth that can be defined and defended leads to a dependence on words and concepts and rational formulations. Over the years these formulations become rigid because of the authority of the community that accepts them. The forms in which Truth is expressed and the ways in which it is accepted become institutionalized and are often regarded by the community as more important than truth itself. Creeds become substitutes for truth, and confessions prevent conversations that might lead to the emergence of the new.

"No other religion has a record of theology," writes David L. Edwards, "reducing the greatest metaphysical mysteries of God, about man and about the unique 'god-manhood' of Jesus Christ to simple seeming sentences which could be adopted by a council or other authoritative body and made compulsory for all believers by anathematising the slightest disagreement as heresy most foul."[12]

This is in striking contrast to the Hindu and Buddhist attitudes in India or that of Confucianists and Taoists in China. Not that they underestimate the power of reason, language, words, and concepts to mediate truth, but there is always a feeling that truth is greater than formulations of truth and that therefore *tarka* (logic) must be subordinated to *anubhava* (experience). This is one reason there are no heretics in India, in the Western sense of the term. The manner in which a community of faith treats dissent within its own community may be an indication of whether or not its claim to possess truth is justified or whether it is truth that possesses it. The either/or way of thinking and its dependence on credal formulations make it impossible for Christianity to coexist with people of other faiths. "Christianity either dominates others or is isolated from them. The exclusive character of "either/or" thinking has made inclusive exclusive."[13]

Because the either/or way of thinking distinguishes sharply between the knowing subject and the known object, science and technology become possible, with all their benefits to humankind. It would be most unwise to emphasize only the dangers of technology. But over the centuries this way of thinking has also led to serious dichotomies between God and creation, between humanity and nature, between transcendence and immanence, between body and spirit. This should not be understood as Eastern criticism of the West, because in recent years the dangers of these dichotomies have been recognized by Western scholars themselves. During the conference organized by the Church and Society department of the World Council of Churches at the Massachusetts Institute of Technology in 1979, quite a few scientists, if not Christian theologians, evinced keen interest in the perspectives of other religions on the relation between humanity and nature, science and religion.[14]

The concern here goes much deeper than ecological questions and touches the relationship between Christianity and the religions of Asia because of their different approaches to truth. Thomas Berry remarks:

> Our present Christianity is overly committed to biblical revelation rather than to revelation in the natural world; to the salvific process rather than the creative process; to the human rather than to the

earth-community as the norm and reality of value; to progress as increased human well-being rather than an advance in the well-being of the entire life community; to a sense of the individual historic Christ of the Synoptic gospels, rather than the sense of Christ as a dimension of the entire order of the universe.[15]

This heightened sense of need to overcome dichotomies and accept relationships demands an urgent search for a larger global framework which can hold together those matters that are now divided and kept separate, namely, God and the world, humanity and nature, science and religion, transcendence and immanence, body and spirit, Christianity and other religions. The quest for a revised christology in this larger, more inclusive framework is obviously focused on Jesus Christ, in whom God is not separated from the human or the human from God. Jesus Christ is divine because he is human and human because he is divine.

There is another matter which is often neglected but is important to the shaping of revised christologies in a religiously plural world, particularly in Asia. This is the role that signs, symbols, and images play in religious life. The Roman Catholic and Orthodox heritage is very rich in this area. Protestant life, partly because of historical reasons and partly because of an overemphasis on rational or propositional theology, is poor in this respect. Protestant christologies, bereft of this profound dimension and dependent on intellectual formulations and verbal proclamations and brought into the living context of Asian life that is so rich and full of sound and color, signs, symbols, and images, have made little impact on the hearts and minds of people in Asia.

The reasons behind such theological poverty and spiritual barrenness are now slowly being recognized. During the colonial period, Christians in Asia rejected Indian art and symbols and signs as Hindu or Buddhist and therefore non-Christian. Contemporary distortions of language and the abuse and misuse of words in the media, make people look for other means of receiving and sharing truth and values in life. Modern science, in its demand for accuracy, precision, and practical usefulness, has led to a technological culture that discourages openness to symbols and images. Realms of meaning beyond the ken of the literal are often regarded as confusions to be cleared up by logical thinking. Worse still, they are suspected of leading the clear stream of reason away from scholarly objectivity, into the marshlands of emotionalism. Even though the importance and significance of myths and the mythical way of thinking to the understanding of religions have received scholarly attention during recent years, many theologians do not seem to be sufficiently aware of their importance to christology. One should not be surprised, therefore, to discover that Protestant Christianity in Asia is so barren in this area.

THE UNITIVE VISION OF *ADVAITA*

The cumulative effect of all these factors demands a new conceptual framework for revised christologies in a religiously plural world; ones that can hold together elements that are diverse but not contradictory to one another. With all the diversity of races, languages, religions, and ideologies in Asia, there is still, particularly in the cultures of India and China, a sense of an all-embracing unity that holds together nature, humanity, and truth or *Dharma* or God in a larger harmony, within which diversities do not lead to debilitating conflicts but creative tensions. This is not to underestimate in any way the terrible economic, social, and political conflicts that are going on in most of the countries of Asia today; nor does it point accusing fingers at conflicts elsewhere in the world. But it does point to the sense of an all-pervasive unity whose roots go deep into the metaphysical soil that refuses to take exclusive positions and either/or attitudes.

Most of the religions in Asia take this for granted. The most conspicuous doctrine of Jainism is perhaps *Syadavada* (from Sanskrit root *as* = to be, the doctrine of "may be"), which maintains that because of the indeterminate nature of Reality, different viewpoints are possible, that none of them can provide final knowledge, and that all viewpoints are conditional.[16] The Buddhist doctrine of *pratitya samutpada* (dependent origination, the interconnectedness of all things) is well-known.[17] In China, the book *I Ching* or the *Book of Changes*, one of the five classics of Confucianism, provides the common source for both Confucian and Taoist philosophy. Its central emphasis is on the harmony between *yin* and *yang* held together in tension.[18] In his foreword to a translation of this book, C. J. Jung remarks that while the Western mind "carefully sifts, weighs, selects, classifies and isolates, the Chinese picture of the moment encompasses everything down to the minutest non-sensical detail, because all the ingredients make up the observed moment."[19] That the *yin-yang* principle of holding opposites together is not just a sectarian religious symbol but encompasses all life became very visible during the Olympic games in Seoul, South Korea (September 1988), where it provided a visual symbol to hold together sportsmen and women of so many nations in tense competition with one another.

One of the main strands of India's classical thought so pervasive even to this day is *advaita*, the roots of which go back to the *Upanishads*, the *Brahmasutra*, and the *Bhagavadgita* and which has a grand vision of unity that encompasses nature, humanity, and God. In my earlier writings I have given reasons why no emerging theology and christology in India can afford to ignore the power and enduring influence of *advaita* on the Indian mind.[20] While recognizing the developments during recent years of liberation theology in Latin America, *minjung* theology in South Korea, and the *Dalit* theology in India, I find no substantial reason to change my earlier emphasis on *advaita*. In recent years several Roman Catholic theologians in India have also drawn attention to this matter.[21]

To translate *advaita* with the English word "monism" is quite wrong. It misses the profound subtlety of the term, which avoids dichotomies. It may be translated as "not twoism." It is often forgotten that all the three great *acharayas*, Sankara (eighth century), Ramanuja (twelfth century), and Madhwa (thirteenth century) stand within the tradition of the *Vedanta*, the latter two only qualifying *advaita* in important ways. To criticize *advaita* as being "elitist" is to forget that it is not just a philosophy in the Western sense of the term, but a *darshana*, a vision of or an insight into reality. It does not remain on the conceptual level but is also a *sampradaya*, a way of life and conduct that is being followed even to this day by millions of people. To criticize that it lacks social and ethical concern is to misunderstand Hindu life and practice. What Hindus themselves have to say about the matter should be taken into account before such criticism from the outside.

B. K. Matilal, at present the Spalding Professor of religion and ethics at Oxford, has on the basis of careful textual studies, rejected R. C. Zaehner's criticism questioning the value of Vedantic mysticism and expressing misgivings about "the implicit amorality of a monistic metaphysical tradition." Matilal points out that this is a misunderstanding of the texts, and is quite wrong.[22] In a more recent study, Debabrata Sinha remarks:

> The value attitude, so markedly present in *Advaita*, has to find its root deeper than what might be called just "ethical" (as Kant and Kierkegaard would have it). It may, after all, be questioned as to how far the said "ethical" could truly represent the total "metaphysical demand" of human nature as argued by Kierkegaard himself. The absolute value-demand, it is evident, cannot be fulfilled on the level of action on prescription, but rather on the level of truth, where the pathway of knowledge (*jnana*) consummates.[23]

The point is not that ethical and social concerns are unnecessary or unimportant, but that they do not exhaust the Mystery of God or Ultimate Reality. Perhaps these criticisms of a bygone era, which always tried to prove the inadequacy of other religions on the basis of criteria derived from within Western Christianity, should be abandoned once and for all. In any case, for Christian thinkers in India to ignore *advaita* and its enduring influence on the life and thought of people is the easiest way to commit theological suicide.

That the *advaita* vision of a grand unity that holds together diversities in harmony and tension is not just a narrowly sectarian religious doctrine but a view of life, the consequences of which have a pervasive influence on the larger life of the nation, is not always recognized. It has an enduring influence on the cultural life of India, enabling people to hold together diversities in languages, races, ethnic groups, religions, and more recently in different political ideologies as well. Uma Shankar Joshi, the noted Gujarathi writer who won the National Academy Prize in 1984, points out how the *acharayas* speak of the *ekavakyatva* ("one sentenceness") of the great epic *Mahabharata* even though it contains over 100,000 *slokas* (verses). The emphasis is on its power to hold together the varieties of human experience within one all-embracing unity of poetry and Truth.[24]

There is a further point to which insufficient attention has been given: the political implications of the pervasive influence of *advaita* in holding together diversities within a larger unity. *Political unity* is a modern term, but throughout India's history, it was its cultural unity, based on religion, that held together elements of race, ethnic groups, and languages and diversities of, and within, different religions. It seems a miracle that during the four decades of post-independence India has succeeded in being geographically and politically one country, in spite of all the tensions, conflicts, and tragedies of life in the secular state.

Nirad Choudhuri, no lover of India, sarcastically remarks that there is "a clayey core within the cavernous foundations of India,"[25] which is most irritating and painful to people who seek criteria for choice and demand a "rocklike hardness" toward all ambiguities. But maybe it is this refusal to choose when choice itself becomes ambiguous that holds together contradictory things, although it can be irritating and painful. Even in the matter of such different religions as Hinduism and Islam, with immense theological distance between them and all the difficulties and tensions through the centuries, there are Muslim theologians who point out that at higher levels there is no incompatibility between *advaita* and *tawheed* (the unity of God). Learned theologians like Allam Mashriqui and Kwaja Hassan Nizami accepted some of the gods of Hinduism, such as Rama and Krishna, as prophets. Sufi poet Maulana Hastrat Mohani held Krishna in such high respect that he used to go to Mathura every year during Krishna *Janmastami* (birthday celebrations). Maulana Abul Kalam Azad, a colleague of Mahatma Gandhi and Nehru, maintained that while on the level of *Sharia* (law) Islam is incompatible with Hinduism, on the deeper level of *din* (faith) there need not be any contradiction between them. Sufism of Islam and Bhakti of Hinduism helped to bridge the gap between Muslims and Hindus through the centuries in the struggle to build national harmony.[26]

Political thinkers like Rajni Kothari point out that unlike China, which had a clear political center with an empire and an emperor, India has never been a well-defined, centralized nation. Indian nationalism has always flourished through the acceptance of a plural society. Unlike certain other more orderly countries, "India can live with a certain amount of chaos. It might be described as a functioning anarchy," remarks the well-known journalist Mark Tully, who has observed life in India for more than twenty years for the British Broadcasting Corporation in New Delhi. "A plural society can never be a neat affair; but it can be very strong. The Afghans, the Moguls and the British all tried to put their stamp on India; but they found that it was like punching cotton wool. They made an impact, but they could not dent the essential India whose culture has the inner strength to resist invasions, even to be generous to them."[27]

Romila Thapar, the noted Indian historian, points out that throughout history, unlike some other countries, in India the state was never the *only* institution. Religious institutions were always parallel to it, functioning as a brake on state power. Even after 1947, when India became independent and the state in India had a government of its own, Mahatma Gandhi, until his death, functioned as a parallel authority to the state. In the earlier history of India, although there were tensions, for example, between Hindus and Buddhists, society was held together and a cultural unity maintained through certain acts of the rulers and people. The notion and practice of *dana* (religious gift) given by ordinary people and those in power to different religions also has this underlying sense of accepting differences within a larger unity. Even to this day, when a church is being built or renovated, Hindus and Muslims offer donations without the slightest hesitation. Romila Thapar points out, "where (Hindu) Kings presided over Brahmin *yajnas* (sacrifices) their wives and sisters made donations to Buddhist monuments," thereby lessening the tensions and contributing to harmony in society.[28]

This is not to see the hidden hand of *advaita* in every nook and corner of India or to glorify the political indecisiveness that fails to take prompt decisions to ensure a measure of social and economic justice when the state has power to do so. Neither is it to condone the social injustice of the caste system and untouchability in the interests of a larger political unity. These evils are being fought against now by people of diverse religious beliefs and secular convictions, including Christians and *advaitins*. *Neo-advaitins* take into serious account the urgency of social concerns, the challenge of a growing scientific and secular culture, and the dangers of a rising fundamentalism within several religious groups. But the point is that the survival of the political unity of India is based on its cultural unity, within which there persists a core of religion to which the sense of "not-twoism" and the mind-set that holds together diversities by refusing to be exclusive make an enduring contribution.

There are, then, certain elements in the Asian heritage which should help make a larger and more inclusive conceptual framework which can hold together revised christologies that do more justice to new perceptions of religious pluralism in the world today. These are a mood of awe and reverence and silence before the Mystery of Truth or God or Ultimate Reality; a profound hesitation to take any exclusive stance where faith is concerned, and an unwillingness to claim finality to particular responses to Truth; a suspicion of all rational formulations of Truth, even when their necessity is acknowledged; a nontriumphalistic attitude toward other religions and a refusal to destroy dissent as "heresy"; the emphasis on inwardness, meditation, contemplation, and *sadhana* (discipline) in religious life;

and the importance given to signs, symbols, and images, and so to the aesthetic dimensions of life such as art, sculpture, music, and dance, both as providing insights into the depths of Ultimate Reality and as means of mediating Truth. It is within such a dynamic framework that throbs with creative tension in holding together these elements that the components of a revised christology should come together, so that those who live by faith in Christ might become a liberated and liberating community in a religiously plural world.

8

The Making of a Revised Christology

Jesus Christ is the substance of all christologies. New Testament scholars generally agree that although there is but one Jesus, there are several christologies within the New Testament. In subsequent developments over the centuries, including recent decades, several attempts have been made to redefine christology in order to resolve the conflict between traditional christologies and modern realities. These developments in the West have taken into account such matters as the decline in the belief in God, the secularization of life, the challenge of science and the growth of a technological culture, and the emergence of several political ideologies which threaten Christian faith itself.

In all these developments in the West, one factor that is missing is the fact of religious pluralism, the fact that whether Christians like it or not, they *are* living in a religiously plural world in which there are "other lords" and "other saviors" who are accepted by millions of neighbors of other faiths. The theological significance of this fact has not yet entered seriously into christological reflections. It is either ignored or rejected. It is this factor to which pointed attention is being given here. Any attempt toward a revised christology in the world today which ignores the fact of religious pluralism will not only be theologically inadequate but also less than ecumenical.

THE CONTEXT OF REVISION

Granting that the roots of all christologies go back to Jesus Christ, the question must be asked: Who *is* this Jesus Christ? How and what do we know of him? Where do we encounter him today? What difference does faith in God through Christ make to our knowledge of God, our understanding of the human, and to our relationship to nature? In particular, what difference does it make to our relationship to neighbors of other faiths in an interdependent world? While it is obviously impossible to give a systematic and comprehensive answer to such questions, a beginning has to be made to indicate the direction a revised christology should take in a religiously plural world.

The context in which this question is being raised today should be noted. Obviously, the religious dimension is one of the factors in the contemporary global situation. There are secular forces and ideologies based on a scientific and technological culture that touch human life at many points. There are political and economic forces that influence the ferment within religions. It should not be forgotten that religious and cultural factors are the most enduring factors in human history. They influence political, social, and economic life, and the ways in which people respond to the power of science and technology. While the linkage between all these factors should be kept in mind, the emphasis here is deliberately on the religious factor because, for various reasons, it is the most neglected and misunderstood element in the contemporary context.

A consultation on christology organized by the Christian Conference of Asia (CCA) and attended by representatives of ten mainline Protestant churches, the Asia-Pacific region of the World Student Christian Federation, and the Federation of Asian Bishops' Conference, pointed out that in all christological reflections today there should be "a recognition of the ties that link the communities of Christians across the manifold differences of time, space and culture." This means that the urge toward the revised christology in the religiously plural world of Asia is not a matter of misguided national zeal but a serious attempt to grasp those theological moments when the local becomes ecumenical and the ecumenical local. Lest this concern be limited to the narrowly parochial Christian, the statement goes on to add that "the enriching, correcting and sometimes profoundly disturbing wisdom of the faithful and indeed *of those who see Christ through the eyes of other faiths and ideologies* is necessary in order that Christ may not be deformed in any context."[1] In other words, without taking into theological account the responses of neighbors of other faiths to Jesus Christ, no revised christology can become truly ecumenical.

There is a further point in the context that should be noted. At the moment, in most countries of Asia, perhaps particularly in India, there does not seem to be a theological meeting point between those who are actively engaged in political struggles against injustice in society and those involved in serious dialogue with neighbors of other faiths. The former tend to think of the latter as irrelevant, and the latter often regard the former as one-sided in their emphasis, even while recognizing the problem's urgency. *Theoria* and *praxis* are often regarded as alternatives, even as hostile to each other. This leads to a debilitating conflict rather than a creative tension in the ongoing life of the church. This is unfortunate. At a time when there is so much poverty and injustice in society, the stress on social and political activism is indeed justified.

Praxis, in its essence, is a protest against *puja* (ritual) that becomes a substitute for action. It is also a rejection of all abstract theological speculation that is not rooted in the human struggle and which becomes an end in itself. The Buddha, nearly six centuries before Jesus of Nazareth, was certainly in the stream of *praxis*, not *theoria*. But surely, even in the case of the Buddha, *praxis* was not limited to its political, economic, and social expressions.

Dialogue, in the sense of Christian involvement in the religious life of their neighbors, leads to new relationships and helps to transform religious values into social virtues. Thus dialogue is also a form of *praxis*. Dialogue is not a matter of discussing religious ideas with neighbors of other faiths. It includes working together in society. At the same time, it includes sharing of religious life at the deepest level, where elements of meditation and contemplation become important. Without nourishing the deeper roots of life, those immersed in social and political activism are sometimes in danger of spiritual exhaustion. For Christians to be consciously rooted in the life of the crucified and risen Christ is to participate in the being of God and to be sustained by a power that is working in history but is not limited by it. That the situation of dialogue itself could become a revelatory context should not be discounted. Neither *doing* nor *thinking* can exhaust the depth and mystery of God's *being*.

Any revised christology that takes into account both the Christian experience of interreligious dialogue and Christian involvement in the political and social struggle for justice in society must start with the historic person and work of Jesus of Nazareth. The road to a confession of his divinity passes through his humanity. This assumes that the "fact" of Jesus deserves priority over later doctrinal formulations and justifies attempts articulating christology "from below" as opposed to according an absolute priority to a christology "from above." Although the connection between the two in Christian faith is indeed important, the process of development in the New Testament is from the former to the latter.

In developing this point, one obviously has to depend on the enormous amount of work by New Testament exegetes and New Testament theologians. The range of books and articles on the subject is so vast that even to give a list of books consulted would be inadequate. Although one's indebtedness to scholars who have worked in this area should be obvious, the decision to choose among different viewpoints is one's own, and the theological framework within which some of the fruits of New Testament scholarship are interpreted by an Indian may legitimately differ from the framework of the West, within which these scholars have done their investigations. The framework has to take into account the theological significance of the religions of our neighbors, in particular, the plurality of scriptures and the fact that, even as Christians accept the authority of the Bible, neighbors of other faiths live by the authority of *their* scriptures. This is a decisively new factor in christological debates today.

HELICOPTER CHRISTOLOGY VS. BULLOCK-CART CHRISTOLOGY

There are several assumptions behind this discussion. One is that whatever may be the difficulties involved in connecting the developments in Christianity as a historical religious tradition with the person and work of Jesus Christ, one must acknowledge and accept the *fact* of Jesus of Nazareth. "We should not overlook the fact," remarks Ernst Kaesemann, "that there are still pieces of the Synoptic tradition which the historian has to acknowledge as authentic."[2] Another assumption is that while on the basis of the synoptic tradition a recognizable portrait of Jesus of Nazareth is possible, this portrait itself is based on the testimonies of the believing community. The *being* or the *truth* of Jesus behind the testimonies is larger, deeper, and more mysterious than any portrait painted by the brushes of scholarly study. Therefore the being or the truth of Jesus must remain the controlling factor in interpreting the testimonies of writers.

A third assumption on the basis of general agreement among New Testament scholars is that within the New Testament there is *one* Jesus but *several* christologies. If, then, within the New Testament itself people felt free to develop different christologies, why should people today have any hesitation or anxiety in seeking to revise traditional christologies which have served their time and are now not only outmoded but even hindrances to authentic Christian faith, life, and witness? "The real history of Jesus is always happening afresh,"[3] comments Kaesemann. Thus a quest for a revised christology in a religiously plural world is both existentially possible and theologically legitimate.

There is a discernible tension here between New Testament scholars and the theologians and authorities of the church. The church, both in the East and the West, has taken the easy way by starting with christology from above reflected in the classical dogmas. Popular piety has merely followed the orthodox line. However, to ask which is most adequate is not so shocking, particularly when the insights of New Testament scholarship are taken into account when examining what happened during the period from Nicea (A.D. 325) to Chalcedon (A.D. 451) when the classic dogmatic formulae were solidified.

Among many Christians, there seems to be a desperate need to defend and guard the divinity of Christ, lest by starting from below one might compromise the confession that "Jesus is the Christ, son of the living God." Is this fear historically and theologically justified? A *helicopter* christology, in its attempts to land on the religiously plural terrain of Asia, makes such a lot of missiological noise and kicks up so much theological dust that people around it are prevented from hearing the voice and seeing the vision of the descending divinity. A *bullock-cart* christology, on the other hand, always has its wheels touching the unpaved roads of Asia, for without continual friction with the ground, the cart cannot move forward at all. Moreover, a bullock-cart christology has the advantage of having its bullocks move on with a steady pace, even when the driver sometimes falls asleep.

The major difficulties of a christology from above in a religiously plural world should be noted. First, it compromises the very basis of all monotheistic faiths. In all theistic faiths, Ultimate Reality or *Sat* or Truth or the Transcendent is designated by the term *God* or *Theos*. To the Jews this was YHWH. Jesus, as a Jew, was very much part of the Jewish religious life and practice of his time and fully participated in the life of the Jewish home and synagogue. In emphasizing the particularity of Jesus of Nazareth as a Jew, this fact has to be taken into account seriously. "Would it have been possible," asks Joseph Fitzmyer, "in the monotheistic setting of pre-Christian Palestine for a Jew like Jesus to claim openly *ana elaha* (in Aramaic) or *ego eimi theos* (in Greek), that is 'I am God'? . . ."[4] It is difficult to imagine how such a statement would have been understood. In the time of Jesus and his disciples it would have perhaps been possible to say that the God of Abraham, Isaac, and Jacob had been revealed in the person and work of Jesus of Nazareth confessed as the Christ, the Son of the living God. But it would have been quite another thing to say that Jesus of Nazareth *is* the God of Abraham, Isaac, and Jacob. The evidence of the synoptic gospels, as understood and interpreted by New Testament scholarship, is against such a claim. This is not to deny the divinity of Jesus Christ confessed by the believing community but to suggest the need to qualify carefully the notion that Jesus of Nazareth is ontologically the same as God. As has been suggested by Perkins and Fuller, "the God present in Jesus is God himself. It is not that Jesus in his own being is identical with the God who is present in him."[5]

Second, a simplistic, deductive interpretation of christology from above does not do justice to the humanity of Jesus of Nazareth as attested to by the synoptic gospels. At a time when there is so much degrading dehumanization in the world and such a great need to bring out what it is *to be human* in such a world, to minimize the humanity of Jesus is to diminish seriously the resources for supporting the struggles for human freedom, dignity, and self-respect. How can it be forgotten that the synoptic gospels give so much information about the humanness of Jesus, pointing out that he hungered and thirsted and wept and was angry and identified himself so much with ordinary human beings of his time? Furthermore, not only did he himself pray to God, he also taught his disciples to pray to God as "Our Father," without any mediation through the Son. How can God pray to God? He constantly pointed not to himself but to God's Kingdom, all of which becomes very problematic in certain rigid theologies which take wooden approaches to Chalcedonian doctrinal formulae. Even when his disciples tended to be christocentric Jesus was always theocentric. There seems to be no disagreement on this point among New Testament scholars. In the order of development of New Testament christology, christology from below comes first. Reginald Fuller, accordingly, maintains: "From below to above is the *only* acceptable way of doing New Testament Christology."[6] Kaesemann points out that "it is not the Christ-kerygma of Paul and John that constitutes the norm of christology, but rather the Jesus-kerygma accessible through the critical analysis of the synoptic gospels."[7]

Third, over-emphasizing a christology from above seriously underestimates the significance of the historical at a time when historical consciousness is becoming global. Throughout the Bible, faith emerges as the fruit of historical experience. That God is One, not many, that the God of Israel is not the God of the nations but that the God of the nations is also the God of Israel, gradually emerged as a fruit of the experience of the people of Israel in history. So too, Peter's confession, "You are the Christ, Son of the living God" (Matthew 16:16) comes as a confession after a period of association with the human Jesus.

Faith cannot be imposed from above. It is only doctrine and belief, dogma and ritual, which can be imposed upon others by authority from above. Faith is not an answer seeking a question. Faith is a question that receives the answer at the end of a process of living and working together with Jesus of Nazareth, sharing his life in all its humanness in the ambiguities, conflicts and tragedies of history.

This emphasis on the humanity of Jesus anchored in history is particularly important in a country like India where, unlike in China, there seems to be less importance given to facts of historical life. Acceptance of eternal values is often given greater importance than their actualization in the dust and heat of history. Therefore the name Jesus of Nazareth is necessary to prevent the balloon of faith being cut away from its moorings in history, quickly soaring above, and getting lost in the clouds.

> If Jesus had never lived or faith in him were shown to be a misunderstanding of the significance of the historical Jesus the ground would be taken away from under the Christian faith. If it lost its support in the historical Jesus, it would perhaps not be devoid of an object altogether, but it would be devoid of the object that the Christian proclamation has continually put forth as the central object of faith.[8]

Unless the rope of Christian faith in God through Christ constantly feels the tug of the fact of Jesus of Nazareth rooted in the soil of history at some point, it will lose its historic significance, theological credibility, and spiritual power for today.

Fourth, a christology from above makes it impossible for Christians to relate themselves, their faith in God through Jesus Christ, and the liberated and liberating life in the Kingdom of God, to neighbors of other faiths. This is perhaps the major reason why the quest for a revision of traditional christology is so necessary and urgent in a religiously plural world. Christians have nothing to lose but much to gain by inquiring after the basis and source of the Christian movement in history which still constitutes the distinctive reality of the life of the church in the world. Through the centuries the church in the world has acquired "a fractured relationship to this source."⁹ Christian identity has been distorted by emphasizing christology from above and getting it mixed up with dogmas about his person and doctrines about his work. It is this christology, torn away from its historic moorings and mixed up with so many ideological factors in the history of Western culture, that was proclaimed by missions during the colonial era. This Christianity must lose itself as a religion in order to gain itself as a faith.

Ever since the gospel of Jesus Christ was proclaimed in India in recent centuries, one fact stands out clearly: It was not the dogmas about Christ and doctrines about the atonement that touched the heart and mind of India, but the person of Jesus of Nazareth, his life and work and words, his suffering, death, and resurrection. Paul might have been right when he wrote that the word of the cross was "foolishness" to the Greeks and a "stumbling block" to the Jews (1 Corinthians 1:23), but it is certainly wrong in India, and may be in other countries of Asia as well. This is amply illustrated, not just by philosophers and theologians, but also by political, social, and religious leaders, artists, painters, and poets in India. To a person like Mahatma Gandhi, the cross of Jesus Christ was not "foolishness" or "scandal," but provided the inspiration for nonviolent action against all kinds of oppression, political, economic, social, and religious.

What *is* foolishness, and what *is* a stumbling block to neighbors of other faiths, is the Christian claim that *only* in Jesus Christ has God been revealed *once-for-all* to redeem all humanity. This claim has isolated Christians from their neighbors of other faiths in India, led to their theological alienation and spiritual impoverishment, and in a religiously plural society has made it difficult, if not impossible, for Christians to cooperate with their neighbors for common social purposes. The major emphasis of this book is that this exclusive claim is not integral to the gospel or Christian faith in God through Jesus Christ or to the content and practice of mission today.

In theistic religions that accept the doctrine of the incarnation (Christianity and Vaisnavism) it is accepted that the mystery of God is revealed in the incarnation, which also serves as a means of salvation. The incarnation becomes the bridge that connects the divine and the human, and various attempts are made to understand this divine–human relationship in the person of the incarnate God. To Christians, Jesus Christ is indeed "the Word made flesh" (John 1:14). Christian faith is in God through Jesus Christ, sustained and led by the Holy Spirit.

The Incarnation, I wish to suggest, is best understood not solely in terms of "deity," but in terms of "divinity." It is one thing to say that Jesus of Nazareth is divine and quite another thing to say that Jesus of Nazareth is God. That Jesus Christ is divine is the testimony of the gospels. This is recognized by New Testament scholars on the basis of careful historical research and meticulous exegesis of texts. One wonders how its theological implications could have been so distorted in subsequent developments as to lead to a narrow "Christomonism" and, in popular Christian piety, even to an impoverished "Jesusology." Schubert Ogden has very accurately pointed out that "To say that anyone who is uniquely man of God simply is uniquely God is untenable because one cannot apply the term 'deity' to a life qualified by 'divinity'."[10] If Ogden is correct, to claim that God, the Creator of all humanity, is identical with Jesus of Nazareth or that Jesus of Nazareth is ontologically co-equal with the Creator God is not only to go beyond the evidence of the New Testament but also to cut off all conversations with neighbors of other faiths. Observing this, in no way amounts to denying the divinity of Christ: "The God present in Jesus is God himself. It is not that Jesus in his own being is identical with the God who is present in him."[11] Christ is "the exegesis of the Father,"[12] remarks J. A. T. Robinson. The Indian Christian theologian V. Chakkarai, himself a Hindu convert, observes that "to believe that God is best defined by Christ is not to believe that God is confined to Christ."[13] Wesley Ariarajah remarks, "If Christians believe that Jesus became a window into God then the witness to Christ has to do with the nature of God that we see through his life."[14] Those who reject historical and textual criticism of the New Testament will have no use for this kind of argument, but it is still necessary to draw attention briefly to insights from New Testament scholarship to support these christological affirmations.

A question may be raised here: Why is it necessary for an Indian Christian theologian seeking a revised christology in a religiously plural world to quote so many Western New Testament scholars? There are several reasons for this. For one thing, no christology worth its name anywhere in the world can today afford to do without New Testament foundations. Without grounding oneself in the New Testament, christology is likely to become mere speculation with a generous use of the phrase "crucified and risen Christ" mixed up like currants in a vast mass of unleavened dough. For another, no revised christology today can risk being narrowly nationalistic. Even when the cultural distinctiveness of a particular christology is recognized, the need for an ecumenical criterion for christology should be accepted. But in a religiously plural world the term *ecumenical* can no longer be confined to the narrowly parochial Christian community but should embrace neighbors of other faiths as well. Therefore when I, as an Indian, accept and use the insights of New Testament scholars, these points are interpreted and put in a wider framework than the monoscriptural, monoreligious, and monocultural world of the West.

To these may be added a third reason. In raising serious and critical questions about traditional christologies handed over to Asian Christians by the West, and in calling for a revision of inherited christologies, one risks the danger of being accused of heresy. This risk has to be taken for the sake of Jesus Christ, even if it might mean a rejection by one's friends and colleagues. By drawing attention to the fact that there *are* New Testament scholars and theologians, not only in Asia but in other countries as well, who point out that certain christological claims of the church in the West go beyond the evidence of the New Testament, one at least shows that there are solid scholarly warrants for suggesting that Asian christologists may legitimately begin their reflections "from below."

NEW TESTAMENT WITNESSES TO JESUS OF NAZARETH

In developing a revised christology in a religiously plural world, the interplay between the authority of the scriptures on the one hand and that of the creeds on the other becomes difficult and complicated. One reason for this is the fact that the creeds came to be accepted as authoritative by the Western church under very different circumstances than what obtains in the religiously plural world today. Another is the gulf between what the New Testament exegesis affirms about Jesus Christ and what the church has formulated in the creeds as doctrines about his person and work.

It should be noted that some of the problems about the relation between Jesus Christ and God remain unresolved among Christians even to this day. The creeds were formulated and accepted under the constraints of the historical, social, and political needs of the church in the West. For the sake of Christian worship enshrined in the liturgy, most Christians in different parts of the world have learned to recite the creeds and live with them. But when it is a question of revising christology today, in totally different situations, the witness of a variety of high and low New Testament christologies is more important than the later formulae of the creeds. This means that one has to depend on the fruits of New Testament scholarship based on historical, textual, and redaction criticism. Here one must acknowledge one's indebtedness to generations of New Testament scholars who have given many years to historical study, careful research, and meticulous exegesis of New Testament writings.[15]

New Testament scholars are generally agreed on the chronological developments of christologies within the New Testament. The line runs through the book of Acts, which provides information about the experience of the first generation of Christians, to the synoptic gospels, the epistles of Paul, and later on, to the fourth gospel. Although the historical value of Acts is controversial, one does get a sense of the manner in which early Christians looked upon Jesus of Nazareth. Jesus is called Lord after the ascension (1:21) and Christ after the Pentecost (2:36). In the community of believers in Jerusalem, Jesus is called Jesus Christ of Nazareth (3:6), the Holy and Righteous One (3:14), and God's Holy Servant (3:13, 26; 4:27, 30). Jesus is first called Son of God in Syria (9:20). There is thus a distinctive view of Jesus in the early Christian community, but there is no hint of the doctrine of the incarnation. Jesus is not regarded as a preexistent being but a man appointed by God and anointed by the Spirit for a specific vocation and destiny.[16]

The gospels of Matthew, Mark, and Luke strongly emphasize the humanity of Jesus as a special person chosen, raised up, and commissioned by God for a special purpose. The "Messiah" and the "Son of God" in these gospels are generally human, and the "Son of Man," even though described as a heavenly figure, is not regarded as divine. Although to Mark the phrase "Son of God" does sometimes have a divine resonance, Jesus himself appears not to accept the implication of divinity. Matthew and Luke do not go beyond Mark.

The narrative of birth stories may even be regarded as pulling away from any idea of incarnation because they strongly emphasize the human birth brought about by God's Spirit. Matthew gives Jesus a long line of human genealogy which puts him in the long stream of men of God. He is presented as the carpenter's son who is descended from David through his human father. The name Emmanuel (Matthew 1:23), "God with us," does not imply that Jesus is God. In Peter's confession at Caesarea Philippi (Matthew 16:13-20), Matthew certainly goes beyond Mark, but scholars point out that in the context the phrase "Son of the living God" means Messiah and no more. Luke adds little more to this picture of Jesus of Nazareth in the first two gospels. His phrase "God has visited his people" (Luke 7:16) is a traditional metaphor which follows from the previous exclamation: "A great prophet has risen among us." The synoptic portrait of Jesus therefore is that of one appointed by God to bring in the Kingdom of God and to reign over the age of salvation. However, the gospels come nowhere near to saying that he is the credal "Very God of Very God."[17]

When one comes to what are regarded as the authentic epistles of Paul, the historic Jesus has receded from the scene and Christ, crucified and risen, has taken over. To Paul, Jesus is Lord and the Son of God in an exclusive sense, *the* Son, God's heavenly companion, enthroned at the right hand of God. The historical Jesus, his words and deeds and signs, the Kingdom of God he has ushered in, the vocabulary about his humanness and temptations, his prayers and struggles, have all receded to the background. The emphasis is wholly on Jesus Christ, the Son of God, as the exalted cosmic Lord.

It would, however, be a mistake to assume that Paul formally makes Christ co-equal with God. What seems to have happened is a quick and fateful slide from the humanity of Jesus to the divinity of Christ, and later on, to the claim that Jesus Christ *is* God. New Testament scholars point out that it should not be assumed too quickly that Paul identifies Jesus Christ with God. Paul is extremely careful not to simply identify Jesus Christ with God. Throughout his writings, *God the Father* and *the Son, the Lord Jesus Christ*, are always two distinct beings, closely associated, but never identified. No one would deny that to Paul, Christ is central to Christian faith and life. Paul routes all traffic between God and the world through

Christ and affirms that the only way to salvation is through Christ. But Paul, in spite of his radical Christocentrism, is extremely careful to retain the ultimacy of God. It is *God* who "was in Christ reconciling the world unto himself" (2 Corinthians 5:19). It is *God* "who raised up Jesus from the dead" (1 Corinthians 6:14), and it is *God* "who will sum up all things in Christ" (Ephesians 1:10). He reminds the Corinthians, "You belong to Christ and Christ belongs to *God*" (1 Corinthians 3:23). And in his great resurrection text, Paul affirms that when all things are subjected to the Son, the Son also will be subjected to God "until *God* be all in all" (1 Corinthians 15:28).

It is difficult to see how conservative evangelicals who affirm the verbal inspiration and inerrancy of the Bible can get away from the authority of such clear texts in epistles regarded as authentically Pauline. In the doxological formulae that Paul often uses to begin or end his epistles, the context is liturgical. But even here *God the Father* and *the Lord Jesus Christ* (Galatians 1:3) are surely not spoken of as *God the Father* and *God the Son*. To Paul, *Theos* remains the ultimate horizon for faith in *Christos*. The central purpose of Paul in his epistles is not to prove that Jesus Christ is God but to invite people to share in the salvation wrought through him by God. The New Testament seems to be concerned not so much with the ontological status of Christ in relation to God as with the functional nature of his work as Savior of all humanity. Cullmann points out, "The New Testament always speaks of the Son of God (task) and never of God the Son (status), that is the full co-equal deity is never taught in the New Testament."[18] "The total Christian faith, as reflected in the New Testament, is essentially and primarily theistic, that is to say monotheistic, and secondarily christological."[19]

That the fourth gospel is strikingly different from the synoptic is well known. It has moved rather far from the historic human Jesus of the earlier gospels and, in the prologue itself, affirms that Jesus Christ is the Logos or the Word or the Son of God incarnate. It assumes the preexistence of the Son, and even attributes to Jesus this knowledge about himself.

It is rather surprising that this gospel, so full of meditative wisdom about the Son, should be so anti-Semitic. It is remarkable that many Hindus, both those who follow the way of knowledge (*jnana*) and those who are committed to the way of devotion (*bhakti*), find this gospel very attractive, both in English and in translations into Indian languages. Its anti-Jewish attitude has not made the slightest difference to Hindus who appreciate its "wisdom" about Jesus Christ as the incarnation of God. It is a testimony to the tolerant ethos of India that in spite of the attraction Hindus felt toward the fourth gospel, and in spite of its powerful anti-Jewish sentiments, Jews were never persecuted in India.[20] One reason may be that they took the fourth gospel as putting forward a Christian doctrine of incarnation. Another may be its use of the term *logos*. While responding to the Johannine doctrine of incarnation, Hindus have rejected its anti-Semitism and its exclusiveness.

But while the fourth gospel indeed puts forward Jesus as the incarnation of the Word or Son of God, the question must be raised: Does it uphold the view that the Son of God is himself God? Surely, in the fourth gospel Christ is more than a created being; he is indeed divine. But even though Jesus claims, "I and my Father are one" (John 10:30), such statements are balanced by other sayings, such as "My Father is greater than I" (John 14:28). He clearly affirms that God the Father is "the only true God" (John 17:3). All this means that in the fourth gospel the portrait of Jesus is higher than that of the synoptics but lower than that affirmed in the Nicean creed later on. New Testament scholars point out that the well-known translation of the verse in the prologue, "the Word was with God and the Word was God" (John 1:1) is incorrect in its translation of the original Greek. *Theos* with the article is to be translated as God, but the correct translation of *Theos without* the article should be "divine." In other words, the translation should be, "The Word was with God and the Word was divine." Most of the well-known New Testament scholars agree on this.[21]

The Indian Christian theologian A. J. Appasamy, in a study of the fourth gospel, wrote, "Jesus always lived in whole-hearted trust and faith in the Father. He did not consider himself identical with God."[22] Wesley Ariarajah remarks,

> Jesus' own life is entirely God-centered, God-dependent and God-ward. In the synoptic environment it would be strange if Jesus were to say "I and the Father are one," or "I am the way, the truth and the life." There seems to be no claim to divinity or to oneness with God. What we have is the challenge to live lives that are totally turned towards God.[23]

This means that the "co-equal divinity" of Jesus—that is, the claim that Jesus of Nazareth *is* God—is not explicitly taught in the New Testament, although Jesus is described as divine. The closer people came to affirming the full deity of Jesus, the farther they moved away from the historical Jesus. Jesus himself obstinately remained a devout Jew who spoke not of himself but of God. And, as Cupitt says, "the real Jesus is a much more interesting and religiously relevant figure than the divine Christ of later faith, and He has the advantage of having actually lived ... Christendom-Christianity does not work any more. The historical Jesus is the real Christ for today."[24]

The development of the doctrine of Christ in the period after the New Testament, going through the councils of Nicaea (A.D. 325), the first council of Constantinople (A.D. 381), and onward to Chalcedon (A.D. 451) is well-known. So much has been written about the councils that it is not necessary to deal with the well-known points about the relationship between God and Jesus Christ and the question of the Holy Spirit.[25] Any revised christology has to keep in mind this long process of development from the confession that the human Jesus is the Christ to the affirmation that Jesus Christ himself is God.

When the Council of Nicaea met, presided over by Emperor Constantine—who at that time was an unbaptized Christian (he was baptized only in A.D. 337, the year he died)—political considerations were mixed up with matters of doctrine. It may be a bit too late to ask whether a council presided over by an unbaptized Christian is valid. The emperor was most unwilling to have the unity of the empire jeopardized in any way by disunity in doctrine. But even in the Nicene creed, in spite of its emphasis on the "co-equal divinity" of Christ with God with the phrase, "being of one substance with the Father," the distinction between "one God the Father" and the "one Lord Jesus Christ, the only begotten Son of God" is not abandoned.

In subsequent developments in the church, the movement from the Nicene formula to the declaration that Jesus Christ himself *is* God became all too easy. Perhaps in the situation where both the empire and the church were concerned with unity, the one political and the other ecclesiastical, the claim became too easy. In the absence of powerful alternative religions, there was no serious challenge to imperial Christianity. There was an excess of theological confidence over exegetical common sense. Political religion, it can be argued, overcame the religion inspired by Jesus.

This is obviously an oversimplified version of a highly complex process in the history of the Western church. But it draws attention to the historical baggage bequeathed to Christians in Asia and Africa during a particular period in Western history and that has burdened them in their pilgrimage on the way of Jesus Christ in a religiously plural world. Even more unfortunate is the fatal slip into "Jesusology" so common among Asian Christians that prompts them to claim that "Jesus is our God" when faced with the inevitable fact of living together with neighbors who live by faith in other gods and other saviors. Thus the way the claim that Jesus Christ *is* God is understood has led to a sad impoverishment of the profound depth of Christian faith in God through Christ and has hindered Christians from appropriating new insights in christology today that are emerging through the leading of the Holy Spirit.

THE BUDDHA

The entry point into a revised christology is at the intersection where history and faith meet in the contemporary world today, history with all its ambiguities and conflicts, and faith with all its doubts and certainties. In a religiously plural world this converging point is a bit crowded with other "lords" and other "saviors" whose presence cannot be ignored. To do so would amount to self-deception. The moment the gospel was preached in a country like India, Jesus Christ was inevitably placed among others. In Europe this was not so, but in Asia it could not have been otherwise. Many

Christians feel uneasy, hesitant, even fearful talking about these personalities. But there can be no credible christology today without trying to understand not only their theological significance, but also their devotional meaning and ethical guidance to millions of people.

An extensive study of all religious personalities here is obviously impossible. But some reference must be made to the Buddha, Rama, and Krishna. It is perhaps easier to talk about the Buddha and Christ together, partly because the case for the historicity of each is strong, and partly because both Buddhism and Christianity have transcended their particularities and become universal in the sense that they have found themselves at home in different countries and different cultures. However, it looks as if Buddhism has found it easier to shed its "Indianness" than Christianity its "Westernness."

Several Asian Christian theologians have referred to the Buddha and Christ in their writings. Lynn de Silva has written extensively on the subject.[26] Wesley Ariarajah points out that even though the Buddha clearly discouraged his followers from believing in him or worshiping him, in some branches of Buddhism, the Buddha is claimed to be divine. His previous incarnations are described in detail and, as "Lord Buddha," he has become the object of veneration and worship.[27] This means that even when a *dharma* has no theistic foundation as faith develops into religion, the followers of the founder, sometimes against the express wish of the leader, claim divinity for his humanity. To C. S. Song, the cross and the lotus are two powerful symbols representing two different ways to grasp the world of reality behind the world of phenomena. "Asian Buddhists enter human suffering through the lotus, and Christians through the cross. Whether they will meet before the throne of God's salvation and glory is not for mortals to judge."[28]

Today, however, it is as mediators of *liberation* that the Buddha and Christ are recognized as working powerfully in the life of Asia. During the past few centuries the life and work of Jesus of Nazareth provided both an inspiration and an example for reformers working for the liberation of the poor and oppressed in Asian society. In more recent years, it is the Buddha who has provided both a "shelter" (*saranam*) and a dynamic source of power to millions of *Dalits* (formerly untouchables, Harijans) to break the bonds of the caste system. Millions of *Dalits* under the leadership of Dr. Ambedkar, a former member of the Nehru cabinet, have embraced Buddhism, rebelling against and rejecting the Hindu caste system. This means that even as the liberating power of Jesus of Nazareth provides inspiration for liberation theology in Latin America and elsewhere, so does the liberating power of the Buddha continue to be available to following generations.

In such a situation the obsession with the uniqueness of Christ is a false start, remarks Aloysius Pieris. A christology of domination—that is, the theology of the colonial Christ—cannot be "good news" for Buddhists or Christians or for neighbors of other faiths in Asia. Pieris observes that the two dimensions of liberation, one demanding inner liberation and the other liberation from unjust structures of society, meet each other in the Buddhist–Christian pilgrimage in Asia. An Asian theology of liberation evolves into a christology that does not compete with Buddhology but complements it by acknowledging

> the one path of liberation of which Christians join Buddhists in their *gnostic detachment* (or the practice of voluntary poverty) and Buddhists join Christians in their *agapaeic involvement* in the struggle against forced poverty. ... It is only at the end of the path, as at Emmaus, that the path itself will be recognised by name (Luke 24:31).[29]

Even as in Jesus of Nazareth there is a strong note of compassion toward the poor and the oppressed so well attested to in the synoptic gospels, so too in the Buddha, the Buddhists point out, is the attitude of great compassion (*maha karuna citta*). One of the most well-known Buddhist texts states, "Having myself crossed the ocean of suffering, I must help others to cross it. Free, myself, I must set others free. This is the vow which I made in the past when I saw all that lives in distress."[30]

THE HISTORICITY OF RAMA AND KRISHNA

Rama and Krishna are household words in India and are at the center of theistic *bhakti* (devotional religion), at times merging into the larger horizon of *advaita*. Over the centuries the two epics, *Ramayana* and the *Mahabharata*, in original Sanskrit and translations into Indian languages, have exercised an enduring influence over generations of Indians. There are festivals connected with them, celebrated at different times in the year, in which millions of people take part with great joy. It is rather significant that at present, when the heroes of modern India such as Mahatma Gandhi and Nehru seem to recede into the background, it is these ancient gods that come to the forefront of people's lives and consciousness, reemphasizing values considered necessary to contemporary life in India.

At the time of this writing (October 1988), a television serial on the great epic *Mahabharata*, in which Krishna, the incarnate god, is the hero, is being telecast every Sunday. The series is being directed by a well-known director, B. R. Chopra, and is produced at a cost of 40 million rupees (2.85 million U.S. dollars). Fifty-two episodes, each of 47 minutes duration, are planned. Already several episodes have been televised, and the estimated number of viewers on Sunday morning is put at 50 million. The scholarly research for the re-creation of dialogue, historic details, and scenes was done by the well-known Bhandarkar's Institute of Oriental Research, Pune, and put in 28 volumes in the director's office. Pandit Narendra Sharma is in charge of the script, lyrics, and dialogue.

In 1987 the other great epic, *Ramayana*, the story of Rama, was serialized on television on fifty-two Sundays.[31] A great deal of the epic *Mahabharata* revolves around Krishna, the charioteer of the great warrior Arjuna, who fights the battle against evil. Noted poet Krishna Chaitanya describes Arjuna and Krishna as "partners in history."[32]

The question of the historicity of Rama and Krishna has always been a complex question and needs some attention. This is bound up with the date of the two epics, and is so complicated that it is almost impossible to indicate dates with some measure of certainty. Some scholars are of the opinion that both the *Mahabharata* and the *Ramayana* reached their rounded forms between 400 B.C. and A.D. 400.[33]

One must note, however, that the investigation into the historicity of the founder of any religion is a recent phenomenon. The quest for the historical Jesus began in the West only after European developments in historiography, when methods of historical investigation began to be applied to the Bible. Asking the question, "Who was Krishna?", a Western scholar remarks, "If one expects a historical answer the question is not foolish; it is merely difficult to answer."[34] A. D. Pusalker, an Indian scholar, observes that "an ordinary Hindu is never concerned with the historicity of Krishna; to investigate the problem is a sacrilege to him."[35] One must note that this has been, and even to this day continues to be, the attitude of followers of other religions to any investigation into the historical sources of their respective founders. There are many Christians who reject the results of historical criticism of the Bible. However, in the cases of Rama and Krishna, it is generally agreed that there was originally a real man, as indicated by evidence, in the pre-epic period. The *Rig Veda* refers to Krishna *Angirasa* (VII, 85:3-4) and in the *Upanishads* there is a reference to Krishna *Devakiputra* (*Chandogya* III, 17:6). The Greek ambassador Megasthenes, who visited India in the fourth century B.C., refers to Krishna *Vasudeva*.[36]

Krishna

Among Christians there is a great deal of ignorance about Krishna. Probably no other Hindu god is more vilified by them than Krishna. There is a refusal even to study the story of Krishna objectively. There are at least three strands in the Krishna story which often merge into one. There is the Krishna, the chief of the Yadava clan, who liberates his people from oppression. There is the Krishna who is described as *gopala* (the protector of the cows) who in *Bhakti* literature is adored as the mischievous child, multiple lover, and eternal paradox of flesh and spirit, living in dance, music, poetry and festivals. There is also Krishna, the *avatara* in the *Bhagavadgita* who, as the teacher, charioteer, and lord of Arjuna exercises enormous influence over millions of people even to this day. It is difficult to separate these strands, either in doctrine or in religious practice. The line of demarcation between them is noted, but traffic across the border is heavy.[37]

The *Bhagavadgita* is to the Hindus what the New Testament is to the Christians: the source of faith in a personal God, the basis for a theology of *Bhakti* (devotion), and a guide for ethical conduct in the day-to-day life of the world. In the *Gita* (short form, literally the song) Krishna urges Arjuna to do his duty as a warrior to fight against evil, and points to his own function in the world as an *avatara* of Vishnu, assuring him that whenever there is a decline of *dharma* and a rise of *adharma*, *avataras* intervene in history. "To protect the righteous, to destroy the wicked, and to establish the kingdom of God, I am reborn from age to age" (*Gita* IV:8).[38] And to reassure his devotee Arjuna, he also grants him the Cosmic Vision containing within himself all the worlds (chapter 11).

There are three major points in Krishna's teaching in the *Gita* which are constantly being reinterpreted to provide the basis for a theology of action. These are (a) the ideal of the *sthitiprajna*, or *gunatita*, the person of calm detachment, of perfect poise, whose mind is "like a flame that burns steadily in a place protected by the wind"; (b) the doctrine *nishkama karma*, the call to act without personal involvement in or desire for the fruits of one's actions; and (c) the principle of *lokasangraha*, the welfare of the whole world, accepted as the goal toward which all activity should be directed. Thus the *kurukshetra* (the battlefield) also becomes the *dharmakshetra* (the field of *dharma*). Perhaps one reason for the tremendous response to the Krishna of the televised series today is its blend of the revelation of God and liberation of the human, and a longing for a new *avatara* to destroy the evil of corruption so blatantly present in political, economic, social, and religious life.

Rama

Probably no other figure in the history of India embodies the traditional notions of Indian *dharma* so powerfully as the story of Rama. He furnishes an ideal for Indian ethics and morality as a dutiful son, faithful husband, loving brother, and a responsible king, elements which lift him up above normal humanity in the hearts and minds of people. Rama probably reached the status of divinity earlier than Krishna. His influence extends beyond the borders of India, reaching out to Southeast Asian lands such as Indonesia and Thailand. The original story of Rama by Valmiki, the *Ramayana*, has been translated from Sanskrit into almost every language in India, and in story, poetry, drama, painting, and temple sculpture exercises an enormous influence on people even to this day.[39]

If one follows the different translations and adaptations of the story of Rama during the long centuries, the stages in the growth of an ideal through literary, symbolical, and theological interpretations become fairly clear. Originally Rama was a folk hero, a human figure. Until the tenth century A.D. there were no temples erected to Rama in India. The earliest temple was set up in Java in the ninth century. One notes the developments through which Rama, as the ideal human being, moves into the role of an *avatara* of Vishnu, and then even further into identification with the Brahman. In the original *Ramayana* by Valmiki, Rama is depicted as the ideal son, brother, husband, and king. The author stresses the *human* nature of Rama, and points to *Ramarajya* (the kingdom of Rama) as the social ideal toward which history moves. In the *Dharma* of *Ramarajya* there is an emphasis on the social dimensions of community life which combines spiritual nurture and social renewal. It is not surprising that to Mahatma Gandhi, *Ramarajya* was the ideal social, economic, and political order for India.

Within a few centuries, however, the *Adhyatma Ramayana* (a medieval work) makes Rama the symbol of ultimate Being. Rama becomes Brahman in all his fulness. Rama's character as an *avatara* is transcended by his being identified with the Brahman himself. While Valmiki stresses Rama's human nature, with all its goodness and its weakness, the *Adhyatma Ramayana* goes to the extreme of overemphasizing his *nirguna* nature (without qualities) beyond his *avatara* character. That is, Rama becomes the symbol of Ultimate Reality itself. A few centuries later there is a swing back to his personal nature, and Rama becomes the center of a *bhakti* movement. Tulsi Das's (1763-1843) great devotional work *Ramacharitamanas* (The Holy Lake of Rama's History) makes him the personal center of Hindu devotional religion, and it is in this form that today millions of Hindus worship and follow Rama.

In the development of Rama's person and work through the centuries it is possible to identify three *levels* of meaning: the human level as a model or ideal for moral conduct in daily life; as an *avatara*, one who has crossed over or descended to earth in order to destroy *adharma*, and so has become the object of prayer and devotion; and at the deepest level, as the *Brahman*, both immanent and transcendent (*saguna* and *nirguna*). And yet, no exclusive claims are made for any one interpretation of Rama. On the contrary, there is a feeling that Rama *bhakti* may not be the only way to God, and that the validity of other ways need not be denied. In a multireligious culture, this recognition of a plurality of ways developed over the centuries should be seen as a serious theological alternative to any exclusive claim. Frank Whaling observes:

> It bears witness to the fact that the God revealed by Christ is a God who seeks all men in mercy and love, and is therefore able to inspire and save the Rama bhakta through the lotus feet of Rama just as he is able to save the Christian through the cross and resurrection of Christ. It bears witness to the fact that God has a mission to the world that does not wait for Christian missionaries to arrive before it can operate and does not cease to operate when they leave.[40]

There are two points in the story of Rama to which particular attention should be given. One is his picture as the "renouncer," as one who sacrifices those things which are usually held dear by people: power, money, land, human relationships. The other is the transformation, even the elevation of grief, through which ordinary sorrow is given religious significance. The tragic sense of grief overcomes the pain of ordinary sorrow by giving it religious significance. This is particularly visible and touching in Valmiki's *Ramayana*, the original story of Rama. Rama had a great deal to renounce: his kingdom (in order that his father might keep his word), the ease and pleasures of life by going to the forest, and the power that is universally recognized as the source of all corruption. The element of grief becomes strong when, along with his wife and one brother, Rama takes leave of his father and mother and the vast throng of people who would have been his subjects. Later on, in another version of the story, Bhavabuti's *Uttara Rama Charitra* (The Later History of Rama), where Rama sends his own wife, Sita, to the forest rather than offend his people, one sees an ambiguous act which is a combination of renouncement and grief. This act itself has led to serious criticism in subsequent centuries. There is also an element of grief in the Krishna story, the consequence of being separated from the loved one. This is quite different from Rama's grief. This is the *viraha* (sorrow in being separated from the lover), which is given a religious significance as the longing of the devotee for the object of his devotion. But when one listens to these lamentations of Radha and other women over the absent Krishna, one senses that the dimension of the tragic is absent.[41]

It is often claimed that Christians have a story to tell to the nations. No one denies that Christians do have a great story to tell in the life and work, death and resurrection of Jesus Christ. No one denies Christians their right and freedom to tell their story. But do neighbors of other faiths also have their stories to tell? When this question is put privately or publicly to some well-known Christian theologians, the answer invariably is one of indifference or total silence, a refusal to even consider the question. Do our neighbors also have the right and freedom to tell the stories—for example, of the Buddha and Rama and Krishna? If Christians expect their neighbors to listen to the Christian story, should not Christians also be willing to listen to the stories of their neighbors?

As one follows the long evolution of the stories of the Buddha, Rama, and Krishna, among others in Asia, three points stand out. The first is the combination of revelation and liberation in the life and work of each of these personalities. In the case of the Buddha, of course, there is no revelation of God, but the message of enlightenment leads to a different kind of *jnana* that liberates. In the case of Rama and Krishna, as *avataras* of Vishnu, they serve as revealers of God's grace, being available particularly in moments of trouble and trial. And "liberation," whether understood as *nirvana* or *moksha*, has the double emphasis of being liberated from bonds within and from oppression in society. This latter should not be understood as equivalent to contemporary theologies of liberation. But surely the contrast between "prophetic spirituality" in Christianity and "ascetic spirituality" in Buddhism and Hinduism is overstated and cannot stand careful scrutiny.

Second, in spite of the differences between them, and even though the evolution of religious thought takes place approximately during the same centuries, there is no attempt on the part of the followers of the Buddha or Rama or Krishna to claim superiority over the others. There have indeed been attempts to suppress Buddhism by Hindus. Certain Hindu kings, following one *sampradaya* (way of life, religious tradition), for political reasons have tried to overcome those following another. But, by and large, exclusive attitudes are avoided. The theory of multiple *avataras* seems to be theologically the most accommodating attitude in a pluralistic setting, one that permits recognizing both the Mystery of God and the freedom of people to respond to divine initiatives in different ways at different times.

Third, there is the fact that the evolution from initial humanity to later divinity takes a long time and is generally open-ended. In the case of Christianity, one notes that the slide from open-ended christologies in the New Testament to the authoritative formulations of the creeds takes place within a few centuries. Criteria for orthodoxy were set and limits of doctrines determined rather too quickly, and the slightest deviations were doomed to be suspected as heresies. Perhaps this setting up of norms for belief and criteria for purity of doctrine has its merits. But all too often heresies of the past have been accepted as valid in later years, which of course is of no help to those already burned at the stake. Maybe this mood of open-endedness in complex matters of faith has some merit where such ultimate matters as the generosity of God's love and the infiniteness of God's mystery are concerned. It may even help people of different faiths live together in harmony while being committed to their respective faiths and, at the same time, being open to those of their neighbors.

9

The Substance of a Revised Christology

Taking into account the testimonies of the earliest New Testament documents and recognizing the presence of other "lords" and "saviors" who cannot be ignored without unethical indifference to neighbors of other faiths, it is now necessary to make certain christological affirmations to emphasize the identity and distinctiveness of the Christian faith in a religiously plural world. Since this is more in the nature of a confession of faith, this chapter will be uncluttered by footnotes, but my indebtedness to New Testament scholars and theologians is gratefully acknowledged. These affirmations hold together the Jesus of history and the Christ of faith in a historical relationship by confessing with the church that Jesus of Nazareth is the Christ, the son of the living God, and Lord and Savior of the world.

FAITH AND HISTORY

As one stands within the tradition of the New Testament and shares in the life and worship, service, and witness of the church, it is not enough to merely repeat and proclaim that Jesus Christ *is* Lord and Savior. He must be free to *become* Lord and Savior—*in the life of concrete people.* Firmly based on faith in God through Jesus Christ and led by the Spirit into new avenues of thought and expression, Jesus Christ *becomes* a *darshana* (vision) of God and leads to a new *dharma* (a way of life) that marks people who follow him as unmistakably Christlike. Christian faith is faith in God through Jesus Christ. Christians worship, obey, and serve God in the world through Jesus Christ. For Christians in the world there is no other way to live a life that points unmistakably to the Kingdom of God and shares in the power of the Kingdom in history.

A christological formulation of this faith today is bound by the limits set by our knowledge of the historical Jesus, as far as his portrait can be recovered faithfully through the study of the New Testament and its testimonies.

At the same time, lest this portrait of Jesus become distorted through open or hidden ideological assumptions, this knowledge of the historical Jesus is controlled or put in its proper perspective by faith-directed interpretation. Historical investigation and theological imagination influence each other in guarding the wholeness of Christian faith in a religiously plural world. This combination saves christology from being uncritically bound to the mere fact of Jesus on the one hand and the inflated claims made by people about him in subsequent generations. It holds them together in critical tension so that in a religiously plural world, commitment does not lead to fanaticism or tolerance to shallow friendliness. The Jesus of history and the Christ of faith should not be set against each other. They refer to one and the same person. Faith therefore becomes a question seeking an answer, not an answer looking for a question.

In order to avoid any misunderstanding, it must be stated as unequivocally as possible that the purpose of this discussion is not in any way to deny the centrality of Jesus Christ in Christian faith and life. It is not this faith, but the inflated claims made for Jesus Christ—claims unsupported by New Testament evidence—that hinder genuine relationships between Christians and their neighbors of other faiths. These claims do not provide any basis for genuine relationships and therefore have to be discarded as excess baggage in order to recover the original purpose and message of Jesus in the New Testament, which alone can provide the necessary theological basis.

The humanity of Jesus was not *maya* or an illusory "fact." It was real and genuine. The whole emphasis here is that the New Testament *does* provide a basis that is historically recoverable, exegetically correct, and theologically sound for new relationships with neighbors of other faiths. This does not, however, mean discarding the creeds and the tradition of the church. They are valid and helpful within the liturgical life and worship of the believing community. The proper place for affirmations of faith, insofar as they are expressions of commitment and not negative criticisms of neighbors of other faiths, is *within* the life and worship of the community as confessions of faith. As such, they should not be extended beyond the faith's boundaries.

MARKS OF A REVISED CHRISTOLOGY

What then are some of the elements in the historical portrait of Jesus Christ, his words and deeds and example, his life and death and resurrection, that contribute to the making of a christology that is spiritually satisfying, theologically credible, and ethically helpful to people in a religiously plural world? Certain elements in the portrait of Jesus of Nazareth stand out:
- his pointing to the Kingdom of God as the very center of his message, so that his whole ministry, his words and deeds, his life and death and

resurrection, together actualize the values of the Kingdom in history;
- a total commitment to a vocation accepted as having been entrusted to him by God, together with an abiding trust in God as Father;
- a sense of freedom from all kinds of attachment to things of this world, such as family, money and security; an absence of worry and anxiety to such a degree that his whole attitude was marked by the quality of *abhaya* (fearlessness);
- a deep compassion for the *anawim*, the poor of Yahweh, a concern for and active participation in the life of the marginalized, dispossessed, and oppressed people of his time;
- an obedience to the distilled essence of the *Torah* as summarized in the twin commandments to love God wholly and the neighbor as oneself;
- an acceptance of the critical realism of the Wisdom tradition of his time that comes close to the *jnana* tradition of the Eastern sages; and
- a willingness to be obedient to God even unto death in fulfilling his vocation as the "suffering servant."

The distinctiveness of Jesus is that he not only fused these elements in his own person in a creative synthesis but was also recognized as having actualized them in his own life and work. What was vindicated at Easter was not so much his status in relation to God as his function as liberator in relation to human beings.

THE KINGDOM OF GOD

The Kingdom of God is the central message of Jesus. The content of his message was not himself, but God. The very first words of his preaching recorded in the synoptics are, "The time is fulfilled, and the kingdom of God is at hand; repent and believe in the gospel" (Mark 1:15). His mission was to usher in the Kingdom and invite people to enter it. Nowhere does he ask people to work for the Kingdom. He asks his disciples to pray for the coming of the Kingdom. Nowhere does Jesus define the Kingdom or set limits to its boundaries. Through words and deeds, through signs and parables, and through his own example and attitude toward different kinds of people, he indicates its characteristics. There are three characteristics to be noted about the Kingdom. One is its *comprehensiveness*. The other is its corporate character, the sense of *community* inherent in it. And the third is the question of *power* and power relationships within the Kingdom.

If the notion of the Kingdom of God is taken seriously, it can never be exclusive. No one can set limits to the Kingdom of God. "And men [people] will come from east and west, and from north and south, and sit at the table in the kingdom of God" (Luke 13:29). The Kingdom of *God* cannot but be truly ecumenical. It is the Kingdom of God that constitutes the larger horizon within which the person and work of Jesus Christ have to be situated. The *Kingdom* of God can never be a collection of "saved" individuals. It has a sense of corporateness, a feeling for community, without which it may remain *within* the hearts of individuals, but can never work *among* people.

One of the historic consequences of the life and death and resurrection of Jesus was the emergence of a community of people, "a little flock" (Luke 12:32) that remembered him and followed him and, in doing so, created traditions about him. This community was open-ended. Anyone who followed Jesus, anyone willing to walk along his *marga*, (in his way), became part of the community. Following was prior to believing. One came to know of him as the truth by following him as the way. Further, the notion of the Kingdom, along with the necessity of the community, inevitably brings in the dimension of *power*. There can be no Kingdom without power relationships, the only question being what kind of power and how it is shared and exercised by different people within the larger community. The Kingdom of God as Jesus preached was not just spiritual, but also political.

THE FREEDOM CHRIST BRINGS

This leads to an important consideration to which some reference was made earlier. Any revised christology today has to take into account both the quest for a theology of religions and the struggle for justice in society. Even as there is economic injustice in the relationship between the rich nations of the North and the poor countries of the South, there is also theological injustice in the relationship between Christianity as the religion of the rich and powerful North and the religions of the poor and weak in the South. Therefore, any revised christology today should stand at the point where these two concerns meet. The portrait of Jesus sketched above on the basis of testimonies in the New Testament meets this point. Unless the freedom that Jesus Christ brings saves individuals from sin within the heart and also brings about changes in power relations among people where the two injustices mutually support each other, any christology today would become an exercise in futility.

Much has been written about liberation theology in Latin America and the significant contribution it has made in the working out of christologies of liberation in other parts of the world. Latin American theologians themselves admit, however, that the dimension of religious pluralism so conspicuously present in Asia is missing in their context. If this factor is taken into serious consideration in the global setting, two elements in the life and work of Jesus of Nazareth need to be held together: one is the freedom he gains for himself as a renouncer, and the other is the freedom he brings to others as liberator. Both are rooted in his life in God.

To anyone who lives with neighbors of other faiths in Asia, the first thing that strikes you about Jesus is his character as one who renounced his home, family, and possessions in order to be free to do God's will and invite people to enter the Kingdom of God. A simple life is a free life. A minimum of possessions gives a maximum of freedom. "The Son of man has nowhere to lay down his head" (Matthew 8:20).

This mark of Jesus brings him closer to other liberators of the world. In the history of Western Christianity there are many individual Christians who have followed Jesus in this way. The monastic movement itself was an example of such renouncing, a protest against the power and pomp of the church and state mutually supporting each other. Jesus became *self*-less to the point of being *nothing* (*sunya*). In terms of Indian values, he became a *jivan-mukta*, one who is totally liberated while being alive in this world. The true meaning of *kenosis* is not that he was first divine and then became human in order to regain divinity. He rejected that kind of humanness which refuses to be "empty," so that by becoming perfectly selfless he could become the instrument of God's compassion and justice in society and the revealer of God's love to all humanity. The very absence of divinity-providing deeds on his part indicates the measure of the fullness of divine self-emptying in Jesus.

In the long history of Asia, even to this day, persons who are really held in esteem and veneration are not people of power and wealth, but those whose lives are marked by *tyaga* (renunciation), not *bhoga* (enjoyment). It is the quality of *aparigraha*, nonattachment to things of this world, that enables one to be truly free. This was true of the Buddha in ancient times. It was true of Mahatma Gandhi in more recent times. When Mahatma Gandhi was assassinated (1948) there were only four things in his possession: a pair of wire-rimmed spectacles, a fountain pen, a watch attached to a chain tucked in his *dhoti* (waist cloth), and a pair of chappals (leather sandals). When Jesus died on the cross all that he had was a loincloth. Surely, *kenosis* could not go beyond that.

This mark of Jesus brings him in relation to other liberators in the world. This does not diminish him. On the contrary, it enhances his power to extend the role and influence of the renouncer by recovering that inner freedom which, because it is rooted in God, enables him to free others. Only the renouncers, not the possessors, can truly become the bearers of the gospel to the poor and the weak. Only this kind of christology can truly become a christology *in* and *for* Asia. The "conquering" Christ has no place in the religious landscape of Asia.

THE CROSS-RESURRECTION EVENT

It is at this point that the profound meaning of the cross and resurrection of Jesus has to be noted. They occupy such a central place in the accounts of the New Testament and in the life and worship of the church that the question of their meaning in a religiously plural world cannot be ignored. It would, however, be a serious mistake in Asia to think of the cross as the culmination of the *sanyasi* (ascetic) ideal. Although the element of renunciation and self-sacrifice are indeed important, according to the New Testament, the death of Jesus was not the ascetic surrender of life by an individual. It has a corporate significance, both as an act on the part of Jesus and as an interpreted event in the life of the believing community.

In interpreting the death and resurrection of Jesus in a religiously plural world, one has to be rigorously critical of popular interpretations and, at the same time, more open to new meanings in different social, political, and religious settings. Unfortunately, in Asian Christian popular piety there are two trends which drain the cross of its theological strength and spiritual depth. One is the highly sentimentalized version of the gruesome details of his sufferings and crucifixion manifested sometimes in the long three-hour services on Good Friday. The other is the secularized version of the cross which tends to discover the cross in almost every human situation of sickness or grief or poverty or natural calamity and makes "carrying the cross" a cheap affair, robbed of its power and depth. To avoid these temptations it is necessary to emphasize at least three elements in the New Testament accounts of the cross and the resurrection.

One is the close relationship between the two. It was only after the experience of the resurrection that the disciples looked at the cross once again and were empowered to preach the good news. In the understanding of the believing community, the cross points to the resurrection and the resurrection illumines and vindicates the cross. One has therefore to speak of the "cross-resurrection" event, rather than of two separate incidents, and of Jesus as "the crucified-and-risen One."

Second, they should be seen within the total perspective of the life and work and deeds and teaching of Jesus Christ. The tendency to isolate the cross and resurrection from the totality of the life of Jesus of Nazareth has no support in the New Testament, even though all the gospels give proportionately large space to passion narratives and the accounts of the resurrection.

Third, it is impossible to ignore the fact that not only in the life and work of Jesus of Nazareth, but also in his death and resurrection, the testimony of the New Testament is that it was *God* who was active. The earliest *kerygma* was that "the Jesus you crucified and killed" (Acts 2:23) "God raised up, and of that we all are witnesses" (Acts 2:32). It is therefore within the larger horizon of the activities of the Creator and Redeemer God that the cross and resurrection have to be interpreted. Christology is larger than soteriology, and theology larger than christology. If this is forgotten, one not only isolates the cross from the life of God but also from the life of all humanity, for God alone is the source of all salvation.

Although there is a consensus among Christians that Jesus Christ is Lord and Savior, in the history of the church, the connection between salvation and the cross, and the nature of salvation he brings, are dogmatically left undefined. The gospels keep to a minimum any reference to the saving nature of Jesus' death. To Paul, of course, the cross is at the very center of salvation (1 Corinthians 1:18) and is God's act of reconciling the world unto God's self (2 Corinthians 5:18-19).

In the tradition of Europe, there seem to be two major trends. To the Latin West, led by Paul and Augustine, the cross was the point of contact between God and humanity. Through the cross, God reconciles the world unto God's self and the *suffering* of Jesus is taken up into the heart of God. The major soteriological emphasis falls on the cross. To the Greek East, with such theologians as Clement and Origen, the cross became the manifestation of the *glory* of God. Through his passion, followed by the resurrection, Jesus enters into his glory.

This is obviously an oversimplification of highly complex developments, but it indicates that although Christians are unanimous in confessing that Jesus Christ is Lord and Savior, they disagree as to how that salvation is wrought and what exactly its nature is. Western Christians who brought the gospel to Asia generally agree that salvation is from sin and guilt and the threat of damnation, with the promise of eternal life in the risen Christ. But such a consensus was not prevalent in the New Testament or in the early church, nor does it, when stated in such exclusive terms, prevail uniformly among Christians of the world today. When the Christian message of salvation is brought into a religiously plural world, still different experiences and expressions of salvation are to be expected.

Thus the predicament from which salvation is sought may be described as sin and guilt or *ajnana* (ignorance) or *dukkha* (suffering), and the state into which the saved enter may be described as salvation or *moksha* (deliverance) or *nirvana* (extinction of desire). Thus the Christian question, "Is there salvation in Hinduism?" should be reformulated to mean "Is there in Hinduism the kind of salvation from sin and guilt and damnation which Christians believe to have been wrought by Jesus Christ on the cross?" The obvious answer is no.

The Hindu might ask, "Is there *moksha* in Christianity? Does Christianity provide deliverance from the bondage to *Karma-samsara* (the cycle of births and rebirths) into a state of union of the *atman* and the Brahman?" The obvious answer is no.

How can it be otherwise? Today, both in the East and the West, as a result of economic, political, scientific, and cultural developments, there are not only different priorities in salvation, but the very question of salvation *from* what and *to* what has radically changed. Salvation today has to be understood as personal healing, social healing, and cosmic healing within the larger unity of nature, humanity, and God to which the vision of *advaita*, for example, points. Questions born out of ignorance of other religions and cultures and a lack of sensitivity to differences in human need only create theological confusion. Interpretations imposed on the "cross-resurrection" event as norms for others prevent the emergence of new insights out of its profound depths.

Therefore, in a religiously plural world, the "cross-resurrection event" must be allowed to stand on its own within the total life and ministry of Jesus Christ and within the larger Mystery of God's holiness and love, God's compassion and justice. Christians should not impose their interpretations on others. The crucified and risen One is not the possession of Christians. He belongs to the whole of humanity. Christians should let go their possessive and protective hands from the ark of God. If this is taken seriously, at least three points may be made about the "cross-resurrection" event in a religiously plural world.

First, it points to the fact that when faced with overwhelming evil forces, it is both necessary and possible for individuals to resist evil in a nonviolent way, even to suffer unto death when the cause looks utterly hopeless. The cross thus symbolizes the struggle of millions who have died, and of those who even to this day are suffering and dying, unwept, unhonored, and unsung as victims of unjust systems. The crucifixion emphasizes that because of Jesus it is worthwhile to invest one's life in fighting evil and injustice, even if it ends in failure. One must not ignore the fact that there are millions of men, women, children, and political prisoners who are victims of unjust and evil systems, who have no hope of release in their lifetimes. One reason people in different religions and cultures (for example, in India) respond to the crucified Jesus is precisely because in their sufferings they identify with the sufferings of Jesus on the cross. It is not *doctrines* of atonement but the *cross* itself, therefore, which gathers around itself the suffering humanity in all countries through the ages.

Second, the cross exposes the principalities and powers of this world in their unholy collusion against people. At a time when rising fundamentalism in all religions joins hands with corrupt and unscrupulous political leaders, resulting in situations of oppression and denial of human rights, the figure of Jesus—with hands bound behind him, lashes on his back, and a crown of thorns on his head, standing silently before Pilate with the religious leaders accusing him and demanding his death—evokes the most profound feelings of devotion and inspires the poor and the powerless to resist public immorality in religion and politics. At least one major painter in India, Khanna, has given this as the reason why in recent years he has been painting so many scenes from the sufferings and death of Jesus.

Third, when the cross and the resurrection are taken together, the resurrection becomes God's vindication of the life and ministry and death of Jesus. The cross can stand without the resurrection, but the resurrection in itself has little meaning without the cross. Every resurrection has a cross behind it, but not every cross has a resurrection ahead of it. Although the resurrection of the dead was a common belief among the Jews of the time, the New Testament usage of the term resurrection *from* the dead is distinctive and very striking.

The emphasis in the testimonies of the New Testament is not that Jesus raised himself from the dead, but that God raised him up. Therefore in the faith of the community, the resurrection was understood not as a happy ending to a tragic story but God's vindication of the whole ministry of Jesus Christ. It is because God, who is the source of all life, raised Jesus from the dead, that the sting of death is overcome and hope, instead of being an illusion, is grounded in the reality of God. At his death Jesus was not finished and forgotten. The resurrection was an act of remembrance on God's part of the historical Jesus of Nazareth. Jesus lives in God's memory. He becomes the firstborn citizen of the Kingdom of God, and so, its initiator in history. When Christians confess that Jesus crucified and buried was raised on the third day, they affirm that the Kingdom of God, in the preaching of which Jesus began his ministry on earth, has assumed the character and function of the crucified and risen One. His ministry, begun with the preaching of the Kingdom of God, is vindicated in the resurrection, through which his whole life and work, his death and resurrection, are seen as actualizing the values of the Kingdom in history.

These christological interpretations are based on the testimonies of the believing community in the New Testament about the crucified and risen One. But because these are testimonies, the *being* (or truth) of Jesus behind them remains unknown to us. The meaning indeed has been revealed, but the mystery remains. The residual mystery behind the testimonies is perhaps more readily recognized by people in an Eastern conceptual framework, at least in one particular strand of Hindu thought, namely, the *advaita*, because of its emphasis on the unknowability, the unthinkability, and the inexhaustibility of *Sat*, which is both Truth and Being. The distinction between christology and theology is not obliterated but held together in the relationship of their *not-two-ness* within the wholeness of God.

THE CRUCIFIED AND RISEN ONE IN A RELIGIOUSLY PLURAL WORLD

This has at least two consequences for all christologies that seek to interpret Jesus Christ in a religiously plural world. One is that the universality of Jesus Christ cannot be understood as the extension of one particularity—the Greco-Roman-Western particularity—setting itself up as the norm and obliterating all other particularities. It should be understood as bringing out the universally available profound insights in the revelation of God through Jesus Christ for all people in ways as yet unknown in the history of the church. If Jesus Christ is God's gift to the whole world, it would be a serious mistake to insist that the gift should be received, unwrapped, and appreciated only in one particular way.

Second, this recognition of the mystery of Jesus Christ behind the testimonies not only makes different christologies possible but also validates them, because christologies in their essence bear witness to the meaning of Jesus within the larger Mystery of God. This should also serve as a check on the constant temptation to absolutize a particular christology as the norm for all others. Nevertheless, it must be said that the truth or the being of Jesus Christ behind the testimonies can only be *more, not less*, than the marks of the portrait of Jesus of Nazareth in the New Testament cumulatively suggest.

10

Mission in a Religiously Plural World

The fiftieth anniversary of the world missionary conference held at Tambaram, India, in 1938 is an appropriate occasion to examine the content and practice of mission in a religiously plural world. The new debate has to take place in the light of the many changes that have taken place in the world during the past fifty years, and demands a drastic revision of the conceptual framework in which these matters were debated at Tambaram in 1938.

THE HISTORIC CONTEXT

The historic context in 1938, when the International Missionary Conference met at Tambaram, should be noted. In Europe, war clouds were gathering, to break with terrible fury the very next year. The social and political consequences of the economic depression were threatening the hopes of millions of young people. In India the freedom movement under the leadership of Mahatma Gandhi was gathering momentum. Asian cultures and religions, far from being conquered by the onslaught of the West, were regaining their spiritual power. In addition, fascist ideologies in Europe were threatening not only the cherished values of human freedom but the very foundations of the Christian faith.

Although it was not sufficiently recognized at Tambaram, it was these Western totalitarian ideologies, not Eastern religions, which were the real enemies of Christianity. The significance of Tambaram is that at such a time of confusion and danger a representative group of Christians met together to affirm the fundamentals of the Christian faith. Tambaram was an attempt to recover the spiritual vision, theological strength, moral power, and missionary enthusiasm of the church in the world. Meeting in a multireligious country like India for the first time, one of the obvious themes for discussion was the relationship between Christianity and other religions.

No other name is so closely associated with Tambaram than that of the well-known Dutch theologian and missiologist Hendrik Kraemer, and no other book created so much stir when it was published, and continued to provoke so much discussion in subsequent years, as his volume, *Christian Message in a Non-Christian World*.[1] He based himself on what he described as "Biblical realism," and emphasized the uniqueness of Christ, the necessity of the church, and the obligation to proclaim the gospel to the whole world. Although in subsequent years Kraemer tried to modify his views on religion, and although at certain points he does recognize some positive values in religions, basically his attitude toward all religions is negative. His view can be summed up in his statement that religion is "a fundamental 'being in error'; a field in which we can trace God's own footmarks; noble aspiration and tremendous capacity for creative action; and in the light of Jesus Christ humiliating aberration."[2]

On particular religions he is rather harsh. Hinduism, for example, is regarded as "the outstanding embodiment of primitive apprehension of existence and of naturalistic monism."[3] Hinduism has no order, no consistency, no criterion. "There is a capricious and careless disregard of the real character of a criterion."[4]

He is even harsher on Islam. He remarks:

Islam in its constitutive elements and apprehensions must be called a superficial religion ... The grand simplicity of its conception of God cannot efface this fact and retrieve its patent superficiality in regard to the most essential problems of religious life. Islam might be called a religion that has almost no questions and no answers.[5]

Further, in Islam there is "a stubborn refusal to open the mind towards another spiritual world,"[6] and because of this, "there is also the exceptional stubbornness of Islam towards Christian mission."[7]

Kraemer had a scholarly knowledge of Islam, and this was supplemented by his personal contact with Muslims during many years in Indonesia. He personally knew and was friendly with many scholars of other religions. In view of this, it becomes a serious question whether any scholar can make such heavily negative judgments on other religions whose resources have provided spiritual sustenance, theological direction, and ethical guidance to millions of people through the centuries and have provided foundations for the building of cultures and civilizations that have survived over the centuries. If in Islam there is "a stubborn refusal to open the mind towards another spiritual world," cannot the same observation be made of Western Christianity? If other religions resist Christian mission, does not Christianity also resist other missions? How can what is claimed to be right for Christianity be wrong for neighbors of other faiths?[8]

But it would be a mistake to think that Tambaram 1938 was wholly negative in its attitude toward other religions. Kraemer himself admitted that "the amount of agreement and mutual understanding reached at Tambaram in regard to this problem [how to relate the Christian revelation and Christianity as a historical religion to non-Christian religions] has been *appallingly small.*"⁹

Alfred Hogg had come to Madras Christian College in 1903 and, after thirty-five years of service as professor and principal of the college, had just retired in 1938. He was rightly asked to stay on to participate in the conference. Hogg disagreed with Kraemer, and—with a lifetime of teaching experience with some of the finest Indian students, most of whom were Hindus—he rejected the notion of discontinuity and emphasized the reality of what he termed "non-Christian faith." Hogg writes, "Why then am I so convinced of its actual existence? Most of all because I am sure I have already met with it. I have known and had fellowship with some for whom Christ was not the absolute Lord and only Saviour, who held beliefs of the typically Hindu colour, and yet who manifestly were no strangers to the life 'hid in God'."¹⁰

One should note that Radhakrishnan (1888–1975), the former president of India, was a student of philosophy under Hogg. Referring to the life and work of men like Mahatma Gandhi, Hogg asks:

Why should one feel "a religious concern" at all in respect of anyone who so clearly is "a man of God?" And if, within non-Christian faiths, such fine levels of spiritual life can be reached, why should Christian effort be directed towards getting men to change their religion instead of to make progress within the religion they possess?¹¹

These words, which are seldom quoted, might disturb some Christians, but coming from a person like Hogg, whose intellectual honesty and theological integrity cannot be questioned, can hardly be ignored. They raise a serious question relevant even to this day, fifty years after Tambaram. In such an important and complex matter as the relationship among religions, should not the opinion of a man like Hogg, who had thirty-five years of actual experience of dialogue with Hindu students and scholars, be given far greater theological significance than it seems to have received so far?¹²

Although Hogg wrote these words in 1938 in serious theological opposition to Kraemer, in a later book he seems to have changed his opinion. To a Hindu "caste-convert" he wrote, "The injunction 'Follow Me' includes the further command, 'Join My Church.' "¹³ As one studies these chapters, three questions arise. First, when a missionary scholar with thirty-five years of experience makes a serious theological statement at a world conference and then, after a few years of retirement in his native country, takes the opposite view, how is one to assess the two statements? Does the latter statement annul the theological significance of the former?

Second, does the injunction, "Come, Join My Church" have the same scriptural authority as the command of Jesus, "Come, Follow Me?" Third, is the word *church* in the chapter heading "Come, Join My Church" to be identified with the organized, visible Christian church community? The question is not just whether the church is integral to the gospel, but also what is meant by the "church" which others are called upon to join in a religiously plural world. Can christological affirmations be so easily translated into ecclesiastical demands in the interests of mission?

There were also some Asian Christians present at Tambaram: V. S. Azariah of India, T. Z. Koo of China, and Toyohiko Kagawa of Japan. But they were a minority. More significant was the work of the "Rethinking Group" in Madras, of which P. Chenchiah was the leading light. Chenchiah, in criticizing Kraemer, wrote:

> The Indian Christian can never understand Jesus until he understands the drama of God's dealings with man in and through the other religions of the world ... To us in India the interrelations of religions have become a matter of life and death. We can have no peace here or hereafter and our nation can have no future until we find the key to this mystery.[14]

Even though they were ignored and the "Rethinking Group" did not even get a footnote in the Tambaram documents, the courage, conviction, and theological seriousness with which this lay Christian group did their rethinking should not be forgotten.

CHANGES SINCE TAMBARAM

During the fifty years since Tambaram, many changes have taken place in the world. The major events that erupted onto the surface of history with such cataclysmic force are well known. The second world war (1939-45) brought immense suffering, not just to European nations, but also to millions of people in Asia and Africa who had no part whatsoever in the tribal quarrels of European nations. The Holocaust that took place in a country that gave birth to the Reformation, and the first use of the atom bomb, raised moral and spiritual questions about the effectiveness of Christianity. There are more recent threats of environmental pollution and the danger of nuclear annihilation, the roots of which are not in Asia or Africa but whose people would also be victims of their consequences. The post-Tambaram question therefore is not about the relevance of the Christian message in a non-Christian world, but about the credibility of the Christian message in the Christian world itself.

The emergence of pluralism—religious, cultural, and ideological—is perhaps one of the most important characteristics of post-Tambaram history. The focus here is mainly on religious pluralism. The word *emergence* is probably not the right term in this connection. Plurality of religions and cultures was always a fact in human history, in spite of efforts to ignore it or overcome it as an aberration. India was pluralistic in religions, cultures, ethnic groups, and languages for a few thousand years. Hinduism itself is a monolithic description imposed on a family of religions, obscuring its internal plurality. What is significant today is the new perception of pluralism and its implications for human relations, including the relationships among different religious communities in the world.

Several factors have contributed to this new perception in contemporary history. One is the demise of certainties, the disarray in theological method in the West itself. The other is the emergence of a large number of nations onto the stage of history as a result of the dismantling of colonialism, nations seeking their identity in terms of their own religions and cultures. To these must be added a third factor strikingly different from anything else in previous history: the threat of total annihilation hanging over all life, either through slow environmental pollution or sudden nuclear death. Since this is a threat to all humanity, to claim that one religious tradition has the only answer to such a global problem sounds preposterous. These points have been considered earlier and there is no need to elaborate them here. However, that neighbors of other faiths are also struggling with these questions should not be forgotten.

Christians and their neighbors of other faiths realize that in the contemporary world a plurality of theological methods is not only legitimate but essential. Other religious communities are struggling with new problems and seeking new ways of dealing with them. There is in India a spiritual struggle, maybe a second renaissance, going on within Hinduism, in which Muslims, Christians, Sikhs, and secular people are taking part. This struggle acknowledges that when facing common problems in the larger community, no single religious tradition can claim to have the monopoly on answers and that the right way lies in the pooling of resources.

The politicization of religions in India is a desperately serious matter. Christians cannot afford to stay out of the debate.[15] Amrik Singh, a well-known Sikh educator, writes on "The Crisis of Hinduism," to which there are responses by other thinkers such as R. C. Dutt and Sukdev Singh Sohal. The courage of a Sikh scholar pointing to the crisis within Hinduism at this sensitive time, and the remarkable way in which Hindus responded, is a sign of great hope for the future.[16]

Asghar Ali Engineer, a Muslim scholar and the director of Islamic Studies, Bombay, discusses "Hindu–Muslim Relations in Contemporary India" with case studies of some of the recent Hindu–Muslim riots in different parts of the country.[17] A question like "Meditation" is no more the preserve of *sadhus* and *gurus*, but of serious critical thinkers seeking its meaning and relevance in a technological age. "Logic or science itself," says Sisir Kumar Ghose, "is a close-knit meditation."[18] Perhaps Indian Christians and colleagues in the West who discuss "spirituality" so often might join in and make a contribution to this discussion in a more pluralistic setting, and in the process learn a few lessons themselves.

In any case, Christian theologians cannot afford to ignore these cooperative efforts on the part of neighbors of other faiths to tackle serious problems confronting people in other parts of the world. The political and economic problems of any nation have moral and spiritual roots. This means that there should be far greater cooperation among people of different faiths in order to develop a critical principle that would help them live *in relation* to one another, rather than *against* one another in the global community. Many years ago, Rabbi Berkowitz said, "Judaism does not have the ambition to save mankind because it has never maintained that mankind is lost without it. Judaism is the only possible way of life for Jews. Only Jews are lost without it. As to non-Jews, Judaism maintains that the righteous of all peoples have a share in the world to come."[19] This probably comes close to an acceptable critical principle in a world of plurality.

MAJOR ISSUES

What then of Christian mission in a pluralistic world? If there is to be any breakthrough in the present confusion and difficulty in understanding the nature of mission and its relationship to dialogue, two things are necessary. The first is to accept the plurality of religions and cultures with courage and hope, rather than with hesitation, doubt, and fear. Plurality is the inescapable fact of history. To ignore it and behave as if it does not exist may amount to self-deception. "The Christian faith will have to compete in the market place of religions as never before," remarks David Bosch. "And it will have to do this in total humility, at the same time repenting of the arrogance and intolerance that characterised much of its evangelism in the past."[20]

Second, all religions that make exclusive claims will have to critically reexamine their positions, in the first instance within their own communities of faith and, later on, together with neighbors of other faiths, so that commitment does not lead to fanaticism or openness to shallow friendliness. An exclusive claim is like a bit of rock in a handful of peanuts. It may break a few teeth, but it will never provide nourishment to the body.

Perhaps the first point could be accepted because it simply cannot be ignored, but the second point would be difficult, because it is mixed up with emotional and spiritual factors, along with habits of thought, patterns of conduct, and a network of symbols and meanings that have a powerful hold on people. But in its long history, the church has come to accept as correct positions that for centuries it held to be wrong or false. The six-day-creation theory and the geocentric universe are two examples. It took the church more than nineteen centuries to absolve Jews of their "guilt" for the death of Jesus, although Jews felt that it came rather too late.[21] The frontier of religious pluralism may be more difficult to cross, but without doing so, the church might remain a rock in the world but cannot become the salt of the earth.

Mission and *conversion* are legitimate terms in all religious life. Without conversion there would have been no Buddhism or Jainism, no Sikhism in India, and no Christianity emerging out of Judaism in the first century. Without mission there would have been no Buddhists in Tibet, Thailand, China, Japan, and Sri Lanka, or Muslims in Indonesia and the Philippines. Before the sea route to India was discovered by Vasco da Gama in 1498, Hindu, Buddhist, Muslim, Christian and Jewish traders came together for nearly a thousand years in central Asia for commerce. In the course of this trade, there was an enormous interchange of religious and cultural ideas and experiences leading to mutual enrichment. The results are to be seen in art, poetry, drama, sculpture, and architecture, no less than in dress, food habits, and cooking styles.

Why then are words like *mission* and *conversion* received with such dread in countries in Asia and Africa, even to this day? Two reasons are obvious. First, both Islam and Christianity came to India mixed up with military conquest, political domination, and economic exploitation. Western Christianity came with racial arrogance as well. The rich and the powerful can never be, and have never been, bearers of the gospel to the poor and weak. They could be, and have been, instruments for the expansion of Christianity as a religion.

Second, they came with claims of exclusiveness, seeking to overcome and displace other religions and cultures that provided spiritual sustenance, theological direction, and ethical guidance for millions of people for a few thousand years. They brought in entirely new beliefs, doctrines, and ways of life. The relentless stream of negative judgments passed on the cherished beliefs and practices of people who had their own scriptures, hermeneutics, philosophies, and theologies, their own culture, art, social structures, and civilization, has left deep wounds on the soul of India. Unfortunately, this negative attitude persists among many people even to this day.

This was strikingly different from the earlier "mission" and "conversions" of Buddhism, Jainism, and Sikhism. Christianity and Islam were already in India for many centuries, the former in the first century and the latter before the invasions. Hindu *gurus* had Muslim disciples, and Sufi saints had Hindu disciples. Jews and Zoroastrian refugees came and lived among Hindus without being disturbed. Buddhism, Jainism, and Sikhism did not alienate people from their own culture and community life. They brought in new visions, new ways of life, new insights into the mystery of life and death, and so provided a critical ferment within the larger life of the community. They did not have a "destabilizing effect" on the life of the country. This is one reason why Dr. Ambedkar, the Harijan leader, after pondering for many years whether to embrace Islam or Christianity, finally decided to lead millions of his followers to Buddhism.

Conversion, instead of being a vertical movement toward God, a genuine renewal of life, has become a horizontal movement of groups of people from one community to another, very often backed by economic affluence, organizational strength, and technological power. It also seriously disturbs the political life of the country by influencing the voting patterns of people. Why then should Christians be surprised when the very words *mission* and *conversion* provoke so much anxiety, suspicion, and fear?

Former president of India Zail Singh, when he was still president (1987), gently urged Christians "to declare a self-imposed moratorium on efforts to convert Hindus," stating that they have enough to do "in terms of service to the country's poor among whom God dwells."[22] Bishop S. K. Parmar, the president of the National Council of Churches in India, wrote:

> Christianity in India does not need more members. Numerical growth of the membership of the Church has not brought any significant change in the life of the society. It is a small minority within the Church, who, in the spirit of Christ, ventures out to spread the good news through their humble life-style and service.[23]

During the Anglican Consultative Council held at Singapore April 26–May 9, 1987, the Archbishop of Canterbury is reported to have made a plea in a sermon at the cathedral service "that Christians and churches respect, understand and assimilate with discernment, the cultural and religious heritage of people of other faiths." The Christian churches, however, were silent on this matter. "Once again, an opportunity to explain to a receptive citizenry the positive contribution of the Christian gospel in a multireligious society was lost."[24]

PLURALITY OF METHODS

In a religiously plural world, Christians, together with their neighbors of other faiths, are called upon to participate in God's continuing mission in the world. Mission is God's continuing activity through the Spirit to mend the brokenness of creation, to overcome the fragmentation of humanity, and to heal the rift between humanity, nature, and God.

Christians confess that to them this activity is decisively revealed in Jesus Christ, his life and work and teachings, his death and resurrection. This provides the basis for their faith, strength for their work, and ground for their hope. At the very beginning of his ministry, Jesus proclaimed the coming of the Kingdom of God and pointed to it as the focus of the good news (Mark 1:14). Toward the end of his earthly ministry, he said to his disciples, "Peace be with you. As the Father has sent me, even so I send you" (John 20:21). This gives Christians their unmistakable identity and empowers them to share with their neighbors their faith and vision, their words and silence.

So stated, this affirmation of faith in God through Christ, and the consciousness that the Spirit is perhaps leading them to unfamiliar areas of truth, becomes a joyful confession of faith, an affirmation of commitment rather than a negative judgment on neighbors of other faiths. A recognition of the ontological priority of God, and a more willing acceptance of the guidance of the Spirit, sometimes away from past positions, might deepen Christian commitment to Christ and enlarge the Christian vision of the kingdom.

MISSIONS AND CONVERSIONS

God's creative and re-creative activity provides that larger source from which streams of God's revealing and saving activity flow into the river of history. This creating and redeeming activity of God is prior to and more comprehensive than the church's mission, and directs our attention beyond the church to the Kingdom. This has nothing to do with the expansion of Christianity as a religion or the statistical increase of Christians in the world.

If the perception of the changed historic context of mission that is described here is correct, and if it is affirmed that for Christians all mission is rooted in God's activity to reconcile the whole of creation to God's self in Jesus Christ, then the universality and depth of God's ongoing mission—and, within it, the particularity and distinctiveness of Christian mission—need to be restated in such a way that cooperation with neighbors of other faiths for common purposes in society is not seen as a betrayal of mission but as the context in which the Christian witness to God's saving work in Jesus Christ becomes transparently clear. No one demands that the church abandon this mission. Mission is integral to the gospel. The question is the *kind* of mission to which Christians are committed and the *manner* in which it is to be practiced in a religiously plural world. The distinctiveness of Christian mission lies precisely in its being Christian, that is, in its being rooted in God through Jesus Christ and being active in the world in the power of the Spirit, without denying, however, that neighbors of other faiths have their "missions" in the global community.

THE CONTENT OF MISSION

The spiritual, theological, and ethical dimensions of this mission are all interrelated in Jesus Christ, in whose life and work, death and resurrection these are historically manifested. The components of this mission, its enduring marks, are clear and easily recognizable in the long history of the church. One is to serve the poor in the name of Christ. The removal of ignorance, the healing of the sick, the caring of orphans and widows, and the comforting of those in distress, irrespective of their religious or ideological affiliations, have always been part of the mission of the church. This is rooted not just in the pattern of his ministry but the kenotic life-style that led to his death and resurrection. When this service is done not as an open or hidden instrument for conversions but as the Christian response to God's love in Christ, then *diakonia* becomes *marturia*.

Another component of mission is concern for justice in society, the demand for which is rooted in the righteousness of God as affirmed in the Bible, particularly in the life of the prophets and the ministry of Jesus. This means not only uttering the prophetic *word* against injustice in society but also participating in the struggles of the oppressed against the oppressors. When this means loss of power, prestige, and privilege for the church as an institution, and suffering, even death, to Christian individuals and communities involved in this struggle, then that too becomes not just a protest against injustice but a witness to the liberating truth and all-embracing love of God in Christ.

One should note here the significance of charity (or *dana*), the giving of gifts to the poor and the needy which, as a religious obligation, is a time-honored custom in every religious community. It may be that in certain situations the giving of *dana* might become a substitute for participating in struggles against injustice. In some situations it may even be that works of charity prevent the structures of injustice from being broken, or it may be used to pacify victims of oppression with small benefits. *Dana* is not done just by the rich for the poor. Very often, people sacrifice a good deal to give *dana* to others. The poor themselves give *dana* to the poor, not just in money or things, but in sharing life itself in its suffering and joy. When urgent human needs have to be met, and when the dismantling of unjust structures is a long-term process, one cannot deny the need for *dana*, not as an escape from the demands of justice, but as a religious obligation to God and human beings in society. Therefore, *dana* also can become part of Christian witness.

This brings out another point in a religiously plural world that cannot be ignored. Where service, *dana*, and the struggle against injustice are concerned, not just Christians but also neighbors of other faiths are actively engaged in them, manifesting the same kind of commitment and spirit of sacrifice Christians show on the basis of their faith in the crucified and risen Lord. This means that in a religiously plural society, even though the faith commitments of people are different, where human liberation is concerned, there is a convergence of ethical concerns.

Therefore, at a time when not just countries in Asia but also those in the West are becoming increasingly pluralistic, Christian mission has a specific contribution to make to life in the larger community. This may take several forms: bringing the resources of the gospel to bear on the solution of common global problems; deepening the pool of human values such as justice and compassion, love and truth, which to Christians stem from God's saving work in Jesus Christ, to undergird social and political structures; and encouraging the emergence of new communities of people who, while being rooted in their respective traditions, are at the same time willing and courageous enough to join hands with their neighbors of other faiths in acts of courage and self-sacrifice. To identify them, support them, cooperate with them, suffer with them, pray for them, and even die with them is part of Christian mission.

This leads to what may be regarded as another component of Christian mission in a religiously plural world: the pastoral function of the church in equipping congregations for mission. Without this, there will be no spiritual undergirding of Christian life for the ethical and social concerns of mission and the witness of the church to Christ. Therefore, nurturing people in Christian life, helping them to abide in Christ, providing intellectual nourishment to the members of the church, particularly to younger people so much in need of proper understanding of the fundamentals of Christian faith, are important.

Christians, now alienated from their neighbors of other faiths because of their negative attitudes toward other religions and their distorted notions of mission from a bygone era, need to be reconciled to them, not on the basis of shallow friendliness but on a profound understanding of other religions and the depths of Christian faith. The Orthodox emphasis on liturgy and worship draws attention to a dimension of mission which has been smothered by notions of mission practised as numerous evangelistic activities. What is described as "the liturgy after the liturgy" implies that for Christians to be in worship is to be in mission, because the gathered congregation itself, as the body of Christ, becomes a witness to the glory of God and the saving power of the crucified and risen Lord.

CONTRIBUTION OF CHRISTIAN MISSION

Although there is no need to be unduly concerned with the distinctiveness of Christian mission in the sense of being anxious to put the label *Christian* on the church's activities of various kinds, one should avoid the blurring of distinctions between different communities of faith. Christians need to be quite clear about the basis of their faith, their identity in Christ, and the specificity of their Christian contribution. The distinctiveness of Christian mission becomes alive to Christians, and its motivation transparently clear to neighbors of other faiths, when the ethical and social concerns of the church in the world are recognized as stemming from God's saving activity in Jesus Christ.

This is not another dimension to be added onto other dimensions of Christian mission, but its foundation and the source to which Christian mission points. A one-way proclamation of the name of Jesus without any sensitivity to other faiths alienates Christians from their neighbors and becomes an obstacle to cooperation with them. A one-sided emphasis on struggles for social justice without making clear that for Christians the source and goal of this struggle are in Jesus Christ, obscures Christian witness and fails to recognize that without the mercy and judgment of God, all human efforts are in danger of being infected with human pride and self-righteousness. Ethical insights and activities are dependent on theological insights. Doing does not exhaust being. To hold together the different elements in mission and be constantly aware of their one source in Christ is to witness to Jesus Christ, in whose life and ministry this wholeness of mission was manifest. The mission of Jesus was to draw attention to God and to proclaim the coming of God's Kingdom. This is why christology, to which so much importance is given in this volume, becomes thrustingly relevant to the church's life and witness in the world today.

In discussing the future of Christian mission in a religiously plural world, whether or not the church is to be identified exclusively with the visible and institutional church will become a difficult question. A definite and clear-cut answer might be premature at this moment in history. It is Christ who gives reality to the church, and it is the Spirit who leads the church in the world in its life of worship, service, and witness. Jesus Christ points beyond himself to God and God's Kingdom. In a religiously plural world the mission of the church is not to make other people Christian but to invite people to enter the Kingdom of God. The church is the community of people whose lives are transformed by Jesus Christ, and who, being rooted in him and empowered by him, are committed to move people in the direction of the Kingdom. There are, however, many people, particularly in countries like India, whose lives are also transformed by Christ, who also show the marks of love and self-sacrifice in their commitment of human liberation, but who are not baptized members of the institutional church.

So too, there are many people in different parts of the world who reject religious affiliations of all kinds, whose convictions are secular, and who are engaged in acts of service and struggles against all kinds of oppression in society. Some of these actions may overlap or converge with those of Christians. Some may be tentative, some circumstantial, and some complementary. But as long as they do not contradict the distinctively Christian concern for love and justice manifest in the life and work of Jesus Christ, there is no reason to reject the call to cooperate with neighbors of other faiths and ideological convictions in their efforts to renew and enhance human life.

In a pluralistic world, it is indeed necessary for Christians, as members of the church, to openly affirm and declare the Lordship and Saviorhood of Jesus Christ. The christological substance of Christian faith should be unmistakably clear. Once this is affirmed, the "onlyness" of Christian parochialism should not prevent people from accepting the "manyness" of God's love and concern for all humanity.

All existence is rooted and grounded in a mysterious, transcendent Center, which is the Source of all truth and holds all things together in its embrace. This is the Ultimate Mystery, the Truth of the Truth (the *Satyasya Satyam*), which is the fountainhead of all values and the criterion to judge all human efforts in history to save them from pride and self-righteousness. This language is necessary because in a religiously plural world, the Name of this Mystery is expressed in different ways through different symbols and different words. The distinctiveness of Christian mission is to point to the Mystery of God through the meaning of Jesus Christ. God's revelation in Jesus Christ and the message of Jesus about the coming of the Kingdom of God, the need for repentance, and the good news of salvation constitute the content of Christian mission. A christology that reveals the meaning of God and at the same time retains the Mystery of God provides the basis and power for Christians in their lives of worship, service, and witness in a religiously plural world.

Notes

1. NEW PERCEPTIONS OF RELIGIOUS PLURALISM

1. Ashis Nandy, "Cultural Frames for Social Transformation," *Alternatives* 12 (1987): 113-14.
2. Pascal Bruckner, *The Tears of the Whiteman: Compassion as Contempt*, trans. William R. Beer (New York: MacMillan, 1986), quoted in *New York Times Book Review*, December 4, 1986, p. 4.
3. World Council of Churches, "My Neighbours' Faith and Mine: Theological Discoveries Through Inter-Faith Dialogue" (Geneva: World Council of Churches, 1986), emphasis added.
4. Ignatius Puthiadam, "Diversity of Religions in the Context of Pluralism in Christian Life and Reflection," in Michael Amaladoss, G. Gispert-Sauch, and T. K. John, eds., *Theologising in India* (Bangalore: Theological Publications in India, 1981), p. 438.
5. Hans-Georg Gadamer, *Truth and Method*, trans. Garret Barden and John Cumming (New York: Seabury, 1975), p. 401.
6. Jacques Derrida, "The Principle of Reason," *Diacritics* 13:3, pp. 3-20, cited in the *Journal of the American Academy of Religion* 53 (1983): 440.
7. Nathan Scott, Jr. "The House of Intellect in an Age of Carnival: Some Hermeneutical Reflections," *Journal of the American Academy of Religion* 55 (1987): 14-15. See also Paul Ricoeur, *Essays in Biblical Interpretation* (Philadelphia: Fortress, 1980). Jürgen Habermas, *The Theory of Communicative Action*, trans. Thomas McCarny (Boston: Beacon, 1984). For the Indian understanding of the connection between sound and meaning, see Gopinath Kaviraj, *Aspects of Indian Thought* (Burdwan University Press, 1967) and Bimal Krishna Matilal, *Logic, Language and Reality* (Delhi: Motilal Banarasidas, 1985). See also the review symposium on David Tracy, *Plurality and Ambiguity: Hermeneutics, Religion, Hope* (New York: Harper and Row, 1987) in *Theology Today* 54 (1988): 496-515.
8. Felix Wilfred, "A Matter of Theological Education: Some Critical Reflections on the Suitability of 'Salvation History' as a Theological Model for India," *Vidyajyoti* 48 (1984): 538-56. C. S. Song, "From Israel to Asia: A Theological Leap," in Gerald Anderson and Thomas Stransky, eds., *Mission Trends No. 3* (New York: Paulist Press, 1976), pp. 211-22. Patrick Kaliombe, "The Salvific Value of African Religions," in *Mission Trends No. 5* (New York: Paulist, 1981), pp. 50-68. George Khodr, "The Economy of the Holy Spirit," in *Living Faiths and the Ecumenical Movement* (Geneva: World Council of Churches, 1971), pp. 131-42.
9. See Hendrikus Berkoff, "Crisis in the Authority of Scriptures," *Judson Bulletin* 6 (New Series, 1987): 34-40. Edward Schillebeeckx, *Jesus: An Experiment in Christology* (London: Fount Paper Backs, 1983), pp. 573ff. See also Schillebeeckx's

more recent *Jesus in Our Western Culture* (London: S.C.M., 1987). Don Cuppit, *The Debate about Christ* (London: S.C.M., 1979), pp. 54ff. Albert Nolan, *Jesus Before Christianity* (Maryknoll, N.Y.: Orbis Books, 1985), pp. 3ff. John Hick and Paul F. Knitter, eds., *The Myth of Christian Uniqueness* (Maryknoll, N.Y.: Orbis Books, 1987).

10. See Hans Frei, *The Eclipse of the Biblical World View* (New Haven: Yale University Press, 1974). Edward Farley, *Ecclesial Reflection: An Anatomy of the Method* (Philadelphia: Fortress, 1982). Gordon Kaufman, *An Essay on Theological Method* (Missoula, Mont.: Scholars Press, 1975).

11. See for example C. S. Song, *Third-Eye Theology* (Maryknoll, N.Y.: Orbis Books, 1979). Gavin D'Costa, *Theology and Religious Pluralism* (Oxford: Basil Blackwell, 1986). S. J. Samartha, *The Other Side of the River* (Madras: Christian Literature Society, 1983). S. Wesley Ariarajah, *The Bible and People of Other Faiths* (Maryknoll, N.Y.: Orbis Books, 1989). John S. Mbiti, "Theological Impotence and the Universality of the Church," in Anderson and Stransky, eds., *Mission Trends No. 3*, pp. 6–18. Yung Young Lee, "The Yin-Yang Way of Thinking: A Possible Method of Ecumenical Theology," ibid., pp. 29–38.

12. Bipan Chandra, *Communalism in Modern India* (New Delhi: Vikas Publishing House, 1984), pp. 165ff.

13. Rajni Kothari, "Moving Out of 1984: A Critical Review of Major Events," *Mainstream Annual* (January 1985): 31.

14. John B. Chethimattam, Editorial in *Jeevadhara* 8 (September/October 1978): 352.

15. Paul Knitter, *No Other Name?* (Maryknoll, N.Y.: Orbis Books, 1985), p. 3.

16. John R. Stott, *Issues Facing Christians Today* (Bombay: Gospel Literature Services, 1987), p. 40.

17. Ibid., p. 53. See also chapter 3, "Pluralism," pp. 44ff.

18. Geoffrey Parrinder, *The Christian Debate: Light from the East* (London: Gollancz, 1964), cited by Paul Knitter, *No Other Name?*, p. 20.

19. Karl Rahner, "Towards a Fundamental Theological Interpretation of Vatican II," *Theological Studies* 40 (1979): 716–17.

20. Tom Driver, "Post-Script," in Hick and Knitter, eds., *The Myth of Christian Uniqueness*, p. 207.

21. Heinrich Ott, "The Dialogue between Religions as a Contemporary Theological Responsibility," in C. D. Jathanna, ed., *Dialogue in Community* (Mangalore, India: Karnataka Theological Research Institute, 1982), p. 192.

22. Langdon Gilkey, "Plurality and its Theological Implications," in Hick and Knitter, eds., *The Myth of Christian Uniqueness*, p. 39.

23. See S. J. Samartha, ed., *Towards World Community: The Colombo Papers* (Geneva: World Council of Churches, 1975), p. 120.

2. THE OTHER END OF THE DIALOGUE BRIDGE

1. See *The Journal of Ecumenical Studies*, Temple University, Philadelphia. *Religion and Society* (Bangalore: CISRS). The journal of *Dharma*, Dharmaram College, Bangalore, India, and others have done a great deal of work in this area during these years.

2. For example, in January 1986 the University Grants Commission of the government of India sponsored an international seminar on "Inter-faith dialogue

for national integration and human solidarity." They asked the philosophy department of the Madras Christian College, Tambaram, Madras, to plan and organize the seminar.

3. S. J. Samartha, ed., *Dialogue Between Men of Living Faiths* (Geneva: World Council of Churches, 1971).

4. See Secretariatus pro non-christianis, *Bulletin* 22:1 (1987), for a complete documentation of this event, including the speeches of the Pope, the list of participants, prayers of different religious leaders, a long report on the event by Francis Cardinal Arinze, the President of the Secretariat for Non-Christians, and an assessment by Marcello Zago.

5. Ibid., section 4, "Theological Meaning of Assisi," p. 150.

6. Ibid., pp. 150–51.

7. Ibid., p. 153.

8. Ibid., p. 22. This was spoken on October 22 in general audience in St. Peter's Square in relation to the prayer for peace at Assisi.

9. Ibid., pp. 39, 41.

10. Ibid., p. 22.

11. Dom Bede Griffiths, *The New Leader* (August 9, 1987): 10. See also the issue of August 30, 1987. There were quite a few letters to the editor on the subject in addition to short articles in this Catholic weekly in India.

12. Quoted by Swami Kulandaiswami in *The New Leader* (August 30, 1987): 12. For a Western Protestant view of the meeting, see Paul Crow, "Assisi and a Day of Prayer for True Peace," *Midstream* 26: 2 (April 1987): 253–56. Crow observes that two fears, namely Papal domination and syncretism, did not materialize at Assisi. These are familiar Protestant anxieties. While syncretism was taken care of by the subtleties of the English language, there are others who are not too sure about the first. *Press Service* (October 16):3186. *Time* Magazine, November 10, 1986. Friedrich Meichsner, "Von Assisi nach Kyoto," *Diacritics* 3 (September 1987): 76ff.

13. See "Caught in the Crossfire," *India Today* (August 15, 1982): 62ff. The Indian church has paid no attention whatsoever to the life of the Jewish community in India. They number about 8,000 now, from about 40,000 at the time of independence (1947). The Bene Israel (children of Israel), who number around 7,500, are mostly settled in Bombay. They believe that their ancestors came to the Konkan coast around 175 B.C., fleeing from Galilee, where the Greek overlord Antiochus Epiphanes was persecuting them. The Cochin Jews traditionally trace their origin to A.D. 70, when the Roman emperor Titus destroyed the second Temple at Jerusalem. The oldest Torah in India is at the Cochin synagogue.

14. Schalom Ben Chorin, *Bruder Jesus: Der Nazarener in judischer Sicht*, p. 14, quoted in Hans Küng, *On Being a Christian* (London: Collins, 1977), p. 173.

15. Arthur A. Cohen, "The Temper of Jewish Anti-Christianity: A Theological Statement," in David McKain, ed., *Christianity: Some Non-Christian Appraisals* (Westport: Greenwood Press, 1964), p. 212.

16. Ibid., p. 178. The original essay was written in 1933 in German under the title, "Kirche, Staat, Volk, Judentum."

17. Ibid., p. 180.

18. Ibid., p. 188. On this question see also Krister Stendhal, "Call Rather Than Conversion," in *Paul Among Jews and Gentiles* (Philadelphia: Fortress Press, 1976), pp. 7ff.

19. On this and related questions see Jürgen Moltmann, "New Appraisals of

Israel," in *The Church in the Power of the Spirit* (London: S.C.M. Press, 1977), pp. 144ff. Hans Küng, "Christianity and Judaism: Future Possibilities," in *On Being a Christian* (London: Collins, 1977), pp. 169ff. Johannes Feiner and Lukas Vischer, "Christ and Israel," in *The Common Catechism* 3:17, iii (London: Search Press, 1975), pp. 379ff. This is the first *common* catechism prepared by Catholics and Protestants since their separation in the sixteenth century. Original edition in German, *Neues Glaubensbuch, Der gemeinsame christliche Glaube* (Freiburg: Verlag Herder, 1973).

20. Jürgen Moltmann, Newsletter of the Churches' Committee of the Jewish People (CCJP) 2 (1977): 15. See Franz von Hammerstein, ed., *Christian Jewish Relations in Ecumenical Perspective* (Geneva, World Council of Churches, 1978). For response to Moltmann by Jewish scholar R. J. Zwi Werblowsky, see ibid., pp. 9ff. For a response by D. C. Mulde, Moderator of the Dialogue Sub-Unit, see ibid., pp. 7ff. In the W.C.C. the Jewish concern was for many years within the sub-unit on World Mission and Evangelism. In 1973 it was lodged in the Dialogue sub-unit. My impression is that Jewish friends would prefer to be related to Dialogue rather than Faith and Order. In the former their identity will be recognized but in the latter the Christian whale might swallow up the Jewish Jonah and digest him.

21. Arthur A. Cohen, "The Temper of Jewish Anti-Christianity," p. 210.

22. Ibid., p. 222.

23. Eugene B. Borowitz, in Donald G. Dawe and John B. Carman, eds., *Christian Faith in a Religiously Plural World* (Maryknoll, N.Y.: Orbis Books, 1978), p. 68.

24. "Jews and Christians on the Way to Vancouver," *The Ecumenical Review* 34:3 (July 1982): 281.

25. Ellen Flesseman-van Leer, "Agenda for Dialogue with the Jews?," *International Review of Mission* 281 (January 1981): 43.

26. Ibid., p. 45.

27. Rabbi Arnold Jacob Wolf, *Christianity and Crisis* (September 28, 1987), quoted in Ecumenical Press Service, January 1–31, 1988, .01.20. Organized Western Christian mission work is strongly resented by the Israelis. The main missionary groups in Israel are the International Christian Embassy, Fellowship of Messianic Believers, and Project Kibbutz, which places young Christians as volunteers in the kibbutzim. Rabbi Moshe Berliner describes such groups as "Trojan horses." Dr. Rossing, Director of the Israeli Ministry of Religious Affairs (1984), remarks that all proselytizing activities violate the atmosphere of mutual respect and mutual acceptance among various cultures and groups in the country. See *New York Times*, January 15, 1984.

28. See Edward Said, *Covering Islam: How the Media and Experts Determine How We See the Rest of the World* (New York: Pantheon Books, 1981).

29. Karen Elliot House and Faud Ajami, "Muslim World in Ferment," *Indian Express* 1 and 2 (August 19 and 20, 1987): 8ff.

30. See A. H. H. Abidi, "Islamic Fundamentalism in West Asia," *Mainstream Annual* (March 19, 1988): 25ff.

31. Abdulla Omar Naseef, *Current Dialogue* 11 (December 1986): 29–32.

32. Maarouf al-Dawalibi, reported in *Dharma World* (July/August 1987): 14–16.

33. Qur'an LX:8.

34. Fazlur Rahman, in Donald Dawe and John B. Carman, eds., *Christian Faith in a Religiously Plural World* (Maryknoll, N.Y.: Orbis Books, 1978), p. 73. The references to the Qur'an are II: 113, 120, 124, 134, 141.

35. Abdulla Omar Naseef, *Current Dialogue*, p. 31.
36. Ibid., p. 30.
37. Nirmal Mukarji and Ashis Banerji, "The Hindus and Their Isms: A Symposium on Some of the Complexities of a Dominant Religion," *Seminar* 133 (September, 1985): 26ff.
38. Karan Singh, "Presidential Address to the Vishal Hindu Parishad at Cochin," *Deccan Herald*, April 14, 1982.
39. Nirmal Mukarji, "The Hindu Problem," *Seminar* 133 (September 1985): 37ff.
40. See M. J. Akbar, *Sunday*, March 14–20, 1982, pp. 20ff. Mohan Deep, "Were Pune Riots a Hindu Revenge?" *Caravan* (April 15, 1982): 24ff. "Politico-Religious Fight for Supremacy," *Deccan Herald*, March 20, 1982. *Organiser*, January 10, 1982. *Dalit Voice* 9 (February 16–28, 1982) and *Dalit Voice* 10 (March 1–16, 1982): 10f., and numerous other writings. For an expression of the view that there is nothing wrong with Hinduism which is not also wrong with Islam and Christianity, see "Why Blame Hinduism," *Probe* 4:6 (August 1982): 77. For a view highly critical of Hinduism, see G. Ramakrishna, "Empty and Black Boxes Explored," *Economic and Political Weekly* 17:31 (July 31, 1982): 1233–36. Walter Anderson and Shrindhar Danle, *The Brotherhood in Saffron* (New Delhi: Vistar Publications, 1987).
41. Swami Chinmayananda, quoted in the *Indian Express*, January 10, 1981, p. 1, emphasis added.
42. *National Christian Council Review* (December 1987): 688.
43. V. A. Devasenapathi, "Hinduism and Other Religions" in Edward Juriji and E. J. Brill, eds., *Religious Pluralism and World Community* (Leiden: E. J. Brill, 1969), pp. 106–28.
44. Anantanand Rambachan, "A Hindu Model for Inter-Religious Dialogue," *Current Dialogue* 12 (June 1987): 7–12. The quotes here are on p. 11.
45. K. L. Seshagiri Rao, in Dawe and Carman, *Christian Faith in a Religiously Plural World*, p. 57.
46. Sundararajan, "The Hindu Models of Inter-Religious Dialogue," *The Journal of Ecumenical Studies* 23:2 (Spring 1986): 239–50.
47. Ibid., p. 246.
48. Ibid., p. 250.
49. Yagi Sei'chi, "An Unhappy Dialogue," *Japanese Religions* 14:4 (July 1987): 2.
50. Mahinda Palihawadana, in S. J. Samartha and Lynn de Silva, eds., *Man in Nature: Guest or Engineer* (Colombo: Ecumenical Institute, 1979), p. 99.
51. Walter Strolz, in *Man in Nature*, p. 95. See also John Cobb, "Can a Christian Be a Buddhist Too?" in G. W. Huston, ed., *Dharma and the Gospel: Two Ways of Seeing* (New Delhi: Sri Satguri Publications, 1984), pp. 1–20.
52. Notto R. Thelle, "The Flower Blooms on the Cliff's Edge," *Japanese Religions* 13:4 (December 1984): 47. See also "From Anathema to Dialogue: Buddhist-Christian Relations in Japan," *Japanese Religions* 10:3 (December 1978): 61ff. "Foe and Friend: the Changing Image of Christ in Japanese Buddhism," *Japanese Religions* 12:2 (July 1982): 84ff.
53. Mahinda Palihawadana, "A Buddhist Response," in Dawe and Carman, *Christian Faith in a Religiously Plural World*, p. 34.
54. See Gunapala Dharmasiri, "Buddhism and Marxism in the Socio-Cultural Context of Sri Lanka," *Dialogue* 12:1–3 (January-December, 1985): 42–65.

55. Osamu Mura, "No Development Without Peace," *Dharma World* 10 (February 1983): 43–44.

56. *Dialogue*, New Series 12:1–3 (1985): 112–15.

57. See K. N. Jayatilleke, *The Message of the Buddha* (London: George Allen and Unwin, 1975), pp. 114–15. See also Gunapala Dharmasiri, *A Buddhist Critique of the Christian Concept of God* (Colombo: Lakehouse Investments, 1974).

58. See Mahinda Palihawadana, "Buddhism and the Scientific Enterprise," *Faith and Science in an Unjust World*, vol. 1 (Geneva: WCC Plenary Presentations, 1980), pp. 138–48. See also Nobuhiko Matsugi, "A Contemporary Buddhist's Critical Evaluation of Scientific and Technological Culture," ibid., pp. 149–51.

59. Ibid., p. 146. See also the section report on "Humanity, Nature and God," pp. 28–38.

60. On this question see also Masahiro Mori, *The Buddha in the Robot: A Scientist Speculates* (Tokyo: Tokyo Institute of Technology, 1986). Saon Patumtevapibal, "Ethical Considerations in the Scientific Enterprise," pp. 38–44, and Padmasiri de Silva, "Some Philosophical Considerations," both in *Man in Nature: Guest or Engineer*, pp. 76–88.

61. Tom Driver, "The Case for Pluralism," in John Hick and Paul Knitter, eds., *The Myth of Christian Uniqueness* (Maryknoll, N.Y.: Orbis Books, 1987), p. 208.

62. Report of the W.C.C. Conference on Faith, Science and the Future, *Faith and Science in an Unjust World*, vol. 2 (Geneva: World Council of Churches, 1986), p. 36.

63. Robert Jamieson, quoted by Jim Cairney, "The Church Apologises to Native Americans," *Christian Century* (October 8, 1986): 852.

64. Ibid.

3. RELIGIONS, CULTURES, AND THE STRUGGLE FOR JUSTICE

1. "The Final Communique of NAM foreign ministers' meeting in New Delhi," April 16–20, 1986. *Deccan Herald*, April 21, 1986, p. 5. "North-South Dialogue: Retrospect and Prospect," *Mainstream* 23:25 (February 16, 1985): 6ff. "Following the WB and IMF Line," *Economic and Political Weekly* 22:8 (February 22, 1986): 327ff.

2. C. T. Kurien, in Aruna Jnanadason, ed., *The National Situation* (Madras, 1986), pp. 2f, points out that although on the eve of the seventh five-year plan (1985) India produced 152 million tons of grain, compared with only 50 million tons in the early 50s, it has not made any difference to mass poverty because the poor have no purchasing power. During the past three years the price of rice has gone up by 70 percent and wheat by 61 percent.

3. See Kurien Mathew, "Asian Issues in Perspective," in *Out of Control* (Delhi: Asia Youth Assembly, 1985). In 1948, just a year after independence, the total private foreign capital in India amounted to about Rs.2650 million but has now (1986) risen to Rs.15,000 million. According to British Information Services (release B–246), Britain agreed to give Rs.19.5 million in aid to finance a pilot project to provide computers in 250 Indian secondary schools to cover 25,000 secondary schools by 1990. The computer chosen for the program was Acorn. According to M. Nanda, *Indian Express*, August 15, 1984, Acorn is reported to have netted a profit of Rs.30 million already from the Indian pilot project. According to Chris Miller, British industry benefited by 46.8 million *pounds* in November and Decem-

ber 1980 through orders arising out of grants and loans to developing countries (Chris Miller, *Community Development Journal* 18:1 [1983]: 42–49). Quoted by Krishna Kumar in "Educational Recovery," *Seminar 1985 Annual* (January 1986): 53–59, this shows "the vulnerability of our educational and developmental interests to the interest of foreign corporate capital."

4. Quoted by A. W. Clausen, *Deccan Herald*, April 18, 1986, p. 5, in a speech to the German Foreign Policy Association in Bonn. V. P. Singh also said that when the policy of a government fails, it has to pay the price at the time of elections. But when the advice of international organizations fail, to whom are they accountable?

5. William E. Smith, "Transition," *The New Yorker*, March 3, 1986, pp. 72ff.

6. George Aiyitty, "To End Hunger Set the Peasants Free," *London Times*, May 27, 1986, p. 12. In the U.N. General Assembly's special session on Africa (May 28, 1986), George Schultz of the U.S.A. and Georges Howe of Britain urged Africa to help itself. In response to the request of African nations to grant 80 billion dollars as aid over the next four years, only two nations responded. The Netherlands agreed to cancel payments of interest and principal for 5 years ($80 million) and Canada promised sub-Saharan countries a 15-year moratorium on repayment of loans ($25 million). This is true of many nations in Asia as well. *The Guardian*, May 29, 1986, pp. 1, 32.

7. Yushi Tsurumi, "The Future of American Trade," *New York Times*, January 4, 1984. See also Barry Bluestone and Benner Harrison, *The Deindustrialization of America* (New York: Basic Books), and Jerome E. Deal and Allan Kennedy, *The Corporate Cultures* (Reading, Mass.: Addison Wesley Publishing Co., 1982). See also the article by Peter Wilsher, "The New Continents," *London Sunday Times Magazine*, October 12, 1985, pp. 42ff.

8. "Social Development in Asia: Retrospect and Prospect" (New York: United Nations, 1971), pp. 1ff.

9. Ajit Singh, *Economic and Political Weekly*, vol. 20, no. 1, p. 26.

10. Indira Gandhi, in a speech delivered on December 6, 1976, quoted in *Mainstream* 24:32 (April 12, 1986): 9.

11. The UNESCO Mexico City Declaration on Cultural Policies, *Cultures: Dialogue Between Peoples of the World* 9:1 (1983):1.

12. See David Barrett, "Five Statistical Eras of Global Mission: A Thesis and Discussion," *International Bulletin of Missionary Research* 8:4 (December 1984): 160–68. Barrett suggests how "instant surveys" could be made of the "unreached two billion." He writes, "One would have to resist the temptation to ask sensitive or loaded questions like 'Are you saved?' or 'What think ye of Christ?' and to ask instead "guarded questions which do not reveal one's evangelistic objectives."

13. In recent years several thoughtful studies have been made on this complex subject. See Asghar Ali Engineer, ed., *Communal Riots in Post-Independence India* (Hyderabad: Sangam Books, 1984). Several case studies are included in this volume. Bipan Chandra, *Communalism in Modern India* (New Delhi: Vikas Publishing House, 1984). Also see Kishan Swarup Thapar, "Genesis of Partition," *Mainstream* 22:48 (August 18, 1984): 10ff. Nirmal Srinivasan, "Majority Communalism versus Minority Communalism: Is It a Threat to Indian Secularism?" *Religion and Society* 30:3, 4 (September/December 1983): 138–46.

14. Quoted by Theodore de Bary, *Sources of Chinese Tradition* (New York: Columbia University Press, 1961), p. 274.

15. Wing-Tsit Chan, "The Historic Chinese Contribution to Religious Pluralism

and World Community," in Edward J. Juriji, ed., *Religious Pluralism and World Community* (Leiden: E.J. Brill, 1969), p. 115.

16. Wilfred Cantwell Smith, "Traditions in Contact and Change: Towards a History of Religion in the Singular," in Peter Slater and Donald Wiebe, eds., *Selected Proceedings of the XIV Conference of the International Association for the History of Religions* (1983): 12ff.

17. For a brief discussion on Edward Said's book *Orientalism*, 1978, see Frank Whaling, ed., "The Humanities," vol. 1, *Contemporary Approaches to the Study of Religion* (Amsterdam: Mouton Publishers, 1984), pp. 394–97.

18. Jacques Waardenburg, *Classical Approaches to the Study of Religion* (The Hague: Mouton, 1973) begins with F. Max Müller (1823–1900) and ends with Baston Berge (1896–1900). In the introduction to his book in the same series, published in 1984, p. 5, Whaling writes: "The books are written by an authentically international team and our only *slight* regret is that it has not been possible to include a non-western scholar" (italics mine). How can a team be *authentically* international without a single scholar from the South, particularly when the book deals with *contemporary* approaches to the study of religion? Drawing attention to such matters should not be misunderstood as "clobbering" or "lambasting" the North, but as a plea for greater collaboration in a common academic task.

19. Ibid., p. 12.

20. Santosh Chandra Sen Gupta, "The Misunderstanding of Hinduism," in John Hick, ed., *Truth and Dialogue in World Religions* (1974), pp. 96ff.

21. K. Satchidananda Murthy, ed., *Readings in Indian History, Politics and Philosophy* (Bombay: Allied Publishers, 1967).

22. Subhas Anand, "Women in Hindu View of Life and Way of Life," *Jeevadhara* 22:92 (January 1987):51–63. Published in English and Malayalam. There are a number of journals devoted to the question of women in the religions of India and in Indian society today. See Madhu Kishwar, ed., *Manushi*. See also many other journals noted for their intellectual and scholarly quality, such as Nikhil Chakravarthy, ed., *Mainstream*, which has significant articles written by women contributors. *Religion and Society*, published by the Christian Institute for the Study of Religion and Society, Bangalore, from time to time publishes articles and books on women's questions. For example, *Religion and Society* 32:2 (June 1985) is on the theme "Religions and the Women's Status." There are articles by women writers, for example, Ranjana Kumar, "Femaleness: The Hindu Perspective"; Doris Franklin, "Impact of Christianity on the Status of Women." *Religion and Society* 31:1 (March 1984), on the theme, "The Law, The Oppressed and Women," has articles by Noorjehan Razah, "Muslims and the Civil Code," and Lotika Sarkar, "Women's Rights." There are many other Hindu, Muslim, Christian, and Sikh women writing scholarly articles on their concerns critically referring to their respective religious traditions. The references here are to the Indian situation only because the author is more familiar with it. There are surely other women writers in other countries of the South. In view of this, a "lack of suitable contributors" can hardly be the reason Arvind Sharma's *Women in World Religions* (Albany, N.Y.: SUNY Press, 1986) has *all* Western contributors.

23. K. L. Seshagiri Rao, "Human Community and Religious Pluralism: A Hindu Perspective," in C. D. Jathanna, ed., *Dialogue in Community* (Mangalore: Karnataka Theological Research Institute, 1982), p. 162.

24. See Charles H. Kraft and Thomas N. Wisely, eds., *Readings in Dynamic*

Indigeneity (Pasadena, Calif.: William Carey Library, 1979), p. 259f. Jacques Derrida, *Writing and Difference*, trans. Alan Bass (Chicago, 1978), pp. 280ff. Paul Ricoeur, *Essays in Biblical Interpretation* (Philadelphia: Fortress Press, 1980), p. 4.

25. J. A. B. Van Buitenen, in Milton Singer, ed., *Krishna: Myths, Rites and Attitudes* (Honolulu: East-West Centre Press, 1984), pp. 35-36.

26. See Gopinath Kaviraj, *Aspects of Indian Thought* (Burdwan University Press, 1967), pp. 41ff. C. S. Kashikar, *Preface to the Rig Veda Samhita*, vol. 4 (Poona: Vaidika Samshadhana Mandala, 1946), with the commentary of Sayana edited by N. S. Sontakke and C. G. Kashikar.

27. Attempts are being made in this direction, some tentative and preliminary, some more ambitious. To give some examples, Samartha and de Silva, *Man in Nature*, "A Preliminary Enquiry by Christians and Buddhists" (Colombo: Ecumenical Institute for the Study of Dialogue, 1979). A large conference called by the World Council of Churches to meet at the Massachusetts Institute of Technology, 1979, on the theme: "Faith and Science in an Unjust World" brought together scientists, theologians, and historians of religions, including Buddhists and Muslims, which produced a statement on this question. See Paul Albrecht, ed., "Reports and Recommendations," vol. 2, *Faith and Science in an Unjust World* (Geneva: World Council of Churches, 1980), p. 36. A more systematic and carefully prepared recent work is "Peace-Experience in Religions," *Journal of Dharma* 11:2 (April-June 1986). This was published in collaboration with Sri Aurobindo Research Academy, Pondicherry, India; Department of Asian Studies, Seton Hall University, South Orange, N.J.; Department of Religious Studies, University of Lancaster, U.K.; and the Dharma Research Association, Centre for the Study of World Religions, Dharmaram College, Bangalore, India. A good example of Southern initiative and Northern cooperation.

4. RELIGIOUS IDENTITIES IN A SECULAR STATE

1. Rikhi Jaipal, "India Against Herself," *Mainstream* 26:31 (May 14, 1988): 10.

2. Swami Agnivesh, "Vedic Socialism," *Seminar* 339 (November 1987): 18.

3. See note "The Unknown Ghazni," *The Week* (December 13-19, 1987): 54. Many recent studies of India's history bring out the need to revise earlier estimates of Hindu-Muslim relationships. For example, Muhammed of Ghazni, who invaded India seventeen times between 1001 and 1021, is usually portrayed as an idol breaker whose purpose was supposedly to destroy Hindu temples and Buddhist viharas. But he was more a plunderer than a fanatic. He converted only one person, Prince Sukupal, by offering him a governership. A whole section of his army was Hindu. Of his forty wars, twenty-three were against Muslim princes. He was greatly influenced by Hindu pandits, a large number of whom were taken to Ghazni. On his coin are the words "Avyaktamekam Muhammad," that is, "Allah" is rendered as "Avyakta." See also other more recent histories of India. Romila Thapar, *Cultural Transaction and Early India: Tradition and Patronage* (Delhi: Oxford University Press, 1987), pp. 21ff.

4. John Bradford, "Worship Assembly in the Multi-faith School," *Discernment* 2:2 (Autumn 1987): 13-20.

5. See Stephen Fuchs, *Rebellious Prophets* (New Delhi: Asia Publishing House, 1965). S. J. Samartha, "Religious Imperatives and Social Concerns," *Religion and Society* 30:3 and 4 (September-December 1983): 110ff. K. C. Abraham, "Role of

Religion and Culture in Action and Politics," *Faith, Action and Politics* (1984): 93ff.

6. Surinder Suri, "Roots of Communalism: A Socio-Historical Analysis," *Religion and Society* 31:4 (December 1984): 79.

7. C. T. Kurien, *Meadows* 3:6 (November 1985): 17.

8. Ashis Nandy, "An Anti-Secularist Manifesto," *Seminar* 34 (October 1985): 20.

9. See Rajni Kothari, "End of Secular Credo," *Express Magazine* (August 10, 1986): 1ff. See also Arun Shourie, "Secularism under Siege," *The Illustrated Weekly of India* (August 31 and September 6, 1986).

10. Kothari, p. 2.

11. See Rajni Kothari, *State Against Democracy: The Search for Humane Governance*, and *Transformation and Survival: In Search of Humane World Order* (New Delhi: Ajanta Publications, 1988). See also Jen-Alphonsue Bernard, *L'Inde: Le Pouvoir et la Puissance* (Paris: Librarie Artheme Fayard, 1985). Ashis Nandy, *Traditions, Tyranny and Utopias: Essays in the Politics of Awareness* (Delhi: Oxford University Press, 1987). Also M. V. Kamath, "The Nature of Leadership," *Organiser* (May 29, 1988):4.

12. P. R. Rajagopal, *Communal Violence in India* (New Delhi: Uppal Publishing House, 1987), quoted in *Book Review* 9:5 (September/October 1987): 10.

13. See Bipan Chandra, *Communalism in Modern India* (New Delhi: Vikas Publishing House, 1984). Asghar Ali Engineer, "Bombay-Bhiwandi Riots in National Political Perspective," *Economic and Political Weekly* 19:29 (July 21, 1984): 1134ff.

14. Bipan Chandra, "Communalism: The Way Out," *Mainstream* 24:38 (May 24, 1986): 11ff.

15. Ibid., p. 12.

16. Kuldip Kumar, et al., "The Angry Hindu," *Sunday* (October 25–31, 1987): 25ff. Madumata Majumdar, "Conspicuous Conspiracy," *The Week* 8–14 (1987): 5.

17. Report of a Workshop on How To Meet the Communal Challenge, *Mainstream* (August 1–2, 1987): 16–17.

18. Krishnan Kant, "Nationalism or Composite Culture," *Mainstream* (September 5, 1987): 5.

19. S. Wesley Ariarajah, *Current Dialogue* 13 (1987): 3.

20. See Stephen Fuchs, *Rebellious Prophets* (New Delhi: Asia Publishing House, 1965). F. Houtart, *Religion and Ideology in Sri Lanka* (Bangalore: St. Peter's Seminary, 1974). S. J. Samartha, "Religious Imperatives and Social Concerns," *Religion and Society* 30 (1983): 109–14.

21. Aloysius Pieris, "The Place of Non-Christian Religions in the Evolution of a Third World Theology," *The Bulletin of the Commission on Theological Concerns* 3 (August 1982): 43–61.

5. SCRIPTURE AND SCRIPTURES

1. In my native language, Kannada, spoken by about 42 million people (1986) in the southern state of Karnataka, with a literary history of about 1,500 years, the title page of the Bible describes the book as *Satya Veda*, that is "True Veda," implying that the four Vedas of the Hindus are false. The earlier edition in 1865 was printed in England, and the same title page was printed in the Indian edition in 1951.

2. Theodore de Bary, *The Sources of Chinese Tradition* (New York: Columbia University Press, 1961), p. 17.

3. Ibid. See also Herrlee Glessner Creel, "Literature," in *The Birth of China: A Survey of the Formative Period of Chinese Civilization* (New York: Frederick Unger Publishing Co., 1961), pp. 254ff. The *Book of Changes* was probably the first complete work of Chinese literature, p. 267. See also Peter N. Gregory, "Chinese Buddhist Hermeneutics," *The Journal of the American Academy of Religion* 51 (1983): 231ff.

4. Ibid., p. 350.

5. Quoted by de Bary, *Sources of Chinese Tradition*, pp. 317-18.

6. Ibid., p. 314. Quoted from *Hung-ming chi*, in *Raisho daizokvo* LII 1-7.

7. Lao Tzu, *Mundaka*, III, ii, 9.

8. Quoted by de Bary, *Sources of Chinese Tradition*, pp. 53ff.

9. Ibid., p. 56.

10. Wilfred Cantwell Smith, "Scripture: Issues Seen by a Comparative Religionist" (Claremont, Calif.: Claremont Graduate School, 1985).

11. Marvin Pope, *Song of Songs: A New Translation*, with interpretive commentary (New York: Doubleday, 1977).

12. Patricia Cox Miller, "Pleasure of the Text and Text of Pleasure," *Journal of the American Academy of Religion* 2 (Summer 1986): 241-56.

13. Ibid., p. 242.

14. Krishna Chaitanya, *The Gita for the Modern Man* (New Delhi: Clarion Books, 1987), mentions that he himself has counted over 2,000 editions of the *Gita*.

15. Alladi Mahadeva Sastri, trans., *The Bhagavadgita with the Commentary of Sankaracharya* (Madras: Samata Books, 1897, 1985). See also V. N. Apte, ed., Sankara's *Gitabhasya*, vol. 34 (Bombay: Anandashram Sanskrit Series, 1936).

16. V. N. Apte, ed., Ramanuja's *Gitabhasya*, vol. 34 (Bombay: Anandashram Sanskrit Series, 1936), pp. 9ff.

17. See Balgangadhar Tilak, *Srimad Bhagavadgita Rahasya or Karma Yoga Sastra*, trans. Balchandra Sitaram Sukthankar (Pune: Arya Bhusana Press, 1936).

18. S. Radhakrishnan, *The Bhagavadgita* (London: Allen and Unwin, 1948), with an introductory essay, Sanskrit text, English translation and notes.

19. Ibid., p. 6.

20. J. A. B. Van Buitenen, in Milton Singer, ed., *Krishna: Myths, Rites and Attitudes* (Honolulu: East-West Centre Press, 1984), pp. 35-36.

21. Jacques Derrida, *Writing and Difference*, trans. Alan Bass (Chicago: Chicago University Press, 1978), p. 280f.

22. Paul Ricoeur, *Essays in Biblical Interpretation* (Philadelphia: Fortress Press, 1980), p. 4.

23. Uma Shankar Joshi, *Book Review* 10:1 (August-December, 1985): 8f.

24. See Bimal Krishna Matilal, *Logic, Language and Reality* (Delhi: Motilal Banarasidas, 1985). The notion of a *vakya*, pp. 398ff., following Kumarila Bhatta, *Mimasa-Sloka vartikka codana-sutra* 2, verses 33-61 (Banaras: Chokadamba 1989). Panini (fourth century B.C.), the great grammarian, and Amarasimha (A.D. fourth century) have discussed the relation between metaphysical concepts and semantic forms and the ontological meaning of grammar.

25. J. M. Shukla, ed., Bhartrahari's *Vakyapadiya* (Ahmedabad: Institute of Indology, 1984), is one of the basic works in Sanskrit on the philosophy of Word and Meaning. He identifies the word *Sabda* with *Brahman* and shifts the emphasis from grammar (*vyakarana*) to *tatparya* (meaning). See also Ananda E. Wood, *Knowledge Before Printing and After* (Delhi: Oxford University Press, 1985), pp. 183ff.

26. Saphir P. Athyal, in Douglas J. Elwood, ed., *Asian Christian Theology* (Philadelphia: Westminster Press, 1980), p. 69.

27. For a preliminary investigation see S. J. Samartha, *The Search for New Hermeneutics in Asian Christian Theology* (Madras: C.L.S., 1987). See also S. Wesley Ariarajah, *The Bible and People of Other Faiths* (Maryknoll, N.Y.: Orbis Books, 1989).

28. Samartha, *The Search for New Hermeneutics*, p. 233.

29. Aloysius Pieris, "Toward an Asian Theology of Liberation: Some Religiocultural Guidelines," in Elwood, *Asian Christian Theology*, pp. 235–253. Also see "Linguistic Heterogeneity," ibid., pp. 240ff. J. G. F. Collinson, "Issues in the History of Biblical Hermeneutics: A Protestant Perspective," *The Indian Journal of Theology* 31:314 (July–December, 1982): 335.

30. In addition to numerous articles, Kosuke Koyama has written the following books: *Water Buffalo Theology* (1974), *No Handle on the Cross* (1977), *Three Mile an Hour God* (1980), all published by Orbis Books, Maryknoll, N.Y. See also his new book, *Mount Fuji and Mount Sinai* (Maryknoll, N.Y.: Orbis Books, 1985).

31. Kosuke Koyama, "Theological Perspectives to Jesus Christ Frees and Unites," *North East Asia Journal of Theology* (March 1976): 39ff.

32. Koyama, *No Handle on the Cross*, pp. 1f, 23f.

33. Koyama, *Three Mile an Hour God*, passim.

34. Kosuke Koyama, in Emerito P. Nacpil and Douglas J. Elwood, eds., *The Human and the Holy* (Maryknoll, N.Y.: Orbis Books, 1978), pp. 36–61.

35. Ibid., p. 62.

36. Among C. S. Song's many books and articles, special mention must be made of the following. *Third-Eye Theology* (1979) and *The Compassionate God* (1982), both published by Orbis Books, Maryknoll, N.Y. *The Tears of Lady Ming* (Geneva: World Council of Churches, 1981, and Maryknoll, N.Y.: Orbis Books, 1982). *Theology from the Womb of Asia* (Maryknoll, N.Y.: Orbis Books, 1986). "New China and Salvation History—A Methodological Enquiry," in S. J. Samartha, ed., *Living Faiths and Ultimate Goals* (Maryknoll, N.Y.: Orbis Books, 1974), pp. 68–89. "From Israel to Asia: A Theological Leap," *Mission Trends* 3 (New York: Paulist Press, 1976), pp. 211–22. "Opening the Stone Gate of Religions with a Golden Key," in C. D. Jathanna, ed., *Dialogue in Community* (Mangalore: Karnataka Theological College, 1982), pp. 199–222.

37. Song, *Third-Eye Theology*, p. 103.

38. Song, *The Compassionate God*, p. xiii.

39. For a discussion on transpositional theology, see C. S. Song, *The Compassionate God*, pp. xiff. See also "Transposition of Power," pp. 222ff. There are a number of illustrations where Song puts biblical selections alongside stories and poems from Asia. For example, "The Cross and the Lotus," in *Third-Eye Theology*, pp. 101ff; a poem by a young widow in Vietnam entitled "The First Tragedy," and Psalm 137; "By the Waters of Babylon We Wept," a poem of Love by a Chinese woman poet, and parts of the *Song of Songs*, pp. 120f; a poem by a seventeen-year-old girl, Lai Leng Woon, from Singapore, entitled "I Believe" and the heavenly chorus in the Book of Revelation, 5:12—"Worthy is the Lamb that is slain . . ." p. 243.

40. Song, *Third-Eye Theology*, p. xi. See also "The Hermeneutical Circle and Active Theology," pp. 80ff.

41. See Mar Gregorios, "Hermeneutics in India Today," *The Indian Journal of*

Theology 31 (1982): 153ff. See also Mar Gregorios, "Issues in the Hermeneutical Discussion in the West: Some Notes," ibid., pp. 156–65.

42. Gregorios, "Hermeneutics in India Today," *The Indian Journal of Theology* 31 (1982): 153.

43. Gregorios, "Hermeneutics in India Today," p. 12.

44. Gregorios, "Hermeneutics in India Today," p. 155.

45. Carlos H. Abesan, S.J. "Doing Theological Reflection in a Philippine Context," in Douglas J. Elwood, *Asian Christian Theology*, p. 94, italics mine. There are a number of other Roman Catholic scholars in Asia, particularly in the Philippines, Sri Lanka, Indonesia, and India writing on this subject to whom greater attention needs to be paid by Protestant scholars inhabiting the same *oikoumene*.

46. For example, Francis X. d'Sa, "Christian Scriptures and Other Scriptures," *The Indian Journal of Theology* 31 (1982): 236ff. P. M. Thomas, "The Authority of Hindu Scripture," *The Indian Journal of Theology* 23 (1974): 85ff. The Indian Roman Catholic journal, *Word and Worship*, has published many articles on the subject of nonbiblical scriptures. See also *Jeevadhara* 14: 80 (March 1984). The whole issue is devoted to the theme, "Bible and World Religions." See articles there by E. C. John, "Israel and Inculturation: An Appraisal," pp. 87ff; Lucius Neraparampil, "Jesus and the Nations," pp. 136; Joseph Pathrapankal, "Paul and his Attitude Towards the Gentiles," pp. 162ff. See also "Indian Lines of Approach to the Bible," *Indian Theological Studies*, 21 (September/December 1984). This volume has important articles by Roman Catholic scholars in India on Hindu, Neo-Hindu, Buddhist, and cross-cultural hermeneutics. See especially "Conclusions," pp. 398ff.

47. D. S. Amalorpavadass, ed., "Statement on Non-Biblical Scriptures" (Bangalore, 1976), p. 8.

6. CHRIST IN A MULTIRELIGIOUS CULTURE

1. Karl Rahner, "Basic Theological Interpretations of the Second Vatican Council," in *Concern for the Church* (New York: Crossroad, 1981), pp. 81–82.

2. *Guidelines on Dialogue* (Geneva: World Council of Churches, 1982).

3. William R. Burrows, "Tensions Within the Catholic Magisterium about Mission and Other Religions," *The International Bulletin of Missionary Research* 9 (1985): 3. The same point is made by other Catholic scholars. Paul Knitter remarks that "Christians should seriously consider whether this opening has been toward more abundant life or has now arrived at dead ends." "Roman Catholic Approaches to Other Religions: Developments and Tensions," *International Bulletin of Missionary Research* 8 (1984): 53.

4. See "Inter-Religious Dialogue Today," *Jeevadhara* 9:65 (September-October 1981). See John B. Chethimattam, "Christian Theology and Other Religions," *Jeevadhara* 8 (1978) 352–66.

5. Quoted in "The Extraordinary Synod" (editorial), *Vidyajyoti* 49 (1985): 106.

6. Allan R. Brockway, "Questions after Vancouver," *Ecumenical Review* 36 (1984): 184, emphasis added.

7. See "Gospel and Culture," *International Review of Mission* 74:294 (April 1984).

8. See World Council of Churches, *Guidelines on Dialogue*, pp. 12–13 for a list of concerns and study questions. It must be pointed out, however, that the WCC Working Group on Dialogue, in its March 1985 meeting, decided to launch a sub-

stantial study extending over a period of four to five years on the theological significance of other faiths.

9. Arthur F. Glasser, "A Paradigm Shift? Evangelicals and Inter-religious Dialogue," in Arthur F. Glasser and Donald A. MacGavran, eds., *Contemporary Theologies of Mission* (Grand Rapids, Mich.: Baker Book House, 1983), p. 206.

10. John Stott, "Dialogue, Encounter, Even Confrontation," in Gerald H. Anderson and Thomas F. Stransky, eds., *Faith Meets Faith: Mission Trends No.5* (New York: Paulist Press, 1981), p. 168.

11. Asghar Ali Engineer, "Bombay–Bhiwandi Riots in National Political Perspective," *Economic and Political Weekly* 19 (1984): 1134ff. "Communalism is a modern phenomenon with medieval trappings to enhance its national appeal. The use of medieval symbolism ensures a relative autonomy to it ... and creates the illusion in the minds of common people about the causative efficacy of religion in the whole conflict" (p. 1136). Muslim, Hindu, Sikh, and Christian writers, political scientists, sociologists, and theologians have emphasized this point, which should not be forgotten lest religions be blamed for all the ills of Indian society. See also Kishan Swarup Thapar, "Genesis of Partition," *Mainstream* (August 18, 1984): 10ff. S. Tasmin Ahmed, "Second Thoughts on Secular Democracy," ibid., pp. 15ff. Nirmal Srinivasan, "Majority Communalism versus Minority Communalism: Is It a Threat to Indian Secularism?" *Religion and Society* 30 (1983): 138–46. Bipan Chandra, in a major study, clarifies "the misconception of religion as the sole determinant of communalism" in *Communalism in Modern India* (New Delhi: Vikas Publishing House, 1984), p. 165. "Communalism was the false consciousness of the historical process of the last 150 years because, objectively, no real conflict between the interests of Hindus and Muslims existed ... seeing religion as the main inner contradiction in social, economic, and political life was certainly an aspect of false consciousness" (p. 167).

12. Rajni Kothari and Shiv Vishwanath, "Moving out of 1984: A Critical Review of Major Events," *Mainstream Annual: India, 1984*, no. 305 (January 1985): 31.

13. See the long footnote by Wilfred Cantwell Smith in *Faith and Belief* (Princeton, N.J.: Princeton University Press, 1979): "The famed 'religious tolerance' of Hindus, their acceptance in principle of pluralism as something not merely inescapable but right and proper, has become explicit as a formulated affirmation only gradually and especially perhaps in relatively recent times ... The spirit of recognizing religious life as polymorphic is, however, ancient in India" (p. 215). See also Hajime Nakamura, in Philip Wiener, ed., *Ways of Thinking of Eastern Peoples* (Honolulu: East-West Centre Press, 1978), p. 170: "Generally speaking *we cannot find in any Indian religion the conception of the 'heretic'* in the sense of Western usage."

14. In its original context it was a problem that arose within the Brahmanic consciousness, although even to this day this solution is suggested as a way out of tensions between different religions. The full text reads: "They call him (*Sat*) Indra, Mitra, Varuna, Agni, or the heavenly sun-bird Garumat. The seers call in many ways that which is One; they speak of Agni, Yama, Matarisvan" (*Rig Veda*, I 164, 460). In another well-known verse, when the sage Yajnavalkya was asked: "How many gods are there, O Yajnavalkya?" the long answer leads the student through the many to just the One — and yet, not just the One, but the One without a second (*Ekam Evadvitiyam Brihad*, III, 9, 1–9, and *Chandogya* VI, 2, 1–3). See Theodore de Bary, ed., *Sources of Indian Tradition* (New York: Columbia University Press, 1958), pp. 5ff.

15. See Lal Mani Joshi, *Studies in the Buddhist Culture of India* (Delhi: Motilal Banarasidas, 1977), pp. 177–78. There are others who maintain that the ideas of Buddhism are not original but are dependent on Hinduism. See T. M. P. Mahadevan, *Gaudapada: A Study in Early Advaita* (Madras: Madras University Press, 1960), pp. 84, 226. Radhakrishnan argues that what the Buddha did was "to democratise the lofty teachings of the Upanishads." S. Radhakrishnan, *Indian Philosophy*, 2nd ed., vol. I (London: Allen and Unwin, 1931), p. 471. Although it is extremely difficult to reconstruct past relationships among different religious communities, and while one should be careful not to exaggerate the "tolerance" of Hindus, it remains true that when two Chinese travelers, Fa-Hein (fifth century C.E.) and Hieuen-Tsang (seventh century C.E.) traveled in India they reported that Buddhism was flourishing in northern India with several kings as its patrons. In spite of continuing tensions, "mutual toleration of prevailing faiths was the general rule of the country during the Gupta period" (seventh century C.E.). See R. C. Mujumdar, ed., *History and Culture of the Indian People*, vol. 3 (Bombay: Bharatiya Vidya Bhavan, 1964), p. 397.

16. The *Bhagavad Gita*, faced with the possibility of many *margas* (paths to God), suggested that those who worship other gods in reality worship Krishna alone, but not properly (IXX:23), or worship him unknowingly (IX:24). Does this not remind one of certain Christian attitudes today? The *Gita* goes even further. Krishna says, "Whatever form any devotee wishes to worship, I make that faith of his steady" (VII:21). Also, "In whatever way persons approach Me, in the same way do I accept them" (IV:II). If Christians can speak of the "unknown Christ of Hinduism," Hindus can talk of the "unknown Krishna of Christianity." See Daya Krishna, "Religion and the Critical Consciousness," *New Quest* (July-August 1978): 144.

17. Perhaps one has to reassess the lasting effect of the movement led by Ram Mohan Roy in this last regard. Mulk Raj Anand, the noted novelist, remarks that the Samaj movements led by Ram Mohan Roy, "Passed over the ocean of Hinduism and produced some ripples but not deep currents." Quoted by Guru Dutt in "Will Hinduism Survive?" *Institute of World Culture Bulletin* 5 (1985): 1ff.

18. In recent years, much valuable research on Sanskrit works has been done. See the excellent work by Richard Fox Young, *Resistant Hinduism: Sanskrit Sources on Anti-Christian Apologetics in Early Nineteenth Century India* (Leiden: E. J. Brill, 1981). In the year 1939 John Muir, a servant of the East India Company, published a volume in Sanskrit entitled *Matapariksa*. It consisted of 379 terse lines in the form of a dialogue between a guru and a *sishya* to prove the superiority of Christianity as the only way. Three conservative Hindu pandits took up the challenge and published their answers, also in Sanskrit, because at that time Sanskrit was still the language of scholarship and theological discourse. These were Somanatha (Subaji Bapu), *Matapariksasiksa* (1839); Harachandra Tarkapancanana, *Matapariksottara* (1840); and Nilankanta Goreh, *Sastratattvavinirnaya* (1844–1845). This exchange was a genuine theological and philosophical debate reflecting a serious attempt to come to grips with the central claims of Christianity and the mood of Hinduism. It was probably far more influential on the minds of people than the English controversy between Ram Mohan Roy and the Serampore missionaries.

19. Soli Sorabji, "Politics," *Illustrated Weekly of India*, January 27 – February 2, 1946, p. 34. The Constituent Assembly was formed on December 9, 1946. The draft constitution, prepared by the committee headed by Dr. B. R. Ambedkar, was submitted to the Assembly on February 21, 1948. The amendment to delete the word

"propagate" was forcefully pressed by Loknath Mishra on the ground that "religious propagation had been responsible for the unfortunate division of the country into India and Pakistan and that its incorporation as a fundamental right would not therefore be proper" (p. 34).

20. Lest this be misunderstood as an uncritical exaggeration of Hindu "tolerance," it should be pointed out that there are Hindu organizations that indeed manifest a decidedly intolerant attitude toward other religions. The Arya Samaj, the Ramakrishna Mission, Rastriya Svayam Sevak Sangh, the Vishwa Hindu Parishad, and many others are not particularly tolerant of Muslim and Christian efforts to convert Hindus. Earlier, Hindu violence was directed at Jains, particularly in the eighth century C.E. See Burton Stein, *Peasant State and Society in Medieval South India* (Delhi: Oxford University Press, 1980), p. 80. Romila Thapar, "Syndicated Moksha?" *Seminar: The Hindus and Their Isms*, no. 313 (September 1985): 14–22. There has indeed been violent and intolerant resistance to Islam and Christianity, but these were often defensive reactions against both the religious and political implications of conversions. I have drawn pointed attention to these movements in some of my writings, such as "Indian Realities and the Wholeness of Christ," *Missiology* 10 (1982): 301–17, "Dialogue and the Politicisation of Religions in India," *International Bulletin of Missionary Research* 9 (1984): 104ff.; "Dialog statt Kreuzzug," *Evangelische Kommentare* (February 1985): 75–77.

21. See Charles H. Kraft and Thomas N. Wisely, eds., *Readings in Dynamic Indigeneity* (Pasadena: Wm. Carey Library, 1979), pp. 259f. Jacques Derrida, *Writings and Difference*, Alan Bass, trans. (Chicago: University of Chicago Press, 1978), pp. 280ff. Paul Ricoeur, *Essays in Biblical Interpretation* (Philadelphia: Fortress Press, 1980), p. 4.

22. See D. S. Amalorpavadass, ed., *Seminar on Non-Biblical Scriptures* (Bangalore: National Biblical-Catechetical-Liturgical Centre, 1974), p. 707. I have just completed a manuscript on "The Search for New Hermeneutics in Asian Christian Theology," drawing attention to the attempts being made in different countries in Asia to shake off dependence on Western hermeneutics and work toward a more relevant Asian Christian hermeneutics. See also Gopinath Kaviraj, *Aspects of Indian Thought* (Burdwan: University of Burdwan, 1967), pp. 41ff. G. Kashikar, *Preface to Rigveda Samhita* (with the commentary of Sayana), N. A. Sontakka and G. Kashikar, eds., vol.4 (Poona: Poona Vaidika Samsadhan Mandala, 1946). Thomas B. Coburn, "Scriptures in India: Towards a Typology of the Word in Hindu Life," *Journal of the American Academy of Religion* 52 (1984): 435ff.

23. The International Theological Commission appointed by the Pope in 1969 has brought out two volumes on this matter: *Select Questions of Christology* (1980), and *Theology, Christology, Anthropology* (1983), both published by the Publications Office, United States Catholic Conference, Washington, D.C. The quotations given above are from *Theology, Christology, Anthropology*, pp. 3, 11.

24. The full text now reads: "The World Council of Churches is a fellowship of churches which confess the Lord Jesus Christ as God and Saviour according to the Scriptures and therefore seek to fulfil together their common calling to the glory of God, Father, Son and Holy Spirit." See "Ecumenical Foundations: A Look at the WCC Basis," *One World* 107 (July 1985): 11.

25. *Ecumenical Review* 37:2 (April 1985), is devoted to a discussion of the WCC basis. Two writers, Konrad Raiser and Werner Loeser, S.J., draw pointed attention to the need to take into account the dialogue with persons of other faiths in this

connection. Raiser describes this as one of the two "crucial challenges" (p. 18), and Loeser observes that the most central question here is "that of the picture of God" (p. 237). Thomas Stransky goes even further in calling for "a basis beyond the basis." He repeatedly refers to Jesus Christ as "Lord and Saviour" rather than "God and Saviour" (p. 21).

26. A far more careful and systematic exegesis of related texts within a new hermeneutical framework is called for here. New Testament scholars identify five texts in this connection: Titus 2:13, John 1:18, John 5:20, Romans 9:5, and 2 Peter 1:1. In the text from Titus the use of a single word in the original Greek alters the meaning: "the appearing of the glory of *our* great God and Saviour Jesus Christ." The alternative reading, equally justified on the basis of the Greek text, would be: "*our* great God and *our* Saviour Jesus Christ." Even Paul, with his radical christocentrism, is extremely careful in his christocentric statements. He reminds the Corinthians, "You belong to Christ, Christ belongs to God" (1 Corinthians 3:23). "The total Christian faith, as reflected in the New Testament, is essentially and primarily theistic, that is to say monotheistic, and secondarily, Christological": F. C. Grant, *Ancient Judaism and the New Testament* (New York: Macmillan, 1959), p. 130. For a fuller discussion, see A. W. Martin, " 'Well Done, Good and Faithful Servant'?" "Once More the W.C.C. Basis," *Journal of Ecumenical Studies* (1981): 251–66. Referring to "the continued use of a seemingly heretical formula," Martin asks: "Is it time to retire the formula with the judgment of more or less 'well done'?" (p. 266).

27. Manjeshwar Govinda Pai, *Golgotha* (Mangalore: Baliga and Sons, 1948). It was written in Kannada, the language of Karnataka, one of the southern states, spoken by about 36 million persons.

28. Muliya Keshavayya, *Maha Chetana: A Drama on the Life of Christ* (Mangalore: Kodialbail Press, 1976).

29. Gopal Singh, *The Man Who Never Died* (London: Macmillan, 1969). The poem has also been published in German translation.

30. Ibid., p. 77.

31. Jyoti Sahi, "Trends of Indigenisation and Social Justice in Indian Christian Art," *Indian Journal of Theology* 31 (1982): 89–95. See also Masao Takenaka, "Christian Art in Asia: Signs of Renewal," in Elwood, *Asian Christian Theology*, p. 169.

7. TOWARD A REVISED CHRISTOLOGY

1. Thomas Merton, quoted in *One World* (July 1988): 9.
2. See "Proposal on Inter-Faith Dialogue Prompts Debate in WCC Committee," Ecumenical Press Service, August 88.8.78.
3. David Jenkins, *Mowbray's Journal* 131 (Summer 1988): 27, emphasis added.
4. Paul Knitter, *No Other Name?* (Maryknoll, N.Y.: Orbis Books, 1985), pp. 75ff.
5. David Bosch, "Ecumenicals and Evangelicals – A Growing Relationship?" *Ecumenical Review* 40:3, 4 (July/October 1988): 458ff.
6. Charles J. Fenshaw, "The Evangelical – Roman Catholic Dialogue on Mission," *Missionalia* 16:1 (April 1988): 25ff.
7. Ibid., p. 38, emphasis added.
8. Bosch, p. 472.

9. Julius Lipner, "Being One Let Me Be Many," *International Review of Mission* 64:294 (April 1985): 164.

10. See, for example, John Hick, *Truth and Dialogue in World Religions* (Philadelphia: Fortress Press, 1974). W. C. Smith, *Questions of Religious Truth* (London, 1967). Klaus Klostermaier, "A Hindu-Christian Dialogue on Truth," in W. Foy, ed., *Man's Religious Quest* (London: Open University Press, 1978). K. L. Sheshagiri Rao, "On Truth: A Hindu Perspective," *Philosophy East and West* 20:4 (October 1970): 377ff. William M. Pickard, "Truth in Religious Discourse," *Ecumenical Review* 37:4 (October 1985): 437–44. S. J. Samartha, "Ganga and Galilee: Two Responses to Truth," in *Courage for Dialogue* (Maryknoll, N.Y.: Orbis Books, 1982), pp. 142–57.

11. Knitter, *No Other Name?*, pp. 217ff.

12. David L. Edwards, *Religion and Change* (New York: Harper and Row, 1969), p. 205.

13. Jung Young Lee, "The Yin-Yang Way of Thinking," *International Review of Mission* 60:239 (July 1971): 368.

14. Paul Albrecht, ed., *Faith and Science in an Unjust World*, vol. 1 (Geneva: World Council of Churches, 1980). For a Buddhist perspective, see Mahinda Palihawadana "Buddhism and the Scientific Enterprise," ibid., pp. 149ff; Nobuhiko Matsugi, "A Contemporary Buddhist's Critical Evaluation of Scientific and Technological Culture," ibid., pp. 152ff. For a Muslim perspective, see Zakaria, "The Science-Faith Issue in Islam," ibid., pp. 132ff. For an excellent and most helpful discussion, see Mark Spindler, ed., "Asian Theologians on Science and Technology," EXCHANGE 49 (April 1988).

15. Thomas Berry, "Religion, Ecology and Economics: The Relationship Between Religious Traditions, Bio-systems and Economic Consequences," *Breakthrough* 8:1–2 (Fall 1986/Winter 1987):11.

16. See M. Hiriyanna, *Outlines of Indian Philosophy* (London: Allen and Unwin, 1932), pp. 163ff.

17. *Majjhima Nikaya* I.256f; *Digha Nikhaya* 2: 64ff; *Manimegalai* 11: 55–122, quoted in Theodore de Bary, *The Sources of Indian Tradition* (Columbia University Press, 1960), pp. 102ff.

18. *I Ching* or *The Book of Changes*, Richard Wilhem, trans. (London: Routlege and Kegan Paul, 1951).

19. Ibid., p. 8. See section 8, "Pi/Holding together/Union," pp. 35ff.

20. *The Hindu Response to the Unbound Christ* (Bangalore, 1974), pp. 162ff. German edition, *Hindus vor dem universalen Christus* (Stuttgart: Evangelisches Verlagsawerk, 1970), pp. 161ff. "Ganga and Galilee: Two Responses to Truth" in *Courage for Dialogue*, pp. 142ff.

21. Raymond Panikkar has been writing about the theological significance of *advaita* for many years. There are other theologians, such as M. Amaladoss, Sister Sara Grant, Fr. Amalorpavadass, and others who have written on this subject. See Amaladoss, et al., *Theologising in India* (Bangalore, 1981).

22. B. K. Matilal, "The Logical Illumination of Indian Mysticism," in N. J. Allen, et al., eds., *Oxford University Papers on India* 1:1 (Delhi: Oxford University Press, 1986), pp. 273.

23. Debabrata Sinha, *The Metaphysical Experience in Advaita Vedanta* (Delhi: Motilal Banarasidas, 1988), p. 134.

24. *Book Review* 10:1 (August/December 1985): 8ff.

25. Nirad C. Choudhuri, *The Autobiography of an Unknown Indian* (New Delhi: Macmillan, 1951), pp. 205-13.

26. See Asghar Ali Engineer, "Sufism and Communal Harmony," *Mainstream* 26:38 (July 2, 1988): 19ff.

27. Mark Tully and Zareer Masani, *From Raj to Rajiv* (New Delhi: Universal Book Stall, 1988), pp. 162, 163.

28. Romila Thapar, *Cultural Transactions in Early India; Tradition and Patronage* (Delhi: Oxford University Press, 1987), p. 31.

8. THE MAKING OF A REVISED CHRISTOLOGY

1. Christian Conference of Asia NEWS, October 15, 1986, p. 11, emphasis added.

2. Ernst Kaesemann, *Essays in New Testament Themes* (Philadelphia: Fortress Press, 1982), p. 213.

3. Ibid., p. 214.

4. Joseph Fitzmyer, *A Christological Catechism: New Testament Answers* (New York: Paulist Press, 1982), p. 84.

5. Reginald Fuller and Pheme Perkins, *Who Is This Christ?* (Philadelphia: Fortress Press, 1983), p. 8. See also Karl Rahner, *Theological Investigations* (London: Dartman, Longman and Todd, 1981). *Christology Today* 17:24-28.

6. Fuller, *Who Is This Christ?*, p. 7.

7. Ernst Kaesemann, "Die neue Frage," in Jean Dupont, ed., *Jesus aux Origenes de la christologie* (Gimbloux: J. Dulcolot, 1975), p. 47.

8. Gerhardt Ebeling, *Das Wesen des Christlichen Glaubens* (Tuebingen: J. C. Mohr, 1959), p. 51.

9. E. Schillebeeckx, *Jesus: An Experiment in Christology* (London: Collins, 1979), p. 67.

10. Schubert Ogden, *The Point of Christology* (New York: Harper and Row, 1982), p. 81.

11. Fuller, *Who Is This Christ?*, p. 8. See also his *The Foundations of New Testament Theology* (London: Lutterworth, 1965).

12. J. A. T. Robinson, *The Human Face of God* (London: S.C.M. Press, 1973), p. 189.

13. V. Chakkarai, *Jesus the Avatar* (Madras: C.L.S., 1930), p. 210.

14. S. Wesley Ariarajahi, *The Bible and People of Other Faiths* (Maryknoll, N.Y.: Orbis Books, 1989), p. 35.

15. Some of the books consulted are the following. R. Bultmann, *The History of the Synoptic Tradition* (London: Blackwell, 1963). C. H. Dodd, *Apostolic Preaching and Its Development* (London: Hodder and Stoughton, 1936); *Christology of the New Testament* (London: S.C.M. Press, 1959). Don Cupitt, *The Debate about Christ* (London: S.C.M. Press, 1979). Reginald Fuller, *The Foundation of New Testament Christology* (London: Lutterworth, 1965). Reginald Fuller and Pheme Perkins, *Who Is This Christ?* (Philadelphia: Fortress Press, 1983). Joachim Jeremias, *New Testament Theology*, part 1 (London: S.C.M. Press, 1971). Werner Georg Kuemmel, *Introduction to the New Testament* (London: S.C.M. Press, 1966). Kuemmel, *Theology of the New Testament According to Its Major Witnesses: Jesus, Paul and John* (London: S.C.M. Press, 1986). T. W. Manson and Ernst Kaesemann, *Essays on New Testament Themes* (London: S.C.M. Press, 1964); *New Testament Questions Today* (London:

S.C.M. Press, 1969); *Finding Jesus Through Gospel History and Hermeneutics* (New York: Abba House, 1979). Bruce Metzger, *A Textual Commentary on the Greek Testament* (London: United Bible Societies, 1971). Joseph Fitzmyer, *A Christological Catechism: New Testament Answers* (New York: Paulist Press, 1982). Albert Nolan, *Jesus Before Christianity* (Maryknoll, N.Y.: Orbis Books, 1978). Cullen Murphy, "Who Do Men Say That I Am?: Interpreting Jesus in the Modern World," *Atlantic* 258:6 (December 1986): 37–38. *Scripture and Christology* (Washington: Pontifical Biblical Commission, 1984). J. A. T. Robinson, *The Human Face of God* (London: S.C.M.Press, 1971). Philip Schaff, "Nicene and Post-Nicene Christianity," vol. 3, *The History of the Christian Church* (Grand Rapids, Mich.: Eerdmanns, 1981). Thomas Sheehan, *The First Coming: How the Kingdom of God Became Christianity* (New York: Random House, 1986). Edward Schillebeeckx, *Jesus: An Experiment in Christology* (London: Collins, 1979). *Christ: The Christian Experience in the Modern World* (London: S.C.M. Press, 1980). Norman Perrin and Denis Bulig, *The New Testament: An Introduction*, 2nd ed. (New York: Harcourt, Brace, Jovanovich, 1982). Karl Baus, et al., eds., *The Imperial Church from Constantine to the Early Middle Ages*, trans. Anselm Biggs (New York: Seabury Press, 1980). *New Catholic Encyclopedia* (New York: McGraw Hill, 1967). Johannes Feiner and Lukas Vischer, eds., "Nicea, First Council," in *Common Catechism: A Book of Christian Faith* (New York: Seabury and Search Press, 1975).

16. Don Cupitt, *Debate about Christ* (London: S.C.M. Press, 1979), p. 99. C. H. Dodd, *Apostolic Preaching and Its Development*. George Eldon Ladd, *A Theology of the New Testament* (Grand Rapids, Mich.: Eerdmanns, 1974), pp. 342ff.

17. See also Don Cupitt, *Debate About Christ*, p. 103.

18. Oscar Cullmann, *The Christology of the New Testament*, p. 251.

19. F. C. Grant, *Ancient Judaism and the New Testament* (New York: Macmillan, 1959), p. 130.

20. There were about 40,000 Jews in India in 1947 when India gained her independence. Since then many have left for Israel. Today there are only about 8,000 Jews in India (1988). The Bene Israel, mostly settled down in Bombay, believe that their ancestors came to Konkan coast, the west coast of India, around 175 B.C. to escape from the persecution of Antiochus Epiphanes, the Greek overlord who was persecuting them. The Cochin Jews of Kerala traditionally trace their origin to A.D. 70, when Roman Emperor Titus destroyed the second temple in Jerusalem. The oldest Torah in India is at the synagogue at Cochin. See "Caught in the Cross-Fire," *India Today* (August 15, 1982): 62ff.

21. See J. H. Bernard, *The Gospel According to John*, International Critical Commentary Series (Edinburgh: T and T Clark, 1928), p. 2. E. C. Hoskyns and F. N. Davey, *The Fourth Gospel*, vol. 1 (London: Faber and Faber, 1940), p. 136. C. H. Dodd, *The Interpretation of the Fourth Gospel* (London: Cambridge University Press, 1955): "The logos existed as a hypostasis distinguishable from God and yet remained with him," p. 269. Bruce Metzger, *A Textual Commentary on the Greek Testament*, pp. 195ff. Robert A. Spivey and D. Moddy Smith, Jr., *Anatomy of the New Testament* (London: Macmillan, 1974). In the prologue, John can "hardly mean that Jesus of Nazareth was with God before creation and that he was the mediator of all creation," p. 434.

22. A. J. Appasamy, *The Johannine Doctrine of Life* (London: SPCK, 1934), pp. 2–3.

23. S. Wesley Ariarajah, *The Bible and People of Other Faiths* (Maryknoll, N.Y.: Orbis Books, 1989), p. 21.

24. Don Cupitt, *Debate About Christ*, pp. 138–139.

25. See Philip Schaff, "Nicene and Post-Nicene Christianity: From Constantine the Great to Gregory the Great, A.D. 311–600," in vol. 3, *The History of the Christian Church* (Grand Rapids, Mich.: Eerdmanns, 1981), pp. 12ff. Karl Baus, et al., eds., *The Imperial Church from Constantine to the Early Middle Ages* (New York: Seabury Press, 1980), pp. 14ff. "Nicea," in *New Catholic Encyclopedia* (New York: McGraw Hill, 1967), pp. 432ff. Johannes Feiner and Lukas Vischer, eds., *Common Catechism: A Book of Christian Faith* (New York: Seabury Press, 1975), pp. 91ff.

26. See Lynn de Silva, *Buddhism: Belief and Practice* (Sri Lanka: Wesley Press). *Creation, Redemption, Consummation in Christianity and Buddhism* (Ching: Thailand Theological Seminary, 1964). V. Fabella, ed., "Christian Reflection in a Buddhist Context," *Asia's Struggle for Full Humanity* (Maryknoll, N.Y.: Orbis Books, 1974).

27. Ariarajah, *The Bible and People of Other Faiths*, p. 25.

28. Song, *Third-Eye Theology*, p. 123.

29. Aloysius Pieris, "The Buddha and the Christ: Mediators of Liberation," in John Hick and Paul F. Knitter, *The Myth of Christian Uniqueness* (Maryknoll, N.Y.:Orbis Books, 1987).

30. Edward Conze, ed., *Buddhist Scriptures* (Baltimore: Penguin, 1959), p. 54.

31. Ashok Raw Kavi, "An Epic Endeavour," *The Week* (October 9–15, 1988): 30–41.

32. Krishna Chaitanya, *The Mahabharata: A Literary Story* (New Delhi: Clarion Books, 1985), pp. 357ff.

33. This is the date given by A. D. Pusalker, *Studies in the Epics and the Puranas* (Bombay: Bharatiya Vidya Bhavan, 1955) p. xxxi. For a more recent discussion on the dates and historicity of the epics, see P. L. Bhargava, "A Fresh Appraisal of the Historicity of the Indian Epics," *Annals of the Bhandarkar Oriental Research Institute* 62 (1982), pp. 17ff. M. R. Yardi, "Mahabharata: Its Genesis and Growth," *Annals of the Bhandarkar Oriental Research Institute* (1986). Among earlier scholars, A. A. Macdonnel suggests 500 B.C. – 50 B.C. in *A History of Sanskrit Literature* (London: Heinemann, 1913), pp. 377ff. J. N. Farquahar suggests 200 B.C. to A.D. 200 in *An Outline of the Religious Literature of India* (Delhi: Oxford University Press, 1920), pp. 83ff.

34. Daniel H. H. Ingalls, in his foreword to Singer, ed., *Krishna: Myths, Rites and Attitudes*, p.v.

35. A. D. Pusalker, *Studies in the Epics and the Puranas*, p. 49.

36. K. M. Munshi, *Krishnavatara* (Bombay: Bharatiya Vidya Bhavan, 1962–1973).

37. The literature on all these aspects of Krishna is enormous. The classics here are *Harivamasa, Vishnu Purana*, the *Bhagavata Purana*, and, of course, the *Bhagavadgita*. See *Srimadbhagatam* (Bombay: Sri Venkateshwara Press, 1971). Jibananda Vidyasagar, ed., *Vishnu Purana* (Calcutta: Saraswati Press, 1882). Benjamin Preciado, *Krishna Cycle in the Puranas:Themes and Motives in the Heroic Saga* (Banarasidas: Motilal 1984). Noel Sheth, *The Divinity of Krishna* (Delhi: Munnishiram Manohar Lal, 1984). T. K. Venkataram, "The Rama-Krishna Bhajans of South India," in Singer, *Krishna: Myths, Rites and Attitudes*, pp. 139ff.

38. This is the translation by Shri Purohit Swami, *The Bhagavadgita: The Gospel of Lord Sri Krishna* (London: Faber and Faber, 1978), p. 41.

39. The literature here also is very extensive. Only a brief reference to some is

possible here. *The Ramayana of Valmiki*, trans. Hari Prasad Shastri, 3 vol. (London: Santi Sadan, 1962-70). Rai Bahadur Lala Beiji Nath, ed., *Yoga Vasistha Ramayana* (Bombay: Jnansagam Press, 1903). Gilt Bhatt, ed., *The Balakandha* (Baroda: Oriental Institute, 1962). Shripad Krishna Belvalkar, trans., *Bhavabhuti: Uttara Rama Charitra* (Cambridge, Mass.: Harvard University Press, 1951). Rai Bahadur Lala Beiji Nath, trans., *The Adhyatama Ramayana* (Allahabad: Panini Office, 1913). Tulsi Das, *Ramacharitamanas*, Hanuman Prasad Poddar, ed. (Gorakpur: Gita Press, 1947). R. C. Prasad, *Sri Ramacharita-manasa* (Delhi: Motilal Banarasidas, 1988). For Christian scholars and students, perhaps the most helpful book on Rama is Frank Whaling, *The Rise of the Religious Significance of Rama* (Delhi: Motilal Banarasidas, 1980). This work combines sound scholarship with sensitive understanding of the Rama story and is the only book, as far as this writer knows, that has a chapter on "Rama, Krishna and Christ" (chapter 24, pp. 331ff.). It is rather surprising and disappointing that even though this book was published in India nearly eight years ago by well-known publishers, this writer has not come across a single reference to this book in the writings of Indian Christian theologians or historians of religion.

40. Whaling, *Rise of Religious Significance of Rama*, p. 338.
41. See Daniel H. H. Ingalls, *Krishna*, p. xiiiff.

10. MISSION IN A RELIGIOUSLY PLURAL WORLD

The substance of this chapter was delivered as the keynote address at the Madras Christian College, Tambaram, India, on January 23, 1988, on the occasion of the fiftieth anniversary of the International Missionary Conference held at the same place in 1938.

1. H. Kraemer, *Christian Message in a Non-Christian World* (London: Edinburgh House Press, 1938).
2. H. Kraemer, *Why Christianity of All Religions?* (London: Lutterworth Press, 1962), p. 104.
3. Kraemer, *Christian Message*, p. 160.
4. Ibid., p. 160.
5. Ibid., pp. 216-17.
6. Ibid., p. 220.
7. Ibid., p. 353.
8. The negative consequences of such attitudes were brought home to me very sharply during the visit of a World Council of Churches (WCC) delegation to Algiers, April 17-21, 1971, led by the general secretary, Eugene Carson Blake. During our meeting with Dr. Ahmed Taleb, Minister for Religious Affairs, I was asked to explain the purpose of the newly established program of Dialogue in the WCC. Within a few minutes, the minister politely interrupted me and asked how, when the WCC theologians were making derogatory remarks about Islam, there could be any dialogue based on mutual respect. He had a whole string of quotations from Kraemer, *Lettres de Prison, 1957-1961* (Alger: Société Nationale d'Edition et de Diffusion, 1966), pp. 122ff. He presented a copy of the book to the general secretary. Our dialogue ended before it could be born. Copies of my report of these official visits are in the archives of the World Council of Churches, Geneva, and the United Theological College, Bangalore.
9. See H. Kraemer, "Continuity or Discontinuity," in *The Authority of the Faith*,

vol. 1 (New York: International Missionary Council, 1939), pp. 1–21, emphasis added. The negative term "non-Christians" is used here because it was part of the vocabulary of Tambaram. I use the term "people or neighbors of other faiths."

10. A. G. Hogg, "The Christian Attitude to Non-Christian Faith," in Kraemer, *The Authority of the Faith*, p. 101.

11. Ibid., p. 106.

12. A. G. Hogg, *The Christian Message to the Hindu* (London: S.C.M. Press, 1947), p. 42. See esp. the two chapters "Follow Me," pp. 27ff. and "Join My Church," pp. 39ff.

13. P. Chenchiah in D. M. Devasahayam and A. N. Sundarisanam, eds., *Rethinking Christianity in India* (Madras: Hogarth Press, 1938), appendix.

14. See, for example, "Hindus and their Isms," *Seminar* 313 (September 1985).

15. Amrik Singh, "The Crisis of Hinduism," *Mainstream* 25:33 (May 1987): 2, 9.

16. Asghar Ali Engineer, "Hindu-Muslim Relations in Contemporary India," *Mainstream* 25:34, 35 (May 1987): 9, 16.

17. Sisir Kumar Ghose, "Liberation and Consciousness," *Seminar* 311 (July 1986): 14. The whole issue is devoted to the theme of meditation.

18. Eliezer Berkowitz, "Judaism in the Post-Christian Era," *Judaism: A Quarterly* 15:1 (Winter 1966): 81.

19. David Bosch, "Vision for Mission," *International Review of Mission* 76:301 (January 1987): 12.

20. Leonard Levy points out that "A crusader considered himself unworthy of redeeming the Holy Land from Moslems until he first killed a Jew, for the crusader believed that avenging Christ by killing Jews earned a crusader remission of his sins ... During the Shepherd's Crusade in 1251, almost every Jew in Southern France was slaughtered." Leonard Levy, *Treason Against God* (New York: Schocken Books, 1981), p. 115.

21. Ecumenical Press Service 34: 06-16-20 (February 1987).

22. *National Council of Churches Review*, April 1987, pp. 219–20.

23. *The Singapore Strait Times* ran a full-length editorial on the subject under the title, "Love Thy Neighbour." But the Christian attitude to the sermon and the editorial was negative. Both quotes are from the *Christian Conference of Asia News* (May 15, 1987): 151.

24. See "Delhi Riots: An Appeal for Truth," *Mainstream* (New Delhi: 1987): 24.

Bibliography of Works by S. J. Samartha

BOOKS

The Hindu View of History. Christian Institute for the Study of Religion and Society, Bangalore, 1959.
Introduction to Radhakrishnan. Association Press, New York; and YMCA Publishing House, New Delhi, 1964.
Hindus vor dem universalen Christus, Evangelisches Verlagswerk, Stuttgart, 1970.
The Hindu Response to the Unbound Christ: Towards A Christology in India. Christian Institute for the Study of Religion and Society, Bangalore, 1974.
Courage for Dialogue. World Council of Churches, Geneva, 1981; Orbis Books, Maryknoll, New York, 1982.
The Lordship of Christ and Religious Pluralism. Christian Literature Society, Madras, 1981.
The Other Side of the River. Christian Literature Society, Madras 1983.
The Search for New Hermeneutics in Asian Christian Theology. Senate of Serampore College, Serampore, West Bengal, 1987.
One Christ—Many Religions: Toward a Revised Christology. Orbis Books, Maryknoll, New York, 1990.

BOOKS EDITED BY S. J. SAMARTHA

I Will Lift Up Mine Eyes Unto The Hills (Devanandan's Sermons and Bible Studies). CISRS, Bangalore, 1962.
Dialogue Between Men of Living Faiths. World Council of Churches, Geneva, 1971.
Living Faiths and the Ecumenical Movement. World Council of Churches, Geneva, 1972; Unity Books, Delhi, 1973; also in German as *Dialog mit anderen Religionen*. Verlag Otto Lembeck, Frankfurt am Main, 1973.
Living Faiths and Ultimate Goals. World Council of Churches, Geneva, 1973; Orbis Books, Maryknoll, New York, 1974.
Christian-Muslim Dialogue: Papers from Broumana 1972. World Council of Churches, Geneva, 1973.
Faith in the Midst of Faiths. World Council of Churches, Geneva, 1978; also in German as *Denkpause im Dialog*. Verlag Otto Lembeck, Frankfurt am Main, 1978.
Man in Nature: Guest or Engineer. Ecumenical Institute, Colombo, 1979.

ESSAYS

"Jesus Christ" and "Christianity" in *Encyclopaedia of Religion and Culture: Philosophy Section*. Mysore State Government Department of Literature and Cultural Activities, Bangalore, 1964.

"Paul David Devanandan (1901-1962)" and "Modern Hinduism" in *The Concise Dictionary of Christian World Mission*. (Eds.) Stephen Neill et al., Lutterworth Press, London, 1971.

"Contemporary Trends in Hinduism" in *Lexikon Kirchen und Öekumenische Bewegung*. Verlag, Otto Lembeck, Frankfurt, 1982.

ARTICLES

"The Modern Hindu View of History", *Religion and Society*, Bangalore, Vol. 6, No. 3, October 1959; also in German as "Das Geschichtsverständnis im modernen Hinduismus", *Evangelisches Missions Magazin*, Heft 1/1961.

"Recent Christian Theological Publications in Kannada", *Indian Journal of Theology*, Serampore, Vol. 9, No. 3, July-September 1960.

"Basic Beliefs and Practices of Village Religion in South India", *Religion and Society*, Bangalore, Vol. 8, No. 2, 1961; also in German as "Grundzüge dörflicher Religion in Sudindien: Glaube und Praxis", *Evangelisches Missions Magazin*, Heft 1/1966.

"Swami Vivekananda: The Man and His Message", *Aikya*, Bangalore, Vol. 9, No. 2, February 1963.

"Paul David Devanandan (1901-1962)", *International Review of Mission*, Vol. 3, No. 206, April 1963.

"S. Radhakrishnan: Jesus Christ — One Among the Many", *Religion and Society*, Bangalore, Vol. 11, No. 3, 1964.

"Einer Christologie in Indien Entgegen", *Evangelisches Missions Magazin*, Heft 3/1965; also in Norwegian as "Pa vej til en Kristologi in Indien", *Nordisk Missions Tidsskrift*, Oslo, Heft 3/1965.

"Auf dem Wege zum Gespräch zwischen Hindus und Christen", *Der Bleibende Auftrag*, (ed.) F. Raaflaub, Basel, 1965.

"Die wichtigsten Probleme im hinduistisch-christlichen Dialog von heute", *Die Gefährdung der Religionen*, (ed.) Rolf Italiander, Oncken Verlag, Kassel, 1966.

"Major Issues in the Hindu-Christian Dialogue Today", *Inter-Religious Dialogue*, (ed.) Herbert Jai Singh, CISRS, Bangalore, 1967; also in *Man's Religious Quest*, (eds.) Whitfield Foy and Croom Helm, in association with the Open University Press, London, 1978.

"Rethinking Theological Education in India Today", *National Christian Council Review*, Nagpur, Vol. 87, No. 2, February 1967; enlarged and published in *Renewal and Mission*, (eds.) A. D. Manuel and D. S. Lyon, Christian Literature Society, Madras, 1968.

"The Significance of the Historical in Contemporary Hinduism", *Indian Journal of Theology*, Serampore, Vol. 17, No. 1, January-June 1967.

"The Quest for Salvation and the Dialogue between Religions", *International Review of Mission*, October 1968.

"Ist der Dialog von Christen Menschen und anderen Glauben unvereinbar mit

Mission?", *Christ und Welt*, Vol. 22, No. 46, 14 Nov. 1969, pp. 20ff.

"Perennial Springs and Dried up Wells", *Perspective*, Geneva, World YWCA, February-March 1969.

"Mahatma Gandhi: Nonviolence in a World of Conflict", *Journal of Ecumenical Studies*, Vol. 7, No. 1, Winter 1970.

"Christian Study Centres and Asian Churches", *International Review of Mission*, April 1970.

"Is Non-Violence out of Date?", *Religion in Life*, Nashville, Tenn., Abingdon, Autumn 1970.

"The World Council of Churches and Men of Other Faiths and Ideologies", *Ecumenical Review*, July 1970.

"Einige Reflexionen über die Zukunft des Christentums", Stuttgart, *Radius*, No. 4, December 1970.

"More than an Encounter of Commitments", *International Review of Mission*, Vol. 59, No. 236, October 1970; also in Spanish as "Algo mas que un encuentro de convicciones", *Separata de Misiones Extranjeras*, No. 15, 1973.

"Dialogue as a Continuing Christian Concern", *Ecumenical Review*, Vol. 23, No. 2, April 1971; also in *Christianity and Other Religions*, (eds.) John Hick and Brian Hebblethwaite, Collins, London, 1980; also in German as "Dialog", in *Una Sancta* Sonderdruck, Meitingen-Freising, Kyrios-Verlag, 1972; also in Spanish as "El diálogo: un cometido cristiano permanente", *Separata de Misiones Extranjeras*, No. 15, 1973.

"Kein Kampf der Stachelschweine: über den Dialog zwischen den Religionen," *Evangelische Kommentare*, March 1971.

"Religious Pluralism and the Quest for Human Community", in *The Unity of Mankind in the Perspective of Christian Faith: Essays in Honour of W. A. Visser't Hooft for his 70th Birthday*, (ed.) Robert Nelson, Leiden, E. J. Brill, 1971; also in German as "Religiöser Pluralismus und die Suche nach menschlicher Gemeinschaft", in *Um Einheit und Heil der Menschheit*, (eds.) J. Robert Nelson and Wolfhart Pannenberg, Verlag Otto Lembeck, Frankfurt am Main, 1973; also in Spanish as "El pluralismo religioso," *Separata de Misiones Extranjeras*, 1974.

"The Progress and Promise of Inter-Religious Dialogues", *Journal of Ecumenical Studies*, Vol. 9, No. 3, 1972.

"Dialogue: Significant Issues in the Continuing Debate", *Ecumenical Review*, Vol. 24, No. 3, July 1972.

"Die Grenzen geraten in Unruhe", *Evangelische Kommentare*, No. 10, October 1972.

"... and Ideologies", *Ecumenical Review*, Vol. 24, No. 4, October 1972.

"Christian-Muslim Dialogue in the Perspective of Recent History", *Islam and the Modern Age*, New Delhi, Vol. 3, No. 4, November 1972.

"Living Faiths and Ultimate Goals: Introducing a Discussion," *Ecumenical Review*, Vol. 25, No. 2, April 1973.

"Eine neue Gomata: Lebendige Religionssymbole in Sudindien," *Indo-Asia*, Tübingen and Basel, Erdmann Verlag, Heft 3, July 1973, pp. 253-257.

"Dialogue avec les bouddhistes à Bangkok", *Revue Vivant Univers*, Paris, No. 289, November-December 1973.

"The Holy Spirit and People of Various Faiths, Cultures and Ideologies", *The Holy Spirit*, (ed.) Dow Kirkpatrick. Nashville, Tenn., Tidings, 1974.

"Towards World Community: Resources and Responsibilities for Living Together", *Colombo Papers*, Geneva, World Council of Churches, 1975.

"Reflections on a Multi-lateral Dialogue", *Ecumenical Review*, Vol. 26, No. 4, October 1974.
"Mission and Movements of Innovation", *Missiology: An International Review*, April 1975.
"Called to Community", *One World*, No. 7, June 1975
"Führt Dialog zum Syncretismus?", *Konsequenzen*, Stuttgart, No. 1, 1975/9.
"Can Mount Sinai and River Ganga Meet?", *"Aspects of Inter-faith Dialogue"*, Tantur, Jerusalem, Ecumenical Institute, 1976.
"Areas of Concern in Asian Theology", *African and Asian Contributions to Contemporary Theology*, (ed.) John S. Mbiti, Geneva, World Council of Churches, 1977.
"Courage for Dialogue" (An Interpretation of Debate at the World Council of Churches' Assembly held at Nairobi, November 1975, on "Seeking Community"), *World Faiths*, London, Autumn 1976; also in *Religion and Society*, Bangalore, Vol. 23, No. 3, September 1976; and in German as "Ermutigung zum Dialog", *Evangelische Kommentare*, Stuttgart, No. 6, June 1976.
"Religions in the Quest for World Peace" (paper presented in Moscow, June 6-10, 1977); published in German as "Religionen auf der Suche nach dem Weltfrieden", *Evangelische Monatsschrift*, Berlin, Heft 8, August 1977.
"Dialogue in Community: A Step Forward" (an interpretation of the Chiang Mai Consultation), *Faith in the Midst of Faiths*, Geneva, World Council of Churches, 1977; also in: *Religion and Society*, Vol. 24, No. 4, Bangalore, December 1977; also in German as "Ein Schritt vorwärts" in *Denkpause im Dialog*, (ed.) Michael Mildenberger, Frankfurt am Main, Verlag Otto Lembeck, 1978.
"World Religions: Barriers to Community or Bearers of Peace?", *Insight: A Journal of World Religions*, Chambersburg, Penn., Vol. 3, No. 1-2, 1979.
"Multi-religious Dialogue and Action in Conflict Situations" (paper read at the Third Assembly of the World Conference on Religion and Peace, Princeton, 1979); published in *Proceedings*, WCRP, 1979.
"Guidelines on Dialogue", *Ecumenical Review*, Vol. 31, Number 2, April 1979.
"Partners in Community: Some Reflections on Hindu-Christian Relations Today", *Occasional Bulletin of Missionary Research*, Vol. 4, No. 2, April 1980; also in *Mission Trends*, No. 5, (eds.) G. H. Anderson and T. F. Stransky, Paulist Press, New York, and Wm. B. Eerdmans, Grand Rapids, Mich., 1981.
"The Lordship of Christ and Religious Pluralism," in (eds.) G. H. Anderson and T. F. Stransky, *Christ's Lordship and Religious Pluralism*, Orbis Books, Maryknoll, New York, 1980.
"The Kingdom of God in a Religiously Plural World", *Ecumenical Review*, Vol. 32, No. 2, April 1980.
"Ganga and Galilee: Two Approaches to Truth", in *Diversities of Religious Experience*, (eds.) John Hick and Hasan Askari, London, Avebury Publishing Company, 1982.
"Milk and Honey—Without the Lord?", *The National Christian Council Review*, Nagpur, December 1981.
"Indian Realities and the Wholeness of Christ", *Missiology*, Vol. 10, No. 3, July 1982.
"Religious Imperatives and Social Concerns", *Religion and Society*, Vol. 30, Nos. 3 and 4, Sept. and Dec., 1983.
"Publishing for a Pluralist Society", *South India Churchman*, Madras, June, 1983.
"Dialogue and the Politicisation of Religions in India", *International Bulletin of*

Missionary Research, Vol. 8, No. 3, July 1984; also in German as *Zeitschrift für Mission*, Basel, March 1983.

"The Temper of Crusades and the Spirit of Dialogue", *National Council Review*, Nagpur, Vol. 104, No. 9, October 1984; also in German as "Dialog statt Kreuzzug", *Evangelische Kommentare*, No. 2, Feb. 1985.

"Digging up Old Wells: Reflections on the Legacy of the Basel Mission in India" (public address on the 150th anniversary of the Basel Mission in India, Mangalore, October 27, 1984); published as *Souvenir Volume* by the Karnataka Theological Research Institute, Mangalore, 1984.

"Christian Concern for Dialogue in India" (address delivered at the Church of South India Synod Consultation on Dialogue, Oct. 1-4, 1985, Ecumenical Christian Centre, Bangalore); excerpted in Ecumenical Press Service: 1985; also in *Current Dialogue*, Dec. 1985.

"Inter-Religious Relationships in the Secular State" (keynote address delivered at the international seminar on "Inter-Faith Dialogue for National Integration and Human Solidarity" sponsored by the University Grants Commission, New Delhi, and held at Madras Christian College, Tambaram, January 27-31, 1986); published in *Current Dialogue*, Dec. 1986; also in *Star of the East*, New Delhi, Vol. 8, No. 4, Dec. 1986.

"Commitment and Tolerance in a Pluralistic Society" (address, delivered at the convocation celebrations of Serampore College [University], held at Union Biblical Seminary, Pune, February 1, 1986); published in the *National Christian Council Review*, Nagpur, February, 1986; also in *One World*, June 1986.

"Crossing The Jordan: Towards a Christian Theology of Religions", *Wereld en Zending*, Leiden, special issue, 1986.

"The Cross and the Rainbow: Christ in a Multi-Religious Culture" in (eds.) John Hick and Paul F. Knitter, *The Myth of Christian Uniqueness*, Orbis Books, Maryknoll, New York, 1987; also in (ed.) Somen Das, *Christian Faith and Multi-form Culture in India*, Bangalore, The United Theological College, 1987.

"Religions, Cultures and the Struggle for Justice, Aspects of North-South Dialogue" (lecture delivered at the 350th anniversary celebrations, University of Utrecht, Netherlands, June 6, 1986); published in *Journal of Ecumenical Studies*, Vol. 25, No. 3, Summer 1988.

"Christians and Neighbours of Other Faiths in Asia, A Search for New Relationships" (paper read at the Joint Seminar of the Federation of Asian Bishops' Conference and the Christian Conference of Asia in Singapore, July, 5-10, 1987); published in *Ching Feng*, Hongkong, Vol. 30, No. 3, Sept. 1987.

"Religious Identity in a Multi-Faith Society" (keynote address for multi-lateral dialogue organized by the WCC in New Delhi, Nov. 22-28, 1987); published in *Current Dialogue*, Geneva, No. 13, Dec. 1987; also in German as "Religiöse Identität in einer multi-religiösen Gesellschaft," *Una Sancta*, Vol. 43, No. 3, 1988; also in *Silsilah*, Islamo-Christian monthly publication, Vol. 2, No. 14, Aug. 1988, Zambouaxo City, Philippines; also in *Studies in Sikhism and Comparative Religion*, New Delhi, Guru Nanak Foundation, Vol. 6, Oct. 1987.

"A Hindu-Christian Funeral", *Theology Today*, Vol. 44, No. 4, Jan. 1988.

"Mission in a Religiously Plural World: Looking Beyond Tambaram, 1938", *International Review of Mission*, Vol. 78, No. 307, July 1988.

"Dialogue As a Quest for New Relationships" (public address, Mangalore University, Mangalore, South India, delivered Feb. 18, 1989); published in *Journal of the Chair in Christianity*, Mangalore University, Vol. 1, November 1989.

"On Being Human in A World of Science and Technology: A Religious Perspective" (paper read at the Second Yoko Civilization International Conference, Oct. 28-Nov. 1, 1989, Takayama, Gifu, Japan); published in *Proceedings*, Takayama, 1990.

"The Holy Spirit and People of Other Faiths" *Bangalore Theological Forum* (double number) Vol. 21, No. 4, Dec. 1989 and Vol. 22, No. 1, March 1990; also in *Ecumenical Review*, Vol. 42/43, No. 3/4, 1990

"The Future of the Church in India" (theme address, Platinum Jubilee of the NCCI, Madras, Dec. 3, 1989), *NCC Review*, March 1990.

BIBLE STUDIES, SERMONS, AND POEMS

Bible Studies

"Ecumenical Boasting" No. 94 *One World*, Sept. 1979.
"To Suffer Outside the Gate", *One World*, No. 56, May 1980.
"Hidden from the Wise, Matthew 11: 25-30", *One World*, No. 90
"Advent: the Beginning of a Pilgrimage, Luke 12:35-37", *One World*, No. 100, Nov. 1984.
Three Bible studies on the theme "Religion, Culture and Power" at the Biennial Meeting of the Christian Institute for the Study of Religion and Society, New Delhi, Nov. 26-28, 1985: No. 1, *Naboth's Vineyard* - 1 Kings 21:1-7; No. 2, *Christ and the Powers* - Colossians 1:15-26; No. 3, *By What Power* - Acts 3:1-10. All in *Religion and Society*, Bangalore, Vol. 34, No. 1, Nov. 1987.

Sermons

"In Memory of Jawaharlal Nehru" (sermon preached at his memorial service in St. Mark's Cathedral, Bangalore, on June 8, 1964), *Aikya*, Journal of the Student Christian Moves India, Bangalore, Vol. 10, No. 6, June 1964.

"Other People's Faiths" (sermon preached to the Sixth Public Relations World Congress, Geneva, April 1973), *Frontier*, London, Vol. 17, No. 2, Summer 1974.

"What is Repetitive and What is New in Life", *South India Churchman*, Madras, September 1981.

"This is Eternal Life" (sermon on John 17:3 preached at the Chapel of the United Theological College, Bangalore, on October 14, 1984), *South India Churchman*, Madras, Dec. 1984.

"On Love and Truth" (sermon preached at a service of blessing an inter-religious marriage in St.Mark's Cathedral Bangalore, on April 8, 1985), *National Christian Council of Churches Review*, Nagpur, June-July, 1985; also in *Current Dialogue* No. 8, June 1985.

"Watchman and Shepherds" (an ordination sermon, All Souls' Church, Bangalore, Church of South India, May 24, 1987), *National Christian Council of Churches Review*, Nagpur August, 1987.

"What Kind of Joy" (a Christmas meditation), published as *Christmas Souvenir*, Bangalore, Dec. 6, 1987.

Poems

"The Pillar of Salt Speaks", *One World*, No. 123, March 1987.
"Pharaoh's Daughter", "The Prodigal Son's Mother", and "Timothy's Father", *One World*, No. 130. November 1987.

"Ambiguous Christians", *One World*, No. 143, March 1989.
"Pisgah and Saturday", *One World*, No. 154, April 1990.

BOOK REVIEWS

"Contact, Controversy and Communication", review article on Carl Hallencreutz, *Kraemer Towards Tambaram*, in *Indian Journal of Theology*, Serampore, Vol. 17, No. 1, January-March 1968.

Review of Josepy M. Kitagawa, *Religion in Japanese History* (Columbia University Press, New York, 1966) in *International Review of Mission*, Vol. 58, April 1969.

"Meaning of Mission in a Changing World", review of J. Rossel, *Mission in a Dynamic Society* (London, SCM Press, 1968), *International Review of Mission*, Vol. 58, July 1969.

Review of Jacques Waardenburg, *Classical Approaches to the Study of Religion*, 2 vols. (The Hague, Mouton, 1973), *International Review of Mission*, Vol. 64, Jan. 1975.

Review of (ed.) Charles J. Adams, *A Reader's Guide to Great Religions*, 2nd ed. (The Free Press, New York, 1977), *Ecumenical Review*, Vol. 30, No. 1, January 1978.

Review of Donald K. Swearer, *Dialogue: The Key to Understanding Other Religions* (Westminster Press, Philadelphia, 1977), *Religious Education*, Vol. No.73, Sept./Oct. 1978.

Review of Richard Fox Young, *Resistant Hinduism: Sanskrit Sources on Anti-Christian Apologetics in Early Nineteenth Century India* (E. J. Brill, Leiden, 1981), *Religion and Society*, Vol. 28, No. 4, Dec. 1981.

"The Unknown Christ Made Better Known", review article on Raimon Panikkar, *The Unknown Christ of Hinduism*, rev. ed. (Orbis Books, Maryknoll, New York, 1981), *Religion and Society*, Vol. 30, No. 1, March 1983.

ARCHIVED WORKS

Handwritten and typed texts both of unpublished works and published works, notes of lectures, reports, articles, Bible studies, sermons, memoranda, etc. are in the archives of United Theological College, Bangalore, India. Similar original materials for the period 1968-81 are in the archives of the World Council of Churches, Geneva, Switzerland. All published works and much of the archived materials are also in the library of the University of Utrecht, Netherlands.

Index

Abesan, Carlos H., 71-72
Abraham, K. C., 69
Activism, 113-14
Adharma, 128, 129
Adhikara, 25, 81
Adhyatma Ramayana, 129
Advaita, 25, 63, 83, 107-10, 138, 140
Agnivesh, Swami, 46
Aiyitty, George, 34-35
Amalorpavadass, D. S., 68, 72
Ambedkar, Dr., 125, 148
Analects, 60
Anand, Subhas, 41
Anawim, 134
Anubhava, 5, 61, 67, 83, 99, 105
Appasamy, A. J., 123
Ariarajah, S. Wesley, 55, 119, 123, 125
Arjuna, 64, 127-28
Art, 90-91, 106
Ashoka, 51
Assisa, day of prayer, 14-15, 157n12
Atman, 138
Aurobindo, Sir, 56, 63
AUM, 61
Authority, 58, 62, 69, 71, 75, 85
Avatara, 74, 81, 128, 130-31
Azad, Maulana Abul Kala, 109
Bangladesh, 53, 54
Berkowitz, Rabbi, 147
Bernard of Clairvaux, 62
Berry, Thomas, 105
Bhagavadgita, 2, 59, 63-64, 73, 74, 107, 127-28
Bhakti, 122, 126, 127-28, 129
Bhavabuti, 130
Bhave, 59, 63
Bible, 58, 59, 64, 65, 67, 72
Borowitz, Eugene B., 18
Bosch, David, 97-98, 147

Brahman, 61, 129, 138
Brahmanism, 80
Brahmasutra, 59, 107
Brockway, Allan R., 78
Bruckner, Pascal, 3
Buber, Martin, 17-18
Buddha, 26, 28, 43, 52, 114, 124-26
Buddhism, 26-28, 51, 53, 56, 59, 61, 125, 169n15
Canada, 30
Chaitanya, Krishna, 63, 127
Chakkari, V., 119
Chan, Wing-Tsit, 39
Chandra, Bipan, 50-51
Chathimattam, John B., 8
China, 34, 38, 59, 60, 107, 117
Chinmayananda, Swami, 24
Chopra, B. R., 126
Chorin, Schalom Ben, 17
Choudhuri, Nirad, 109
Christianity, 9, 29-30, 47, 54, 71
Christology, ix, x, xii, 82; helicopter vs. bullock-cart, x, 115-19; revised, 92-111 (chap. 7), 112-31 (chap. 8), 132-41 (chap. 9); theocentric, 89-91
"Christomonism," 86, 88, 119
Church, 11-12
Clement, 138
Cohen, Arthur A., 17
Colonialism, 2-3, 68
Communalism, 49, 50-51, 168n11
Community, 10, 11
Confucianism, 59, 107
Confucius, 59, 61
Constantine, 124
Conversion, 148-50
Cross/resurrection event, 136-40
Cullmann, Oscar, 122
Culture, 36

188   Index

Cupitt, Don, 123
Dalai Lama, 16
Dalit, 52, 125
Dana, 110, 151
Darshana, 99, 108, 132
Das, Tulsi, 129
Devasenapathi, V. A., 25
Da'wah, 22
Derrida, Jacques, 5
Dharma, 8, 14, 23, 24, 27, 28, 43, 50, 56, 61, 81, 107, 125, 128-29, 132
Dharma yuddha, 2, 59, 63
Dialogue, 13-31 (chap. 2), 57, 78-79, 114; Buddhist, 26-29; Christian, 13-16; Hindu, 22-26; Jewish, 16-20; Muslim 20-22
Driver, Tom, 9, 29
Dukkha, 84, 138
Edwards, David L., 105
Engineer, Asghar Ali, 146
Evangelicalism, 78, 96-98, 122
Exclusivism, 96-103, 118
Faith, 46, 56, 117
Fenshaw, Charles J., 97
Fitzmyer, Joseph, 116
Flesseman-van Leer, Ellen, 19
Fuller, Reginald, 116
Fundamentalism, ix, 3, 20-21, 49, 98
Gadamer, Hans-Georg, 15
Gandhi, Indira, 35, 50, 52, 80
Gandhi, Mahatma, 47, 49, 50, 52, 56, 59, 63, 109, 110, 118, 129, 136, 142, 144
Ghana, 34-35
Ghose, Sisir Kumar, 146
God, 18, 46, 56, 57, 71, 80, 87, 107, 110, 116
Gregorios, Mar, 68, 70-71
Gregory of Nyssa, 71
Griffiths, Bede, 16
Gupta, Santosh Chandra Sen, 40
Harijan, 52, 125
Hermeneutics, x, 58, 61, 62-64; in Asia, 66-73
Heschel, Abraham J., 19
Hinduism, 17, 22-26, 50-51, 53, 59, 81-82, 108, 122, 143
History, 10-11
Hogg, Alfred, 144

Hypocrisy, 49
I Ching, 60, 107
Incarnation, 118, 120-22
India, xiii, 2, 7, 30, 34, 38, 40, 45-56, 63, 78, 79, 86, 107, 109, 117
Indonesia, 55, 59
Isaac, Solomon ben, 62, 64
Islam, 20-22, 47, 53, 54, 143
Israel, 17-18
Jainism, 107
Jamieson, Robert, 30
Japan, 35, 60
Jenkins, David, 97
Jesus Christ, 15, 17, 21, 26, 46, 56, 74, 112-13, 133-34, 140; in a multireligious culture, 76-91 (chap. 6); New Testament witness to, 12-24; revised, 92-111 (chap. 7), 112-31 (chap. 8)
"Jesusology," 86, 119, 124
Jivanmukta, 90, 136
Jhana, 41-42, 63, 108, 122, 130, 134
John Paul II, Pope, 78
Joshi, Uma Shankar, 109
Judaism, 17-20, 147, 174n20
Jung, C. J., 107
Justice, 33, 35, 42, 56
Kaesemann, Ernst, 115, 117
K'ai, Chih, 60
Kant, Krishnan, 54
Karma-samsara, 138
Kautilya, 50
Keshavayya, Muliya, 90
Khalistan, 54
Khanna, 139
Kingdom of God, 134-35, 140
Knitter, Paul, 97, 104
Kothari, Rajni, 8, 49, 109
Koyama, Kosuke, 68-69
Kraemar, Hendrik, 143-44
Krishna, 52, 64, 109, 127-28, 169n16
Kulandaiswami, Swami, 16
Language, 67
Lao Tzu, 60-61
Lebanon, 54
Liberation theology, 135
Lipner, Julius, 103
Love, 63, 74
Luke, 121

Madhwa, 108
Mahabharta, 63, 126
Maha karuna citta, 43, 56, 126
Mahavira, 52
Mantra, 65
Marga, 81, 135
Mark, 121
Marxism, 28
Mashriqui, Allam, 109
Mataikya, 81
Matavirodha, 81
Matilal, B, K., 108
Matthew, 121
Megasthenes, 127
Merton, Thomas, 94
Miller, Patricia C., 62
Mishpat, 43
Mishra, Laknath, 82
Mission, 10, 12, 19, 21-22, 53, 78, 101; in a religiously plural world, 142-54 (chap. 10)
Mohammed, 74
Mohani, Maulana Hastrat, 109
Mokksha, 63, 84, 103, 130, 138
Moltmann, Jürgen, 18
Mukarji, Nirmal, 23
Mystery, 83, 85
Nandy, Ashis, 3
Naseef, Abdulla Omar, 21
Nehru, Nawaharlal, 47, 49, 50, 109
Nigeria, 54
Nirvana, 84, 130, 138
Nishkama karma, 128
Nizami, Kwaja Hassan, 109
Northern Ireland, 54
North/South; injustice, ix, 32, 36
Nyerere, Julius, 34
Ogden, Schubert, 119
Origen, 62, 138
Orthodox churches, 71, 152
Ott, Heinrich, 10
Pai, Manjeshwar Govinda, 90
Pakistan, 34, 53-54
Palihawadana, Mahinda, 27, 29
Pancasila, 55
Parmar, S. K., 149
Paul, St., 118, 121-22, 137
Peace, 15, 28, 33, 42-43
Perkins, Pheme, 116

Philippines, 55
Pieris, Aloysius, 125-26
Pluralism, religious, ix, 1-12 (chap. 1); perceptions of, 6-7; roots of, 4-5
Plurality, 47, 80
Politicization of religion(s), 51-53
Prajadharma, 50
Praxis, 113-14
Prayer, 16
Protestantism, 65, 71, 106
Pusalker, A. D., 127
Puja, 52, 114
Qurtan, 21, 59, 62
Radhakrishnan, S., 9 59, 63, 81, 144
Rahman, Fazlur, 21
Rajadharma, 50
Rama, 44, 52, 109, 126-27, 128-31, 176n39
Ramanuja, 59, 63, 108, 126, 127, 129
Rambachan, Anantanand, 25
Religions, ix-x, 4, 35-37, 45-50, 55-57; and natural life, 45-47, 51-54
Ricoeur, Paul, 65
Robinson, J. A. T., 119
Roman Catholic Church, 2-3, 24, 71, 77-78, 86-87
Roy, Jamini, 90
Roy, Raja Ran Mohan, 56, 81
Sabda, 61, 65, 85
Sadhana, 71, 81, 84, 110
Sahi, Jyoti, 90
Salvation, 84
"Salvation history," 6, 104
Sampradaya, 59, 71, 81, 108, 131
Sankara, 59, 63, 108
Sat, 61, 80, 86, 103, 116, 140
Satchidananda Murthy, K., 40
Sat-cit-ananda, 83-84
Sati, 56
Satyasya Satyam, 61, 80, 82, 153
Science, 29
Scripture, x, 10-11; plurality of, 59-61, 62-64, 73-74, 85; and scriptures, 58-75 (chap. 5)
Secular state, 48-49, 51-54, 56
Sei'chi, Yagi, 27
Seshagiri, Rao
Seshagiri Rao, K. L., 25, 41
Shalom, 43

Shanti, 43, 91
Sharia, 109
Sharma, Narenda Pandit, 126
Shlamut, 18
Sikhism, 52, 54
Silva, Lynn de, 125
Sin, 84
Singh, Ajit, 35
Singh, Amrik, 146
Singh, Gopal, 90
Singh, Karan, 23
Singh, V. P., 34
Singh, Zail, 149
Sinha, Debabrata, 108
Sita, 1
Smith, Robert F., 30
Smith, Wilfred Cantwell, 62
Smriti, 41, 61, 63
Sohal, Sukder Singh, 146
Solomon, 62
Song, Choan-Seng, 68, 69-70, 125
Song of Songs, 62, 64
Sorabji, Sola, 82
"Spokenness," 64-65
Sri Lanka, 2, 55
Sruti, 41, 61, 63, 65
Stott, John R., 9
Sundararajan, K. R., 25, 26
Suri, Surinder, 49
Svadharma, 26
Tao, 61
Taoism, 59, 60-61, 107
Tarka, 5, 61, 83, 105
Tawheed, 109
Technology, 28-29

Thailand, 55
Thapar, Ramila, 110
Thelle, Notto R., 27
Theocentrism, 88-91
Theology, 10-11, 87
Theoria, 113-14
Tilak, Balagangadhar, 56, 59, 63, 64
Tolerance, 45, 47, 50, 170n20
Torah, 134
Transposition, 70, 166n39
Trinity, 83
Tripitaka, 59
Truth, 103-10
Tsurwmi, Yushi, 35
Tully, Mark, 109
Tzu, Chung, 60
Tzu, Lao, 60
Tzu, Mou, 39, 60
Upanishads, 59, 107, 127
Vaisnaivism, 118
Valmiki, 128, 130
Van Buitenen, J. A. B., 41
Vedanta, 108
Vedas, 80, 164n1
Viraha, 130
Vishnu, 129
Vivekananda, Swami, 25, 56
Whaling, Frank, 40, 129
Wolf, Arnold J., 19
World Council of Churches, 2-3, 12, 18, 68, 77-78, 86-87, 97
"Writenness," 65, 85
Yin-yang, 107
Zaehner, R. C., 108
Zen, 27

www.ingramcontent.com/pod-product-compliance
Lightning Source LLC
Chambersburg PA
CBHW051739230426
43670CB00012B/2087